# Buddhist-Christian Dialogue as Theological Exchange

## An Orthodox Contribution to Comparative Theology

ERNEST M. VALEA

☙PICKWICK *Publications* · Eugene, Oregon

BUDDHIST-CHRISTIAN DIALOGUE AS THEOLOGICAL EXCHANGE
An Orthodox Contribution to Comparative Theology

Pickwick Publications
An Imprint of Wipf and Stock Publishers
199 W. 8th Ave., Suite 3
Eugene, OR 97401

www.wipfandstock.com

ISBN 13: 978-1-4982-2119-1

*Cataloguing-in-Publication data:*

Valea, Ernest

    Buddhist-Christian dialogue as theological exchange : an Orthodox contribution to comparative theology / Ernest M. Valea.

    xviii + 244 p. ; 23 cm. Includes bibliographical references and index.

    ISBN 13: 978-1-4982-2119-1

    1. Dialogue—Religious aspects. 2. Religions—Relations. 3. Christianity and other religions—Buddhism. I. Title.

BR128 B8 V31 2015

Manufactured in the U.S.A.                                    03/26/2015

# Buddhist-Christian Dialogue as Theological Exchange

To my beloved wife, Cristina,
who taught me to never lose hope.

# Contents

# Acknowledgments

THE FOLLOWING IS AN adaptation of my doctoral dissertation submitted to the University of Wales. Several persons deserve my special appreciation for their help over these last four years. I want to express my gratitude to my director of studies and to my supervisor for encouraging me to undertake this endeavor in the fascinating and (for many) forbidding domain called Buddhist-Christian dialogue. Prof. Dr. Nancey Murphy, my director of studies, guided me in following a clear direction and methodology, as I often found myself side-tracked and lost in details. She helped me to discern what is worthy of exploring in more detail and what to ignore, and so relieved me of the burden of feeling that I needed to know everything on these issues. Prof. Dr. Parush Parushev, my supervisor, kept reminding me to make sure that the whole thesis was well balanced and formed a coherent whole, with proper connections between parts, chapters, and sections, and in the flow of my argumentation.

There are many other people who helped me along the way, of whom I can mention just a few. I want to thank Dr. Jim Purves for his unmerciful criticism when I started this thesis. He has the gift of disclosing very straightforwardly the weaknesses in one's research, which for me had a very sobering effect. And when I (finally) submitted the thesis believing it to be finished, I benefited from the frank but constructive structural criticism of my external examiner, Prof. Dr. Michael Barnes SJ, which resulted in updating my thesis with the most recent developments in comparative theology as well as improving its overall structure.

Since I am not a native English speaker, the entire text was checked by a special friend, Mrs. Danielle Plant, who not only read and proofread the text, but also pointed out several contradictions and asked for clarifications in difficult passages. Any remaining shortcomings are my own. Last but not least, I want to thank my wife Cristina for her patience with me while reading and writing about this strange topic she dubbed "Buddhisms." I ask for her forgiveness for all the time I had to be away from her, even if I was only mentally away, and I thank her for trusting me that I was doing something worthy of this sacrifice. To her I gratefully dedicate this work.

# Introduction

BUDDHIST-CHRISTIAN DIALOGUE IS A vast domain to explore. There can be little doubt that the dialogue between these two seemingly most different religions on earth has drawn more interest than that of any other pairing in interfaith dialogue. We can see it reflected in the huge amount of literature it has produced and the many formal and informal meetings between its representatives. One could wonder, why are Christians more interested in engaging in dialogue with Buddhism, than for instance with Judaism, or Islam, which are much closer to Christianity? A possible answer may be that both are considered missionary religions and as such are not bound to a specific culture or nation (as are Judaism, Hinduism or Shintoism). Another reason could be found in the quite recent meeting of the two religions on Western ground, and in the challenge brought by Buddhism to a traditional Christian culture in addressing contemporary issues. By its very nature as a religion without God and with all the resources one needs to meet its demands to be found in oneself, Buddhism appears to be very attractive to a Western secularized society. As we will see in this book, its philosophical tenets have posed a challenge to Christian theologians as well, and not a few of them have responded by reinterpreting traditional Christian doctrines.

This book does not aim to be an encyclopaedic introduction to Buddhist-Christian dialogue. My goal is twofold. First, I want to bring the rich tradition of Orthodox Christianity into dialogue with Buddhism, and more specifically Romanian Orthodoxy through the voice of its best known theologian—Dumitru Stăniloae. Although the study of world religions is part of the curriculum in Orthodox faculties of theology, Orthodox theologians who have actually engaged in interfaith dialogue are few,[1] and Romanian

1. One exception is the American Orthodox theologian John Garvey. His book *Seeds of the Word*, a welcome engagement of an Orthodox theologian in the field of interfaith dialogue, is mostly a general and descriptive introduction to world religions, and has only a last chapter dedicated to the actual dialogue with other religions.

Orthodox theologians even fewer. In fact I am aware of just one Romanian Orthodox theologian, Nicolae Achimescu, who actually engaged in an academic dialogue with Buddhism, which resulted in a PhD thesis with the University of Tübingen.[2] Given the rich resources of Orthodoxy, it is a pity that it is so weakly represented in interfaith dialogue.

Second, since the three classical approaches to interfaith dialogue—exclusivism, inclusivism and pluralism—have reached an impasse,[3] I felt the urge for a return *ad fontes* in Buddhist-Christian dialogue, and to perform an assessment of its founding fathers. They provide important insights for adopting a new approach in interfaith dialogue called comparative theology. I expect that pursuing this double interest, both in Orthodox theology and in the classics of Buddhist-Christian dialogue, will result in an Orthodox contribution to comparative theology. Hence my research question: What is the possible contribution of Orthodoxy to the approach of comparative theology in Buddhist-Christian dialogue?

An explanatory note is needed here on what kind of "dialogue" I refer to, given the different meanings it bears in interfaith encounter. A first important distinction is made by Michael Barnes between a dialogue centred on content and one centred on form. The first "privileges the meaning of what is said over the act of speaking," while the latter takes "the encounter itself" as of primordial importance over the issues that are actually discussed.[4] I will use "dialogue" in its first meaning, for the participants in Buddhist-Christian dialogue I refer to in this book are mostly concerned with the actual exchange of ideas and concepts expressed in their traditions. Another classification of "dialogue" follows the fourfold distinction stated in the Catholic encyclical *Dialogue and Proclamation*, as four specialized forms of interreligious dialogue:

2. Achimescu, "Die Vollendung des Menschen in Buddhismus. Bewertung aus orthodoxer Sicht" [Human Perfection in Buddhism. An assessment from an Orthodox perspective], University of Tübingen, 1993, translated in Romanian as *Budism şi Creştinism*. The goal of Achimescu's research is to evaluate "whether and to what extent Orthodox mystical theology is echoed in Buddhist mysticism, and more important, whether they are in total divergence" (p. 13). The reference point of his approach is stated as the non-negotiable doctrine of the "true salvation in Jesus Christ," and only from this perspective does he engage in researching a "possible" dialogue with Buddhism (p. 18). Here and elsewhere the translation from Romanian is mine unless otherwise specified.

3. Fredericks explicitly speaks of the "impasse" to which the classic theologies of religions have led in his *Faith among Faiths*, 10.

4. Barnes, *Theology and the Dialogue of Religions*, 20. He affirms that his "interest lies in the second sense, following Levinas" and his emphasis on actually relating to and meeting the "other" (ibid., 20–21).

a. The "dialogue of life" is about cultivating neighbourly friendship among lay adherents of different faiths who share their personal preoccupations and concerns;

b. The "dialogue of action" expresses a shared concern for issues that affect humankind as a whole, such as social justice, the lack of education, the environmental crisis and peace;

c. The "dialogue of theological exchange" is centred upon the actual discussion and debate of doctrinal issues between specialists of each tradition, which can be common or divergent beliefs;

d. The "dialogue of religious experience" takes place between persons who share their personal spiritual experiences (mainly Christian and Buddhist monastics), or engage in common prayer and meditation, while respecting each other's symbols and rituals.[5]

I chose to centre my assessment of Buddhist-Christian dialogue on theological exchange, for this is the primary interest of the scholars I refer to in this book. As representatives of a certain *faith*, our religious experiences and what we think of life and action depends on our foundational beliefs, and we all start with theological assumptions, even if they are not clearly stated. Persons involved in interfaith dialogue first of all represent a *faith*, and only as such express their views of life, action and religious experience. However, I am not suggesting that a dialogue of life or action is not important. Believers of different religions, as well as persons with no religious affiliation at all, should cooperate on social issues despite differences in religious beliefs. They can, and should, cooperate as citizens of the same world. However, my book is focused on a real theological exchange in Buddhist-Christian dialogue. Although there are other issues on which dialogue can be centred, such as "secularization, world peace, human suffering, or the damages visited upon the environment," they are always indebted to theological or philosophical core beliefs.[6] Catherine Cornille affirms that it is easy to proclaim a common interest in world peace, or the environment, but when it comes to finding a theological basis for it in one's own tradition, things get complicated, since "for any believer, the compelling force of a particular criterion will ultimately lie not in its neutrality or commonality, but

5. *Dialogue and Proclamation*, 42. This document was issued by The Pontifical Council for Interreligious Dialogue and the Congregation for Evangelization of Peoples in 1991.

6. Cornille, *The Im-Possibility of Interreligious Dialogue*, 96.

in the fact that it arises from or coincides with one's own deepest religious beliefs and principles."[7]

My guiding thought is that we should not look for a unifying spirituality that would eradicate theological differences, as an alleged guardian of peace and reciprocal understanding. What we should seek instead is a way of dialogue between religious traditions that can respect all, that can deal with disagreements and cherish the religions as they are. Therefore, in the first part of this book, in chapter 1, I will start with a recapitulation of the classic approaches in interfaith dialogue and an evaluation of the impasse to which these approaches lead. Exclusivism, inclusivism and pluralism each follow a set of theological presuppositions and try to formulate an account of how people who belong to other religious traditions can be saved. Since these approaches usually do not encourage an in-depth study of other traditions, they risk forming *a priori* judgements of them, or even (in the case of pluralism) integrating them in a syncretistic scheme that would compromise both the Buddhist and the Christian traditions. Therefore I will explore the new approach of comparative theology, which seems to provide a better solution for building an honest interfaith dialogue by its emphasis on knowing other religious traditions on their own terms and on learning from them in a non-syncretistic way. In chapters 2 and 3 I will describe the view of human perfection as we find it expressed in the traditions of Mahayana Buddhism and Orthodox Christianity and propose it as a criterion for assessing the current positions expressed in Buddhist-Christian dialogue. Since both Christians and Buddhists strive for perfection, the positions they express in dialogue should be consistent with the ideal of perfection stated by the original traditions. In the final chapter of the first part (chapter 4) I will focus on pluralistic views in Buddhist-Christian dialogue and the phenomenon of dual belonging.

As a result of the impasse reached by the current theologies of religions in offering a constructive approach for both Buddhists and Christians engaged in dialogue, in the second part of this book I will explore the thought of several scholars whom I consider to be the founding fathers of contemporary Buddhist-Christian dialogue. These scholars are three important representatives of the Kyoto School: Kitaro Nishida, Keiji Nishitani and Masao Abe, and John Cobb, an American Process theologian.

The start of an academic Buddhist-Christian dialogue was given in Japan at the beginning of the twentieth century when, following the trend of assimilating Western culture, several leading figures of the department of philosophy of the University of Kyoto took the initiative of critically

7. Ibid., 107.

assimilating Western philosophy. As a result, the Kyoto philosophers met Christianity and were drawn into a dialogue with it. This initiative was followed much later in the West at the University of Hawaii's Department of Religion. For the first time Buddhist and Christian scholars formally met at the first International Buddhist-Christian Conference in 1980, which was followed in 1981 by issuing the journal called *Buddhist-Christian Studies*. In 1983 Masao Abe and John Cobb, the pioneers of this dialogue, started the "North American Buddhist-Christian Theological Encounter Group" with 25 theologians, to reach 200 at its 1986 meeting, and 700 at the 1987 meeting.[8] In 1987 was founded the American "Society for Buddhist-Christian Studies" (its Japanese counterpart had already existed since 1982), which was followed in Europe by the establishment of "The European Network of Buddhist Christian Studies" in 1996 at the University of Hamburg's Academy of Mission (now the "European Network of Buddhist Christian Studies"). The scholars involved in these initiatives produced a vast amount of literature over the years, which exceeds by far that of any other pairing in interfaith dialogue.

Although I make references to other scholars involved in contemporary Buddhist-Christian dialogue, in the second part of this book I focus on the four representatives mentioned above and assess their thought in light of what is stated in chapters 2 and 3 to be the ideal of human perfection in the traditions of Mahayana Buddhism and Orthodox Christianity. As my interest lies in a real theological exchange between these traditions, I will then formulate an Orthodox Christian contribution to comparative theology. This contribution can only be imagined if the rich traditions that engage in dialogue are not corrupted by syncretism, but rather respect each other and learn about the other traditions' values on their own terms.

8. Leonard Swidler, "A Jerusalem-Tokyo Bridge," 9–10.

# PART 1

Contemporary Buddhist-Christian
Dialogue and the Issue of Doctrinal
Presuppositions

# 1

# Buddhist-Christian Dialogue in the Context of the Three Classic Theologies of Religions—Exclusivism, Inclusivism and Pluralism—and Comparative Theology as a New Approach in Interfaith Dialogue

Both the Buddha and the Christ sent their disciples to proclaim their message to the ends of the earth.[1] Does this mean that Buddhists and Christians should use dialogue as a means for converting the other to their own views? Seeking the best for one's neighbour as Christian salvation or Buddhist enlightenment is understandable as motivation for those who seek to convert the other, but it is not what defines *dialogue*. In general terms, a real dialogue involves two sides in search of common ground, mutual understanding and peace. In my specific approach of dialogue as theological exchange, I follow James Heisig's definition of dialogue, as it would apply in matters of doctrinal views in Buddhist and Christian traditions, as meaning "arguing, discussing, criticizing, and making up one's own mind in words read and heard, spoken and written."[2] We can discern three well-defined stands currently expressed in Buddhist-Christian dialogue: exclusivism,

---

1. The Synoptic Gospels end with Jesus' Great Commission (Matthew 28:18–20; Mark 16:15–16; Luke 24:46–48) and a similar command is issued by the Buddha in the *Mahavagga* I,11,1: "Go ye now, O Bhikkhus, and wander, for the gain of the many, for the welfare of the many, out of compassion for the world, for the good, for the gain, and for the welfare of gods and men, Let not two of you go the same way."

2. Heisig, *Dialogues*, 115.

inclusivism and pluralism.[3] Fredericks defines them as attempts "to understand the theological meaning of the diversity of religions in keeping with the doctrinal requirements of a home tradition."[4] As such, these three categories are theologies of religions, for they follow a soteriological interest and try to answer the question of how can those of other religious traditions be saved?

1. Exclusivists hold that salvation or liberation can be attained only by following one's own religious tradition. Christian exclusivists see Buddhists as lost and in need of conversion as the only means of avoiding eternal damnation, while Buddhist exclusivists see Christians as lost in ignorance and in need of converting to Buddhism to find enlightenment, as the only way to escape from the maelstrom of rebirth.

2. Inclusivists are more moderate with regard to the other traditions. They acknowledge a salvific or liberating truth in the other tradition, but only as an inferior path to one's own. Christian inclusivists see salvation for Buddhists as mediated by Christ as the Logos at work in all humans. Buddhist inclusivists see Christ as one of the many *bodhisattvas*, who used skilful means for the Jews living in Palestine in the first century AD and for many others who did not come to know the path opened by the Buddha. Although salvation or liberation is possible for people of other faiths, it is nevertheless seen as an exception to the general rule.

3. Pluralists hold that Buddhism and Christianity are both valid as means for attaining salvation or liberation, for neither is superior to the other. Eventually both Christians and Buddhists will reach their expected destinations or even one situated beyond what they currently expect.

These short definitions do not reveal the complexities of each of the three typologies. In the following sections I will briefly summarize the thought of several important participants in Buddhist-Christian dialogue and assess the strengths and weaknesses of exclusivism, inclusivism and pluralism. I will focus as much as possible on Buddhist and Christian authors who have actually engaged in interfaith dialogue and avoid others who do not have a "hands on" approach to it. An exception to this course of action will be the next section, on exclusivism, for its proponents usually have little contact with the other traditions.

3. To my knowledge, this threefold classification of the approaches taken by Christians to define relationships to other religions first appears in Race, *Christians and Religious Pluralism*.

4. Fredericks, "Introduction," in Clooney, *New Comparative Theology*, xiii–xiv.

## 1.1 EXCLUSIVISM IN BUDDHIST-CHRISTIAN ENCOUNTER

Perry Schmidt-Leukel defines exclusivism as the belief that "salvific knowledge of a transcendent reality is mediated by only one religion."[5] All that is needed for salvation or liberation is already there in the tradition itself, and only there, so that any "help" from outside would only corrupt one's way to achieving it. Of the four forms of dialogue mentioned by *Dialogue and Proclamation*, mainly the first two forms (of life and of action) are open for exclusivists.[6] When exclusivists engage in a dialogue of theological exchange, interfaith dialogue can become a means for seeking the conversion of those of other traditions. This is not a negligible aspect. Barnes comments on the enthusiasm for dialogue today, saying that it "does give the impression that it is simply another tool" or "a more subtle way" for proselytising.[7] Although this is a charge brought mainly to Christians, we will see that it applies equally to some Buddhists engaged in interfaith encounter.

Christian exclusivism is linked to the traditions in which no revelation at all is granted to other religions and, as a result, the human being is seen as totally incapable of relating to God. Unlike in Orthodox and Catholic Christianity, which hold that the image given to humans at creation is not completely destroyed by sin, Protestant theology holds that the fall has led to the total corruption of the human being. One of the strong voices of Protestant Christian exclusivism is Karl Barth. His rejection of other faiths as leading to salvation is based on a strong belief in God's sovereignty to reveal himself, and in seeing the act of the creation of the world and of humankind as an act of his absolute free will.[8] Since human beings are sinful and totally incapable of saving themselves by means of their own wisdom and strength,

---

5. Schmidt-Leukel, *Transformation by Integration*, 93–94.

6. Harold Netland, an Evangelical Protestant, argues that exclusivists have four reasons for engaging in informal interfaith dialogue: 1) they need to follow the model of Jesus and Paul to become aware of their audiences" beliefs, 2) to prove that they "take the other person seriously" for they are also created in God's image, 3) to understand the others' values and assumptions in order to be more "effective in evangelism," and 4) as a mark of respect for those of other faiths (Netland, *Dissonant Voices*, 297–9). When it comes to formal interfaith dialogue, Netland follows the missiologist David Hesselgrave and finds five arguments for it: 1) to discuss the nature of dialogue itself, 2) to promote freedom of worship, 3) to promote social involvement for the sake of those unfortunate of every society, 4) to "break down barriers of prejudice, distrust, and hatred," and 5) to better comprehend what separates us and clarify "similarities and differences" to the Christian faith (ibid., 297–301).

7. Barnes, *Religions in Conversation*, 112–13.

8. Barth, *Church Dogmatics*, 1/2, 301.

it is only God who can grant them salvation and only through Jesus Christ.[9] As a result, all religions should be seen as mere human creations aimed at justifying us before God, and religion *per se* is deemed as "unbelief,"[10] for it attempts to replace the divine revelation in Jesus Christ with "a human manufacture."[11] In Barth's theological vision it would be meaningless to search for contact points with other religions, as any such attempt would only minimize the revelation we already have in Jesus Christ, God's special revelation in human history.[12]

Although Barth seems to adopt a more universalistic approach to world religions in the later volumes of his *Church Dogmatics*,[13] a universal redemption is seen as *potential*, and as such must be taken up personally by humans, Christians and non-Christians alike. Barth does not support a Spirit-centred theology according to which the Holy Spirit would provide a sufficient revelation in other religions. When he says that "[I]n this sense Jesus Christ is the hope even of these non-Christians," he refers to a *potential* redemption until a real knowledge of Christ becomes actual in the form of the particular Christian revelation reaching non-Christians.[14] In his words, "It must be said that he (the non-Christian) is not yet these things ('the recipient, bearer and possessor' of the Holy Spirit), because he does not yet know Jesus Christ" and as such the non-Christian "still lacks them."[15] However, before criticizing Barth's position as destructive for interfaith dialogue, we must be aware that his criticism is aimed first of all at man-made Christian traditions which departed from the fundamentals of the Bible, against the liberal theology of the nineteenth century and its compromise to

9. In Barth's words, "everything has actually been done for us once and for all in Jesus Christ" (ibid., 308).

10. Ibid., 300.

11. Ibid., 303.

12. Barth, "Religion as Unbelief," in *Church Dogmatics*, 1/2, 297–324.

13. Barth, *Church Dogmatics*, 4/3.

14. Ibid., 356.

15. Ibid., 355. In other words, "the Holy Spirit, i.e., Christ acting and speaking in the power of His resurrection, is not yet among and with and in certain men, i.e., that He is not yet present and active in them in the subjective realisation corresponding to His objective reality. The Holy Spirit Himself and as such is here a reality which is still lacking and is still to be expected" (ibid., 353). As such, Barth can still be taken as a Christian exclusivist. In the same volume he states very boldly: "Salvation is for all, but the covenant, which as such is God's glad tidings, is not concluded with all. It is the covenant of Yahweh with Israel fulfilled in the Christian community as the body of Christ. Not all peoples are Israel . . . Not every revelation is revelation of reconciliation. Not every attestation of revelation is thus witness of this revelation. Not all knowledge, therefore, is Christian knowledge, nor all confession, however true or significant or clear or brave, Christian confession. Not all men are Christians" (ibid., 222).

rationalistic humanism, and only by extension at other religions (of which he had no close encounter). Although we can easily categorize his position as exclusivistic, he did not aim to write a theology of religions.

It is not only in Christianity that we find exclusivists. Buddhists can be equally exclusivistic in affirming the Buddhist path as the only one effective for reaching liberation. A notorious case of exclusivist Buddhist-Christian encounter is the famous Buddhist-Christian controversy that took place in 1873 in Sri Lanka, known as the Panadura Debate.[16] It was a debate in which the speakers—David de Silva and F.J. Sirimanne on the Christian side, and Gunananda Thera on the Buddhist side—each tried to prove the falsity of his opponent's tradition.[17] As we can expect, such an approach is doomed to fail, for it is based on a wrong methodology. At Panadura each side was "fighting" against the other on the premises of its own doctrinal assumptions, which naturally led to condemning the other as false. Buddhism will always be wrong when seen from the Christian premises of a permanent God, and conversely, Christianity will always be wrong when considered in the light of emptiness as the ground of being. A more promising methodology in interfaith dialogue would suggest that one can be wrong only if not consistent with the premises of his or her *own* religious tradition. In other words, a Christian engages on a wrong path when misrepresenting his or her own premises, and *mutatis mutandis* for the Buddhist. Otherwise one could no longer speak of a dialogue between true Christians and true Buddhists. No wonder then that the Panadura Debate did not lead to further dialogue, but to isolation of the Buddhist and Christian communities in Sri Lanka.[18]

16. Abhayasundara, *Controversy at Panadura.*

17. For instance, David de Silva tried to prove how wrong the Buddhist *anatman* (not-Self) doctrine is, for it would imply that nothing survives death, and as such we are nothing but animals and moral effort is useless. Gunananda Thera in his turn attacked the character of God as displayed in the Old Testament, arguing that God cannot be omniscient, for he was sorry for creating the world (according to Genesis 6:6). These are just two brief examples which prove how superficial each side's knowledge was of the other.

18. It was only with Lynn de Silva that a proper Buddhist-Christian dialogue was reopened in Sri Lanka. He founded the Ecumenical Institute for Study and Dialogue in Colombo in 1962 and one of the first journals on Buddhist-Christian dialogue in 1961, called *Dialogue.*

## 1.2 A FINE BALANCE BETWEEN EXCLUSIVISM AND INCLUSIVISM IN THE DOCUMENTS OF THE CATHOLIC CHURCH FOLLOWING VATICAN II

The Catholic Church is by far the most active of the Christian traditions in interfaith dialogue and in formulating a position on other religions. Following Vatican II, the declaration *Nostra Aetate* states that "the Catholic Church rejects nothing that is true and holy in these religions" and acknowledges that world religions "often reflect a ray of that Truth which enlightens all men."[19] The declaration appreciates in Buddhism that it "realizes the radical insufficiency of this changeable world" and that it teaches its followers how "to acquire the state of perfect liberation."[20] Nevertheless, we are reminded that the "fullness of religious life" is to be found only in "Christ 'the way, the truth, and the life' (John 14:6)."[21]

In order to express what kind of a theology of religions is supported by the *Nostra Aetate*, whether it is exclusivistic or inclusivistic, we need to understand the context in which it was planned and issued. It was first planned as a declaration on the relationship of the Church with Judaism in the aftermath of the Shoah, was then extended to expressing the Church's relationship with Islam, and then extended to other world religions. By its positive tone on other religions, while still proclaiming that salvation is found only in Christ, its real intention is to hold exclusivism and inclusivism in a healthy and creative tension. As such we find the Catholic Church both reaffirming the traditional doctrine of salvation through Jesus Christ alone and a healthy openness towards all people of good will.[22] This dual orientation of the *Nostra Aetate* towards both respecting the freedom and good will of other religionists and against compromising the integrity of Christian teaching can be taken as a strength and an encouragement for interfaith dialogue.[23]

---

19. *Nostra Aetate*, 2. However, nothing is said of what specifically these "rays of truth" may consist of.

20. Ibid.

21. Ibid.

22. In the encyclical *Gaudium et Spes* it is said: "For, since Christ died for all men, and since the ultimate vocation of man is in fact one, and divine, we ought to believe that the Holy Spirit in a manner known only to God offers to every man the possibility of being associated with this paschal mystery" (*Gaudium et Spes* 22).

23. In *Lumen Gentium* we find that salvation is open to people of other religions on two conditions: 1. "through no fault of their own (they) do not know the Gospel of Christ or His Church, yet sincerely seek God;" 2. "moved by grace (they) strive by their deeds to do His will as it is known to them through the dictates of conscience." Therefore salvation is open "to those who, without blame on their part, have not yet arrived

The encyclical *Dialogue and Proclamation* restates both the Church's mission of making Christ known to the world, and that of not holding back from dialogue with other religions. This document explicitly affirms that the two elements, proclamation and dialogue, are "both viewed, each in its own place, as component elements and authentic forms of the one evangelizing mission of the Church."[24] As such they are foundational and uninterchangeable as "authentic elements of the Church's evangelizing mission."[25] At a time when uncritical openness towards other religions was sensed as a threat to the integrity of Christian doctrine the Vatican issued the *Dominus Iesus* declaration. Its purpose was "to set forth again the doctrine of the Catholic faith in these areas, pointing out some fundamental questions that remain open to further development, and refuting specific positions that are erroneous or ambiguous."[26] Properly understood, the *Dominus Iesus* is not a reinstatement of exclusivism. The Church is reminded that "the followers of other religions can receive divine grace," but also that "*objectively speaking*" these religions "are in a gravely deficient situation in comparison with those who, in the Church, have the fullness of the means of salvation."[27] Therefore Christians must be aware that the "solutions that propose a salvific action of God beyond the unique mediation of Christ would be contrary to Christian and Catholic faith."[28] As such, "the elements of goodness and grace which they (the other religions and their scriptures) contain" are received "from the mystery of Christ,"[29] and as a result, the highest value that could be attributed to the religious rituals and prayers of non-Christians would be that "of preparation for the Gospel."[30]

In the official documents of the Catholic Church interfaith dialogue is seen as a missionary tool, a part of the Church's "evangelizing mission"[31] and must not in any way detract the church from proclaiming

---

at an explicit knowledge of God and with His grace strive to live a good life" (*Lumen Gentium* 16). *Dialogue and Proclamation* (29) acknowledges the presence of the Spirit in other religions and the possibility that by a "sincere practice of what is good in their own religious tradition" these people would "respond positively to God's invitation and receive salvation in Jesus Christ."

24. *Dialogue and Proclamation*, 2.

25. Ibid., 77.

26. *Dominus Iesus*, 3.

27. Ibid., 22.

28. Ibid., 14.

29. Ibid., 8.

30. Ibid., 21.

31. Ibid., 22. This view is repeated by Pope John Paul II in his Encyclical Letter *Redemptoris missio*, 55.

that *"salvation comes from Christ and that dialogue does not dispense from evangelization."*[32] Christ is still to be seen as "the one Savior of all" and the fulfilment of history,[33] and thus other ways of salvation cannot be seen as "parallel or complementary to his (to Christ's mediation)."[34] This means that the dialogue initiated by the Catholic Church is one "oriented towards proclamation,"[35] for the Church "*alone* possesses the fullness of the means of salvation."[36] But at the same time dialogue is a "method and means of mutual knowledge and enrichment"[37] and Christians can expect "to be transformed by the encounter."[38] As we can see, dialogue and proclamation, openness towards other religions and holding fast to tradition, represent the two poles between which we find expressed the attitude of the Catholic Church towards interfaith dialogue.

## 1.3 INCLUSIVISM IN INTERFAITH DIALOGUE

Inclusivism acknowledges that salvific or liberating knowledge does not belong to a single tradition, but nevertheless claims that one's own mediates it in a way superior to all others. On the Christian side, inclusivists hold that Christ is the only true way of salvation, while other religions may be acceptable ways towards God for those who never heard about Christ, or were prevented from understanding the gospel by their culture or by Christians who misrepresented the teachings of Jesus. Christian inclusivists can be classified as structural inclusivists and restrictionist inclusivists. According to D'Costa, the first group considers Christ as the "normative revelation of God" but that salvation is still possible for those who haven't heard about him, through participation in their religions. Those in the second group also see "Christ as the normative revelation of God" but non-Christian religions are not salvific, and Christ saves non-Christians despite their religion.[39] A

32. *Redemptoris missio,* 55.

33. Ibid., 6; *Dialogue and Proclamation,* 28.

34. *Redemptoris missio,* 5.

35. *Dialogue and Proclamation,* 82.

36. *Redemptoris missio,* 55. The Catholic Church affirms it must not give up its belief in the uniqueness of Jesus Christ and his indispensable role for our salvation, for "such language is simply being faithful to revelation" (*Dominus Iesus,* 15). In the end, Jesus Christ is "the instrument for the salvation of *all* humanity (cf. *Acts* 17:30–31)" (*Dominus Iesus,* 22).

37. Ibid.

38. *Dialogue and Proclamation,* 47.

39. D'Costa, *Christianity and World Religions,* 7.

similar classification is used by Kristin Kiblinger as "open" and "closed" inclusivism.[40]

The best known form of Christian inclusivism is Karl Rahner's doctrine of "Anonymous Christianity." It is a "structural" or "open" type of inclusivism.[41] On the Buddhist side, inclusivism is the position of the fourteenth Dalai Lama, who holds that Buddhism is uniquely effective in mediating the attainment of enlightenment, while other religions may be seen as skilful means for helping their followers to advance towards it little by little. Another Buddhist inclusivist whose views I will mention is John Makransky.

## 1.3.1 Rahner's "Anonymous Christianity"

Rahner's inclusivism acknowledges salvific value in other religions following two doctrinal assumptions. The first is that the whole creation is sustained in existence by God's grace, and Christ as the eternal Logos is already at work in all humans through the Holy Spirit. For one who has not heard the Christian gospel faith in Christ is present as "the searching memory of the absolute saviour."[42] Since God's love is unbiased, it must be that "a universal and supernatural salvific will of God . . . is really operative in the world."[43] Rahner's second assumption is that a non-Christian can attain salvation "through faith, hope and love" and since these virtues are to be found in other religions as well, they must play a role "in the attainment of justification and salvation."[44] The terms coined by Rahner as "anonymous Christianity" and "anonymous Christian" involve the belief that one can be "a child of God . . . even before he has explicitly embraced a creedal statement of the Christian faith and been baptized."[45] By the work of the Holy Spirit people of other faiths are already connected to the Church of Christ and thus can justly be called by the name of "anonymous Christians."[46]

---

40. Kristin Beise Kiblinger, "Relating Theology of Religions and Comparative Theology," in Clooney, ed., *New Comparative Theology*, 28.

41. Other representatives of Christian inclusivism are Clark Pinnock and John Sanders. Both are Evangelicals and hold a "closed" form of inclusivism. See Pinnock, *A Wideness in God's Mercy*, Pinnock et al., *The Openness of God*, Sanders, *No Other Name*.

42. Rahner, *Foundations of Christian Faith*, 318. This "searching memory" is the capacity of receiving God's gift in Christ, or in his words, "the anticipation of the absolute saviour which searches and watches in history" (ibid., 320).

43. Ibid., 313.

44. Ibid., 314.

45. Rahner, *Theological Investigations*, vol. 12, 165.

46. In other words, anyone who does not suppress the truth of God, "but leaves it free play" is led by "the grace of the Father in his Son," and "anyone who has let himself

Nevertheless, Rahner is keen to remind us that salvation is possible only "in view of the merits of Christ,"[47] who is "the incarnate Logos of God who reaches fulfilment in his earthly reality through death and resurrection."[48] Non-Christian religions should then be seen only as "provisional manifestations, destined to be replaced" by the revelation in Christ.[49] This means that "the historical expansion of Christianity . . . coincides with a progressive abrogation of the legitimacy of these religions."[50]

Several Christian theologians have criticized Rahner's inclusivism for leading to undesirable results. On the one hand it does not encourage one to actually know other religious traditions. Fredericks calls Rahner's inclusivism "praiseworthy," but given its impact on interfaith dialogue it would still be "inadequate to the challenge facing Christians today," for it "does not lead Christians to learn about other religions as a creative response to religious diversity."[51] On the other hand, it would discourage mission. Hans Küng criticizes Rahner's thesis of "anonymous Christianity" for discouraging mission by including non-Christians in the church by simply relabeling them *anonymous* Christians.[52] Henri de Lubac admits that the Holy Spirit is at work in the lives of non-Christians, thus accepting "anonymous Christians," but not "anonymous Christianity," for it makes conversion to Christianity and discipleship in following Christ unnecessary, and it devalues the uniqueness of Christ and the incarnation.[53]

However, when criticizing Rahner's inclusivist views, we must be aware of the limitations he himself acknowledges for his work. He affirms that his inquiry is based on the Bible and the Catholic tradition and therefore must be seen in the context of "an inquiry in dogmatic theology, and not in the history of religion."[54] Therefore he aims to offer only "provisional hints"[55] that theologians involved in the study of other religions must evaluate in further research.

---

be taken hold of by this grace can be called with every right an "anonymous Christian" (Karl Rahner, *Theological Investigations*, vol. 6, 395).

47. Rahner, *Foundations of Christian Faith*, 316.

48. Ibid., 318–9.

49. Rahner, *Theological Investigations*, vol. 10, 47.

50. Ibid.

51. Fredericks, *Faith among Faiths*, 32.

52. Küng, *On Being a Christian*, 97–99.

53. Lubac, *The Church: Paradox and Mystery*, 153–56.

54. Rahner, *Foundations of Christian Faith*, 312.

55. Ibid., see also *Theological Investigations*, vol. 17, 39–40, and vol. 18, 288–300.

## 1.3.2 Orthodox Inclusivism—"Seeds of the Word" in Other Religions

The theological fundament for Orthodox inclusivism is the view that, unlike in Protestant Christianity, the doctrine of the fall allows for some preservation of God's image given to humankind at creation. As a result, an Orthodox theology of religions cannot be fully exclusivistic and allows Orthodox theologians to see other religions, including Buddhism, as "expressions of the human being in search of God, as the human aspiration for salvation."[56] The Romanian Orthodox theologian Achimescu follows the tradition started by St Justin Martyr of recognizing "seeds of the Word" in non-Christian traditions.[57] In Achimescu's words, "all people, be they Buddhists, Christians or otherwise, participate to a so-called 'Cosmic Liturgy,' as all serve—directly or indirectly—God and Jesus Christ and all partake, on various levels, of Jesus Christ."[58]

In a way similar to Rahner, Achimescu speaks of a "'Church' outside Christianity, to which belong Buddhists as well" but which nevertheless should be considered only as a state of "preparation for the true Church of Christ" and as such is a "Church" only in a state of promise of God, awaiting its fulfilment in the actual knowledge of Christ.[59] Although Achimescu's approach appears to be exclusivistic at times,[60] his soteriological convictions

56. Achimescu, *Budism și Creștinism*, 343.

57. In his *First Apology*, St Justin Martyr says: "We have been taught that Christ is the first-born of God, and we have declared above that He is the Word of whom every race of men were partakers; and those who lived reasonably are Christians, even though they have been thought atheists"; (Justin Martyr, *The First Apology*, ch. 46). In his *Second Apology*, chapter 8, he speaks of the Stoics and the poets who wrote "on account of the seed of reason (the Logos) implanted in every race of men." In chapter 13 he affirms that "all the writers were able to see realities darkly through the sowing of the implanted word that was in them." We find a view similar to that in the Catholic decree *Ad Gentes* (11) where it speaks of "the riches which a generous God has distributed among the nations."

58. Achimescu, *Budism și Creștinism*, 334. The concept of the "Cosmic Liturgy" is taken from Stăniloae, who speaks of it in his *Spiritualitate și Comuniune*, 14–16, and in "Liturghia Comunității," 388–9.

59. Achimescu, *Budism și Creștinism*, 336. In a similar way, the American Orthodox theologian John Garvey affirms that "the Buddhist who is moved to compassion by the teaching of the Buddha . . . will be saved because in all these movements of the soul and heart there are seeds of the Word. That Word, we must as Christians insist, is Jesus Christ, who alone is the salvation of human beings" (Garvey, *Seeds of the Word*, 126).

60. For instance, he expresses his firm conviction that "our salvation and the salvation of the whole world has come *only through Jesus Christ*" (Achimescu, *Budism și Creștinism*, 19). Here and elsewhere the emphasis in quotations belongs to the authors quoted unless otherwise specified.

do not give way to intolerance towards adherents of other religions.[61] In a similar way to the thought expressed in the *Nostra Aetate*, he argues that "Orthodox theologians want to take all positive elements in other religions as opportunities for mutual understanding" and as "forms of seeking God."[62] All other religions are said to be driven by the search for the lost paradise and as such "need the true salvation" which is in Jesus Christ.[63] As such Buddhism is seen as a "simple worldview conceived by the means of pure analysis and self-knowledge" while Christianity is "a religion by excellence, which is founded on a supreme authority, that of the revealed God."[64] As we can see, a firm proclamation of Orthodox beliefs is stated as foundational for dialogue with other religions. However, what is lacking is a openness similar to that of the Catholic Church for an actual dialogue with these religions. This is a project to which my book aims to contribute.

### 1.3.3 The Dalai Lama's Openness to All Religions

Buddhist inclusivism originates in the Mahayana doctrine of skilful means, according to which non-Buddhist teachers, whether historical or legendary (for instance the *kami* in Shintoism), are *bodhisattvas* who use skilful means for bringing people closer to enlightenment.[65] This line of thought is followed by Tenzin Gyatso (b. 1935), the 14th Dalai Lama. In his vision, the purpose of different religions is "to cure the pains and unhappiness of the human mind" and therefore each of us needs to pick the one "which will better cure a particular person."[66] In an interview he expressed his view that "Buddhism is the best," but this does not mean it is the "best for everyone."[67]

61. Ibid., 22–23.

62. Ibid., 23. In a similar way to the *Nostra Aetate*'s acknowledging "rays of Truth" in other religions, Peter Bouteneff argues that "Orthodox Christians *admit truth in other faiths*" (Bouteneff, "Foreword," in Garvey, *Seeds of the Word*, 11. However, there is no statement on which these truths in other religions may actually be.

63. Achimescu, *Budism și Creștinism*, 23.

64. Ibid., 25.

65. I will refer to the doctrine of skilful means in section 2.5.

66. Dalai Lama, *Spiritual Advice*, 16. In an interview he expressed his thought that the purpose of all religions is "to make man a better human being" (Dalai Lama, *Universal Responsibility*, 22).

67. Interview taken by James Beverley. The same thought is expressed in an interview published in *Universal Responsibility*, 20. From an ultimate point of view, *nirvana* can be achieved only by Buddhists, for liberation is a state in which "a mind that understands the (empty) sphere of reality annihilates all defilements in the (empty) sphere of reality" (Dalai Lama, "'Religious Harmony' and Extracts from the Bodhgaya Interviews," in Griffiths, ed., *Christianity through Non-Christian Eyes*, 169).

The best religion for Christians is Christianity. From the Dalai Lama's Buddhist perspective, Jesus was a *bodhisattva* teaching a suitable truth for his followers in a particular historical and cultural setting. In his words, "at a certain period, certain era, he appeared as a new master, and then because of circumstances, he taught certain views different from Buddhism."[68] Therefore, Buddhists and Christians should not stumble over philosophical contradictions such as the uniqueness of Jesus or the issue of a creator God. Such contradictions are real, but should not deter us from achieving "permanent human happiness." For some people the idea of a creator God is "beneficial and soothing" while for others the rejection of this idea is "more appropriate."[69] Ultimately, belief in God is just another instance of using skilful means. As a result, the importance of Buddhist-Christian dialogue lies in improving the horizontal dimension of existence. He exhorts us: "Let us just be side by side—helping, respecting, and understanding each other—in common effort to serve mankind."[70]

For the Dalai Lama interfaith dialogue should not be about arguing and proselytising. Religionists should rather exhort each other "to follow their own beliefs as sincerely and as truthfully as possible," for all world religions are helpful ways of guiding people of different inclinations to the best fulfilment.[71] The reason why the Dalai Lama is so confident in affirming that all religious traditions can provide suitable spiritual guiding is his belief in rebirth. He argues that since even Buddhists need many lifetimes to reach *nirvana*, how much more will adherents of other religions also undergo rebirth, so "there is no hurry" to reach liberation.[72] This conviction makes him very respectful towards other religions. However, he is not a pluralist, for he affirms that the many rebirths one has to endure will eventually lead him or her to find enlightenment in a Buddhist tradition. In the specific case of Christians, the Buddhist doctrine of the six realms of rebirth would

---

68. Same interview as above. In one of the sermons delivered at the John Main Seminar in 1994, in which he comments on key passages in the Gospels, he praises Jesus as being "either a fully enlightened being or a bodhisattva of a very high spiritual realization" (Dalai Lama, *Good Heart*, 83).

69. Dalai Lama, "Religious Harmony," 167–68.

70. Ibid., 164. The Dalai Lama is against a syncretistic mixture of Christianity and Buddhism, which would be an attempt "to put a yak's head on a sheep's body" (*Good Heart*, 105. The same warning appears in *Ancient Wisdom*, 237.) However, he argues that Christians can use Buddhist meditation, ideas and practices for "the teachings of love, compassion, and kindness are present in Christianity and also in Buddhism" (ibid., 167.).

71. Ibid., 169.

72. Ibid.

allow them to reach a personal afterlife in the *Tushita* heavens.[73] Nevertheless, immortality in a Buddhist heaven has a limited lifespan, lasting only until one's merits are exhausted, when a new human existence necessarily follows. True liberation can only be *nirvana*, and thus he is consistent with Buddhist inclusivism.

### 1.3.4 John Makransky and the Superiority of Buddhism

John Makransky teaches Buddhism and Comparative Theology at Boston College and is also a Tibetan Buddhist meditation teacher installed as a lama in the *Nyingma* Tibetan tradition. Although, as an inclusivist, he holds that there are countless ways in which truth expresses itself and thus all religious traditions "are limited by historically conditioned assumptions,"[74] he is very clear on the superiority of Buddhism and its unique effectiveness for achieving enlightenment. The practices taught by the Buddha not only lead one to achieving "fullest enlightenment," but among all other versions of salvation the Buddhist path leads to "the most complete form of liberation possible for human beings."[75] Therefore he rejects the pluralist demand that each religion should renounce its claims of superiority "of practice and goal."[76] Even if one would be concerned only with the horizontal dimension of existence, Buddhist practices should be seen as "uniquely effective for undercutting" violence in our world.[77]

Makransky's view is that the ultimate truth on which all religions feed is the *dharmakaya*, as formulated in Mahayana Buddhism,[78] but this does not mean that their followers will all reach "the same soteriological result."[79] A theist's belief in a personal God as Ultimate Reality hinders the realization of emptiness.[80] A Hindu type of yoga practice would allow one to realize some aspect of the Buddha nature, but not the doctrine of not-Self and *shunyata*.[81] Christian rites, such as the Catholic Mass, could be of help in cutting grasping and in raising awareness on human nature, but remain

73. Ibid.

74. John Makransky, "Buddhist Inclusivism: Reflections Toward a Contemporary Buddhist Theology of Religions," in Schmidt-Leukel, ed., *Buddhist Attitudes*, 64.

75. Ibid., 66.

76. Ibid.

77. Ibid.

78. I will refer to this doctrine in section 2.8.

79. Makransky, "Buddhist Inclusivism," 61.

80. Ibid., 61–62.

81. Ibid., 62.

just skilful means which point to the need of realizing the ultimate truth of emptiness.[82] In short, other religious rites and beliefs are of some worth, but cannot provide liberation from rebirth, for only Buddhist practices offer a "direct knowledge of the Absolute."[83]

## 1.3.5 The Paternalistic Character of Inclusivism

In conclusion to this section on inclusivism, I need to note its weakness of forming an *a priori* judgement of other religions and of ignoring what is particular to them. Inclusivists can consider other traditions as being fulfilled by their own only at the cost of ignoring fundamental doctrines that build up those traditions. In the words of Paul Knitter, inclusivists "don't really let that otherness reveal itself to them because they have already *included* the other in their own world of seeing and understanding."[84] It is untenable to claim that one's own tradition can better grasp what all others are really after, especially as most inclusivists have limited knowledge of other traditions. In its essence, to look at Buddhism through the lens of Rahner's inclusivism is to claim that Buddhists do not know that their real goal is Christ and as such that they are anonymous Christians. In a similar way, Achimescu claims that the Buddhist "forgets" that the world is the creation "of the personal God."[85]

There is little doubt on how a Buddhist would meet such a working methodology, for it does not leave much space for dialogue.[86] Although the Dalai Lama seems to have a more balanced position on Buddhist-Christian dialogue by respecting all religious traditions, his inclusivism is as paternalistic as the "Anonymous Christianity" of Rahner.[87] One the one hand,

82. John Makransky, "Buddhist Perspectives," 360. He affirms he attends the Catholic Mass as a Buddhist, despite being aware that it "inscribes fundamental Christian doctrines of the Cross, Resurrection, Body of Christ—the agapeic dynamism of trinitarian reality" (ibid., 360).

83. Makransky, "Buddhist Perspectives," 359.

84. Knitter, *Introducing Theologies of Religions*, 218.

85. Achimescu, *Budism și Creștinism*, 322.

86. In fact, as Achimescu admits, it leaves a very "poor" space for dialogue (ibid., 332). His book is aimed at helping us realize the significant difference between Buddhist liberation and "the real salvation in Jesus Christ" and how far Buddhists are "from the Church of Jesus Christ, in which one can truly be saved" (333).

87. According to D'Costa, the Dalai Lama's position on other religions is a "strict form of exclusivist Tibetan Buddhism of the dGelugs variety" which proves that "inclusivism always finally collapses into exclusivism," and understanding this "helps dissolve the Romantic European view of the 'tolerant' and 'open' 'East'" (D'Costa, *The Meeting of Religions*, 78).

as I argued elsewhere, when assessing the "Jesus as *bodhisattva*" hypothesis from the perspective of history, given all the persecutions, religious wars, hatred and delusion sown in history in the name of Christ, to name him a "*bodhisattva*" would lead us to the contradictory conclusion that he was more a source of delusion than a guide towards enlightenment.[88] On the other hand, Christians cannot accept the "many rebirths" view for reaching salvation. Makransky is even more rigid than the Dalai Lama when it comes to acknowledging the value of other religions. His inclusivism hardly offers space for Buddhist-Christian dialogue, since all religious traditions, not only those of Buddhism, claim to offer a direct knowledge of their Ultimate Reality, and to possess the best means to achieve it.

## 1.4 JOHN HICK'S PLURALISM AS A "COPERNICAN REVOLUTION" IN THE THEOLOGY OF RELIGIONS

Given the non-dialogical nature of exclusivism and the paternalistic tone of inclusivism, it may seem that a better option in interfaith dialogue would be pluralism, for, as Race argues, it "moves beyond the controlling images of any of the religions."[89] There are two major kinds of pluralists. First there are those who attempt to identify a common "something" among religions, a common Ultimate Reality, or a common goal which all pursue. The best illustration of this view is the mountain peak which can be reached by several different paths. Knitter calls them "mutualists"[90] because they not only attempt to reach the same peak, but can also help each other to achieve it. When criticized for being unrealistic, its proponents claim that the true goal of religion is beyond what has been formulated so far by the traditions, i.e., there is a more fundamental Ultimate Reality which makes agreements still possible. As representatives of this group from the Christian side we have John Hick and Perry Schmidt-Leukel. A possible Buddhist candidate for this view is Thich Nhat Hanh.

A second kind of pluralism is one that does not seek for commonalities, and lets each religion define its own path and peak to be reached. Religions should be respected as they are and allowed to be totally different.

88. Valea, *The Buddha and the Christ*, 184–86.

89. Race, *Interfaith Encounter*, 30.

90. Knitter, "Buddhist and Christian Attitudes to Other Religions: A Comparison," in Schmidt-Leukel, ed., *Buddhist Attitudes*, 90. D'Costa calls the first category "unitary pluralism," the second "pluriform pluralism," and adds a third category—the "ethical pluralism" of those who place emphasis not on questions of Ultimate Reality, but rather on ethical concerns such as justice and peace (D'Costa, *Christianity and World Religions*, 9–18).

Knitter calls them "particularists,"[91] for they emphasize and hold dearly to the particular aspects of each religious tradition. A Christian representative of "particularist" pluralism is Mark Heim. In this section I will assess the pluralism of John Hick, and leave the other proposals to chapter 4.

John Hick (1922–2012) went through a dramatic shift in his religious stand towards other religions. At the age of 18, while a law student, he had the religious experience of being "born again" in the Presbyterian church and became a Christian of a "fundamentalist kind."[92] But his certitudes were shaken by his encounter with the plurality of world religions. It led him to leave the "Ptolemaic theology" of the uniqueness of Christ as *the* way of salvation and call for a "Copernican revolution" in the theology of religions in which all gravitate around the same God.[93] For this reason he considers the Catholic attempts following Vatican II, which allow some degree of revelation to other religions, to be unhappy compromises resembling the "epicycles" theory of earlier astronomy to correct the aberrations of Ptolemy's earth-centred universe.

As a result of his interaction with his colleague Abe while teaching at the Claremont Graduate School, Hick realized that he needed to accommodate Buddhism in this theory of religious pluralism and switched from "God-centredness" to "Real-centredness," which would be a more "familiar" term for all religions.[94] His fundamental assumption became that all religions have a partial knowledge of a hidden Ultimate Reality (the "Real") and thus none is entitled to make exclusivistic claims. In Kantian terms, he affirms that religions are "phenomenal manifestations of the noumenal Real-in-itself"[95] or "different ways of experiencing, conceiving, and living in relation to an ultimate divine Reality which transcends all our varied visions of it."[96] As a result, the purpose of every religion, including Christianity, would be "the transformation of human existence from self-centredness to Reality-centredness."[97]

There are two serious issues with Hick's approach. First, since the "noumenal Real-in-itself" cannot be captured in words, his own version of religious pluralism must also belong to the "phenomenal manifestations"

---

91. Knitter, "Buddhist and Christian Attitudes," 90.

92. Hick, *God Has Many Names*, 14.

93. Hick, *God and the Universe of Faiths*, 131.

94. Hick, *An Interpretation of Religion*, 11.

95. Hick, *A Christian Theology of Religions*, 46.

96. Hick, *An Interpretation of Religion*, 235–36.

97. Ibid., 36. In his view, the element that identifies "a religious tradition as a salvific human response to the Real" is the "production of saints," for they all display similar moral qualities (ibid., 307).

of the Real and be seen itself as one of the many which gravitate around it. In other words, it cannot be allowed to offer a higher perspective on Ultimate Reality than all others. Second, Hick found the concept of *shunyata* as taught by Abe to be "remarkably like" his view of "the Real" and "the perfect expression of the key concept that is required for a religious understanding of religious plurality."[98] But by acknowledging that "the Real" is equivalent to *shunyata*, he no longer is consistent with the equal stand of all religions before a common centre. Buddhism would be closer, if not possessing the centre itself.

Referring to the "uniqueness" of Christianity, Hick argues that Christology followed a development similar to that of the doctrine of the Buddha. As in early Buddhism the Buddha was seen as a man who found enlightenment as a result of his earnest search for truth, and only later, in the Mahayana, was proclaimed the incarnation of a pre-existing Buddha,[99] in a similar way the theologians of the early church proclaimed the man Jesus to be the incarnation of a pre-existing Son of God. This parallel development would allow us to find an equivalence between the *Trikaya* doctrine of Mahayana Buddhism, in which "the transcendent Buddha is one with the Absolute," and the Christian doctrine of the Trinity, which proclaims that "the eternal Son is one with the Father."[100] In Hick's view, the proclamation of Jesus to be the Son of God would be a result of "a tendency of the religious mind" of exalting the founder of a certain tradition[101] and therefore language of incarnation should be reinterpreted, for the incarnation is just "a mythological idea, a figure of speech, a piece of poetic imagery."[102] A similar reinterpretation is needed for the story of the resurrection, for in his view one cannot be sure what really happened back then in Palestine.[103]

As we can see, Hick either ignores or plainly rejects essential Christian doctrines. His view of the Real is incompatible not only with all Christian traditions, but with Buddhist traditions as well. As we will see in the next

98. John Hick, "The Meaning of Emptiness," in Abe, ed., *A Zen Life*, 147–48; see also Hick, *A Christian Theology of Religions*, 60–64. However, he is wrong in stating an equivalence between the Buddhist *dharmakaya* and the Hindu *paramartha-satya*, which represents the substantial ground of being (Hick, *An Interpretation of Religion*, 287).

99. Hick, "Jesus in the World Religions," in Hick, ed., *The Myth of God Incarnate*, 169. In his words, "the human Gautama has been exalted into an eternal figure of universal significance" (ibid.).

100. Ibid.

101. Ibid., 170.

102. Hick, *God Has Many Names*, 74.

103. Hick, "Jesus in the World Religions," 170.

chapter, there cannot be any substantial reality in Buddhism which could have the role of Hick's "Real." Therefore Hick's view of religious pluralism is far from being fair to either Christian or Buddhist traditions. In the end, his theory of the "Real" is both paternalistic and unrealistic.[104] It is an unrealistic attempt to formulate a higher ground in interfaith dialogue, above the particular traditions, and thus susceptible to formulating a new one.[105]

## 1.5 COMPARATIVE THEOLOGY AS A NEW APPROACH IN INTERFAITH DIALOGUE

We have seen that the three theologies of religions discussed in this chapter each have their positive and negative aspects in dealing with the tension between commitment to one's own tradition and openness to others. As Cornille observes, "strong religious commitment coincides with religious intolerance, while attitudes of openness toward the truth of other religions somehow go together with a looser relationship to the truth of one's own tradition."[106] In this context we must ask ourselves whether it is possible to find a practice of dialogue which avoids the risk of a particular tradition-centred arrogance (Buddhist or Christian) on the one hand, and an unprincipled accommodation on the other. A possible answer can be found in the new approach of comparative theology, which promotes both commitment to one's tradition, but without being bound to exclusivism, and openness towards other religious traditions, but without compromising one's own. This new approach was started by Francis Clooney and James Fredericks in the late 1980s as an attempt to "suggest a way in which we may rethink faith by means of a critical reflection on the texts and practices of other religious paths."[107]

A fundamental requirement of comparative theology, in Fredericks' words, is "to understand the Other in a way that does not annul the Other's alterity."[108] As such, this approach would leave space to the Other, and not

104. As Fredericks argues,"[P]luralists, like inclusivists, enter into interreligious dialogue knowing more about other religious believers than these same believers know about themselves" (Fredericks, *Faith among Faiths*, 109).

105. For a further criticism of Hick's pluralism see Netland, *Encountering Religious Pluralism*, 231–46.

106. Cornille, *The Im-Possibility of Interreligious Dialogue*, 59.

107. Fredericks, "Introduction," in Clooney, ed., *New Comparative Theology*, ix. The term was already in use in the nineteenth century. Of the history of its use see Clooney, "Comparative Theology," in Webster et al., eds., *Oxford Dictionary of Systematic Theology*, 653–59.

108. Fredericks, "Introduction," in Clooney, ed., *New Comparative Theology*, xiii.

subsume his or her tradition into one's own. Comparative theology avoids the extremes of demonizing the others and withdrawing from dialogue, on the one hand, and that of assimilating other traditions to the extent of forgetting our own identity, on the other. In contrast to exclusivist approaches such as that of the Panadura debate, Clooney emphasizes that "[c]omparative theology is not primarily about which religion is the true one, but about learning across religious borders in a way that discloses the truth of my faith, in the light of their faith."[109] And in contrast to a pluralist approach, one can speak with confidence of a genuine faith to which he or she claims allegiance. As Clooney defines it, comparative theology "marks acts of faith seeking understanding which are rooted in a particular faith tradition" and only from that precise framework does one "venture into learning from one or more other faith traditions."[110] Following this approach, a religious tradition can enrich the other not by syncretistic means, but by providing a better perception of one's own when viewing it in the light of the other. In other words, interfaith dialogue can help us to appropriate the truths of our own religious tradition in a new and unexpected way by looking back on ourselves through someone else's eyes.

A theology of religions is concerned mainly with answering the question of how those of other religious traditions can be saved and less with familiarizing theologians with those traditions on their own terms. In contrast, in the words of Fredericks, comparative theology "does not start with a grand theory of religion in general that claims to account for all religions"[111] and does not look for a "lowest common denominator" of all religions, including Christianity.[112] As a scholar who has applied the method of comparative theology to Buddhist-Christian dialogue, he invites Christians to cross over "into the world of another religious believer," to learn "the truths that animate the life of that believer," and then to return to their home tradition "transformed by these truths now able to ask new questions about Christian faith and its meaning for today."[113] In other words, Christians should "learn something about Buddhism on its own terms,"[114] and only afterwards build a theology of religions. One is entitled to build an exclusivist, inclusivist or pluralist theology of religions only after knowing the "Other" on his or her

109. Clooney, *Comparative Theology*, 15–16.

110. Ibid., 10. As Fredericks argues, "loss of commitment to the home tradition may make the work of comparison no longer theological" (Fredericks, "Introduction," in Clooney, ed., *New Comparative Theology*, xiii).

111. Fredericks, *Faith among Faiths*, 167.

112. Ibid., 167–8.

113. Fredericks, *Buddhists and Christians*, xii.

114. Ibid., and Fredericks, *Faith among Faiths*, 170.

own terms, not just on the basis of a set of strong theological convictions on the "truth" of one's own faith.[115] The outcome of the comparative work is neither an apologetic tool aimed to counteract other religions, nor a syncretistic blend of traditions, but mutual learning across religious borders. As one can expect, Fredericks argues that "sometimes the correlation will be a recognition of similarity, sometimes of difference."[116]

However, we cannot ignore the fact that the comparatist theologian (hereafter called a comparativist) starts to look at other religious traditions with a set of foundational convictions that will influence the outcome of his or her comparative study. Since there always exists a given faith to which the comparativist belongs, even if not explicitly made known, Kiblinger expresses her concern that one's "theology of religions predetermines the outcome" of comparative theology.[117] Therefore a comparativist should disclose his or her theological views in order to be aware and make readers aware of the presuppositions and limitations of this approach. Kiblinger insists that:

> we cannot skip over getting clarity on our theological presuppositions about the other and just jump into the practice of reading, because so much hangs on *how* we read, which is determined by our theology of religions in the first place.[118]

In other words, between comparative theology and the theology of religions seems to exist a reciprocal influence of which we must be aware. A certain theology of religions is already at work when the comparativist performs a comparative study. The two leading figures in comparative theology, both Clooney[119] and Fredericks[120] disclose their views in matters of upholding a certain theology of religions by declaring themselves to be Catholic inclusivists.[121] Therefore I must be aware that in formulating an Orthodox contribution to comparative theology, I must operate on the basis of an Orthodox inclusivism. Following Clooney, I need to "articulate a viable understanding of the 'other,' in which the encountered 'other' is not

115. Fredericks, *Faith among Faiths*, 9.

116. Fredericks, "Introduction," in Clooney, ed., *New Comparative Theology*, xi.

117. Kristin Kiblinger, "Relating Theology of Religions and Comparative Theology," in Clooney, ed., *New Comparative Theology*, 25.

118. Ibid., 29.

119. Clooney, *Comparative Theology*, 16.

120. Fredericks, "Introduction," in Clooney, ed., *New Comparative Theology*, xv.

121. For Clooney the inclusivist position appears as "the most useful" for it maintains a "distinctive tension between an adherence to the universal claim of one's own religion and an acknowledgement of the working of the truth of the Christian religion outside its boundaries" (Clooney, *Theology after Vedanta*, 194–95).

manufactured to fit the comparativist's prejudices and expectations."[122] In my view, in order to meet this demand and to follow a dialogue of theological exchange in which to involve Orthodox Christianity, I need to state a theme of common interest for both Christians and Buddhists which should act as a precise doctrinal lens through which I could appropriately assess Buddhist-Christian dialogue. Although it is not easy to find a theme of equal interest for both Christians and Buddhists, after much pondering I take it to be the concept of human perfection as defined in the tradition of Eastern Orthodoxy,[123] and in the tradition of Mahayana Buddhism.[124] One is called deification (*theosis*) and the other Buddhahood.

There are not many attempts to understand the Christian ideal of perfection by Buddhist scholars. The only one that I am aware of is Medagampala Sumanashanta who successfully completed a PhD thesis on this topic.[125] He compared and contrasted the Theravada Buddhist ideal of perfection as *arhathood*, as presented by Buddhaghosa in the fifth century AD, with the Methodist ideal of perfection as sanctification, as presented by John Wesley, the founder of Methodism in the eighteenth century. His justification for choosing perfection as relevant for both traditions is that "[b]oth Buddhism and Christianity begin with the premise that mankind is imperfect but that Perfection in some sense or other is both a possibility and the true goal or purpose of man's life in the world."[126] As Sumanashanta did, I also assume that perfection is a theme of ultimate importance for all Buddhist and Christian traditions which will be addressed in this book. Buddhists and Christians alike are meant to strive for perfection, and this should bear fruit in their dialogue. Therefore, in the next two chapters, I will perform a study of human perfection in the traditions of Mahayana Buddhism and Orthodox Christianity, but unlike Sumanashanta, who focused on studying perfection *per se* in two traditions, I will use my findings for assessing several important voices in contemporary Buddhist-Christian dialogue and then for formulating an Orthodox contribution to comparative theology.

Another principle in comparative theology, as formulated by Clooney, is that "[b]ecause the comparative theologian is engaged in the study of a religious tradition other than her own, she needs to be an academic scholar

---

122. Ibid., 7.

123. The simple term "Christianity" is used in this book when certain aspects of doctrine are common to mainstream Christian traditions.

124. Although it is notoriously difficult to define *the* Mahayana view on a certain issue all Mahayana Buddhists take Buddhahood as their ultimate goal.

125. Sumanashanta, *A Comparison of Buddhist and Christian Perfection*.

126. Ibid., 1.

proficient in the study of that religion, or at least seriously in learning from academic scholars."[127] In order to make sure that Eastern Orthodoxy will be properly represented in Buddhist-Christian dialogue, and since my contribution to comparative theology is intended as a *Romanian* Orthodox contribution, I will present the Orthodox view of human perfection as I find it expressed by Dumitru Stăniloae, the most significant Romanian Orthodox theologian. However, this will not be a simple descriptive presentation. In order to keep the proper balance in dialogue I will first bring into discussion the Mahayana Buddhist perspective on human perfection, and then present the Orthodox view in both descriptive and comparative terms. I assume that this double perspective will help me ground an informed basis for formulating an Orthodox contribution to comparative theology which would be respectful towards both traditions.

127. Clooney, *Comparative Theology*, 12.

# 2

# An Examination of Doctrinal Presuppositions in Mahayana Buddhism as a Foundation for Assessing Buddhist-Christian Dialogue

## Human Perfection as Buddhahood

IN ORDER TO PRESENT the Buddhist ideal of human perfection I will follow four prestigious British scholars of Buddhism: Rupert Gethin, Steven Collins, Peter Harvey and Paul Williams.

Rupert Gethin is Professor of Buddhist Studies at the Department of Religion and Theology, University of Bristol, Director of the Centre for Buddhist Studies, and President of the Pali Text Society. His area of expertise is the history and development of Buddhist thought in the *Nikayas* (the collections of sutras of early Buddhism) and the *Abhidharma* (the systematization of the doctrines expounded in the Nikayas).

Steven Collins taught at Bristol University (1980–87), Indiana University (Bloomington, 1987–89), and Concordia University (Montreal, 1989–91) before joining the University of Chicago where he currently is Professor in the Department of South Asian Languages and Civilizations. He is also a Council Member of the Pali Text Society. His field specialties include "social and cultural history of Buddhism in premodern and modern South and Southeast Asia" and "Pali language and literature."[1]

1. Source: University of Chicago website, Division of the Humanities/South Asian Languages & Civilizations.

Peter Harvey was Professor of Buddhist Studies at the University of Sunderland, from where he retired in October 2011. He is one of the two co-founders of the UK Association for Buddhist Studies in 1995 and is currently the editor of its journal, *Buddhist Studies Review*, as well as a member of the editorial panel of the internet *Journal of Buddhist Ethics*.

Paul Williams is Emeritus Professor of Indian and Tibetan Philosophy at the University of Bristol and was the head of its Department of Theology and Religious Studies (2000–2003). He was the initiator and from 1993 the co-director of the Centre for Buddhist Studies associated with the University of Bristol and President of the UK Association for Buddhist Studies.[2] While Gethin, Collins and Harvey are specialists mainly in early Buddhism, Williams is a recognized specialist in the Madhyamaka philosophy of Mahayana Buddhism, which is foundational for the traditions of Zen and Tibetan Buddhism, to which most Buddhists engaged in Buddhist-Christian dialogue belong.

In the first four sections of this chapter I will refer to the doctrinal foundations of early Buddhism, which we find represented today by the Theravada school in Sri Lanka and southeast Asia. Theravada Buddhists are a minority among Buddhists who engage in contemporary Buddhist-Christian dialogue. A notable exception follows the initiative of Lynn de Silva and Aloysius Pieris in Sri Lanka, who founded the Ecumenical Institute for Study and Dialogue in Colombo and one of the first journals on Buddhist-Christian dialogue in 1961, called *Dialogue*. Although both de Silva and Pieris are Christians (the first a Methodist and the second a Roman Catholic), they succeeded in engaging Buddhist scholars in Sri Lanka to contribute to a real Buddhist-Christian dialogue. As far as I know, this is the only significant initiative for dialogue between Theravada Buddhists and Christians. Unfortunately, Christian theologians in the West have given little attention to this initiative.

Many if not most Buddhists involved in Buddhist-Christian dialogue belong to either Zen or to Tibetan Buddhism, and their core philosophy depends one way or another on, or derives ultimately from, the Madhyamaka school of Mahayana Buddhism, said to have been founded by Nagarjuna in the second century AD. Madhyamaka was an influential school of Mahayana Buddhist thought in India and crucial in the transmission of Buddhist thought particularly to Tibet but also to East Asia. Therefore I will devote

2. Williams was a practitioner of Tibetan Buddhism himself for more than 20 years, led Buddhist retreats and made many contributions in the media worldwide as a Buddhist scholar. Although he converted to Roman Catholicism, he is still a fine scholar of Mahayana Buddhism whose writings can provide great help in defining the Mahayana Buddhist ideal of human perfection.

the last five sections of this chapter to the Mahayana tradition and its view of human perfection.

## 2.1 THE TEACHING ON HUMAN NATURE. THREE MAJOR DOCTRINES

What makes Buddhism so appealing today in the West is its capacity to be a religion without God, the result of an individual's search for truth, which does not require faith in an unseen God, but only in oneself. The man who opened this path is said to have been Siddhartha Gautama (Pali: Siddhattha Gotama),[3] a man who lived about two and a half millennia ago in the region of today's northern India and southern Nepal. According to the Buddhist tradition, he renounced worldly pleasures and became a *Shramana*, an ascetic who started from the grassroots of ordinary human experience to reach the ultimate truth. He defeated the veil of illusion and ignorance and became the Buddha ("the awakened one"). Any of us can reach the same truth the Buddha discovered if we are willing to engage on the way he opened. In early Buddhism he was seen as the first in status among many equals to follow him, not as the unique revealer, knower and embodiment of truth. This is one of the major differences between the Buddha, the founder of Buddhism, and Jesus Christ, the founder of Christianity. For the first, the message does not depend on the identity of the messenger, while for the second, personal identity and message stand or fall together.

As Rupert Gethin argues, "the story of the life of the Buddha is not history nor meant to be,"[4] and should rather be taken as a hagiography, a story shaped by the needs of the community that the Buddha has founded. A similar view is followed by Peter Harvey, who emphasizes that in reading the Buddha's story one should realize what is the meaning of the Buddha's life for Buddhists and what lessons must be learned from it.[5] All that matters is to have his teaching and to follow it. Therefore I will not follow the classic introduction to Buddhism of starting with the life-story of the Buddha. His teaching is all that counts for attaining perfection.

---

3. When using Buddhist terms I will use the Sanskrit transliterations, except in quotations. In the first four sections, on early Buddhism, whose writings are in Pali, at the first use I will indicate both the Sanskrit and the Pali form, and then just the Sanskrit form. Due to technical limitations I have not used the diacritical marks for Sanskrit and Pali words. Scholars do not need them to recognize these words in their original written form, and the majority of readers have nothing to gain from the diacritical marks.

4. Gethin, *The Foundations of Buddhism*, 16.

5. Harvey, *Introduction to Buddhism*, 15.

The early Buddhist view on human nature is shaped by three major doctrines, also called the three hallmarks of existence (Sanskrit: *trilakshana*, Pali: *tilakkhana*): suffering, impermanence and not-Self. What they mean and how they define human nature is the content of the first of the Four Noble Truths, which are said to have been formulated by the Buddha at his enlightenment. The First Noble Truth states that the whole of human experience is marked by suffering (Sanskrit: *duhkha*, Pali: *dukkha*). According to Collins, it is of three types:

> "Ordinary suffering" is everyday physical and mental pain, contrasted with ordinary happiness, or indifferent feelings. "Suffering through change" is the unsatisfactoriness alleged to be inherent in the fact that all feelings, all mental and physical states are impermanent and subject to change . . . The third form of dukkha is "suffering through (the fact of) conditioned existence."[6]

This quotation introduces us to the heart of the Buddhist view on human nature. Suffering is more than just physical pain; it is a condition inherent to one's unenlightened nature. Its source is the fact that everything we use to define our identity is in a process of constant transformation, being nothing more than an ephemeral product and an ephemeral cause in a very long series of interlinked events. This ephemeral status of any given being, thing or state one could think of expresses the second major doctrine associated with the First Noble Truth, the doctrine of impermanence (Sanskrit: *anitya*, Pali: *anicca*). It affirms that there is nothing in human nature or in the world of unenlightened experience that is changeless and could be called an Ultimate Reality. Everything in our psycho-physical nature or in the outside world is merely a temporary effect of certain causes, and is itself a cause in a series of further transformations.[7]

The third foundational element of Buddhism is the denial of a self as the core element that would define human nature. This is the not-Self (Sanskrit: *anatman*, Pali: *anatta*) doctrine. According to the early *Upanishads*, which were part of the Buddha's religious heritage, the self (*atman*) is an eternal and unchanging essence that represents our true nature and which is passing through innumerable bodies until it finally reaches liberation. Buddhism denies that there is any such unchanging element that could

---

6. Collins, *Selfless Persons*, 191–92. See also Gethin, *The Foundations of Buddhism*, 61 and Williams and Tribe, *Buddhist Thought*, 42–43.

7. A close concept in meaning is that of momentariness, according to which all existence—material or mental, "is produced by a sequence of 'moments' (*khana*), of minute, temporally 'atomic', particles" (Collins, *Selfless Persons*, 226).

define us.[8] What is currently called the "self" is the illusion generated by five interlinked factors called aggregates (Sanskrit: *skandha*, Pali: *khandha*): form (*rupa*), sensation (*vedana*), perception (*samjna*), volition (*samskarah*) and consciousness (*vijnana*). *Form* is the body with its six sense organs[9] and the objects they sense. The senses generate *sensations* of pleasure, aversion or indifference. The process of organizing and labeling them into categories is called *perception*. As a result, *volitional acts* are initiated in response to the objects of sensory experience, which bear consequences in this and further lives. Finally, *consciousness* is "an awareness of ourselves as thinking subjects having a series of perceptions and thoughts."[10] It gives the impression that one is a distinct agent of cognition, that there is a self doing the observing and responding to the objects of perception, when in fact it is only the end result of a process dependent on sensory input.

In a famous discourse the Buddha proceeded to analyze the five aggregates and proved that none of them has the function of the self (*atman*) as found in Hinduism.[11] All five are impermanent and to believe otherwise would generate attachments and only lead to suffering. Therefore one should not speculate on whether the Buddha did or did not actually exclude the existence of a self behind the aggregates.[12] The human being is nothing but a series of impermanent physical and mental processes, a mere heap of five aggregates, or to be technically more precise, "a particular, individual combination of changing mental and physical processes, with a particular karmic history."[13] As Gethin explains: "My sense of self is both logically and emotionally just a label that I impose on these physical and mental phenomena in consequence of their connectedness."[14]

---

8. Buddhism rejects the Hindu view of the self (*atman*) as "something wholly free from phenomenal determination, an entity independent of the process of karmic conditioning" (ibid., 95).

9. There are six senses because in Indian philosophy the mind is also called a sense organ, as it senses the world of ideas and thoughts, just as the other five sense the five aspects of the material world.

10. Gethin, *The Foundations of Buddhism*, 136.

11. *Anattalakkhana Sutra*, in Bodhi, *The Connected Discourses of the Buddha*, 901–3.

12. Collins discusses the views of several Buddhist scholars on the issue of admitting or not a substantial self behind the aggregates. Rhys Davids, R. C. Zaehner, S. Radhakrishnan, and Coomaraswamy do not exclude it (Collins, *Selfless Persons*, 7–9), while Oldenberg and Stcherbatsky view the not-Self doctrine as leading to nihilism (ibid., 11–12). Paul Williams argues that if the Buddha had accepted a self behind the aggregates he would have certainly said it. He could not have omitted such an essential doctrine in his teaching (Williams, *Buddhist Thought*, 60).

13. Harvey, *Introduction to Buddhist Ethics*, 36.

14. Gethin, *The Foundations of Buddhism*, 139.

The "connectedness" that holds human beings together is affirmed by the Buddha as the chain of conditioned arising (Sanskrit: *pratityasamutpada*, Pali: *paticcasamuppada*), a series of twelve links, each generating the next without the need of a permanent self.[15] What truly characterizes human existence is suffering, impermanence and not-Self. They are interconnected and inseparable. Impermanence leaves no room for a self as a permanent entity to define a human being. Since one is not aware of it, he or she suffers. This "unawareness" of how things really are is called ignorance (Sanskrit: *avidya*, Pali: *avijja*), a fundamental concept in Indian philosophy. Ignorance means alienation from the truth, not knowing the world as it is, and having the wrong picture of it. It is the root cause of human existential suffering.

The Second Noble Truth states that the cause of suffering is craving (Sanskrit: *trishna*, Pali: *tanha*), which is the desire to experience (the illusion of) permanence, of having a self and of living in a permanent world. Craving is more than simply wanting something; it is a deep thirst for the objects of sensory experience. This "thirst" for the wrong things has its roots in ignorance. Human beings are craving for the wrong things because they do not know what or how the world really is. In this process the belief in a self (the "I," and what is "mine") as the potential beneficiary of the objects of craving is strengthened. This is so because fundamentally all forms of craving are linked to a hidden belief in a self and its related aspects such as "who am I?" and "what is mine?."

## 2.2 KARMA AND REBIRTH

As in other Indian religions, the result of ignorance is that a mechanism of causality called karma becomes operational. Karma is the mechanism which brings about rebirth (*samsara*), i.e., the enactment of another series of five aggregates in a further existence as a sentient being as a result of one's present ignorance.[16] What one experiences in the present is a consequence

15. The twelve links in this chain are the following: spiritual ignorance, mental constructions, discriminative consciousness, name-and-body, six senses, sensory stimulation, feeling, craving, grasping, becoming, birth, and ageing-and-death ("*Mahanidana Sutta*: The Great Discourse on Origination," in Walshe, *The Long Discourses of the Buddha*, 223–26. See also Gethin, *The Foundations of Buddhism*, 141–42; Harvey, *Introduction to Buddhism*, 54–56; Williams, *Buddhist Thought*, 62–72).

16. The mechanism of karma was first stated by the Upanishads, which see desire as the key element that starts the reincarnation chain: "And (here they say that) a person consists of desires. And as is his desire, so is his will; and as is his will, so is his deed; and whatever deed he does, so will he reap" (*Brihadaranyaka Upanishad* 4,4,5, Navlakha, in *Upanishads*). Here "desire" means thirst for experiencing the illusion of the physical world, and as a consequence what one will "reap" is karma's retribution in a further life.

of past causes, and present mental states expressed as thoughts and deeds become causes which bear fruit in further existences. Conversely, what one will reap in further existences as a sentient being is the result of what was sown in the mind in his or her present life. The teaching of not-Self doctrine does not involve the annihilation of being at death, nor does it make karma unoperational. In Buddhism, karma and rebirth operate without the need of a self. In other words, it is not a self (*atman*) that reincarnates, but the stream of mental flow is reborn in a new temporary form. In other words, only karmic forces pass from one life to another like a force devoid of ontological substance.[17] To say that a certain *person* is reborn as such or such being is a mere convention of speech.[18] The use of pronouns and names is a conventional method of talking about a particular collection of physical and mental states, or a temporary heap of five aggregates. In Buddhist thought, it is the karmically determinative forces within the mind stream that generate another set of aggregates in the form of a new sentient being. But since we must stick to conventions of speech in order to communicate, I will continue to use pronouns and names, and instead of using the complicated formula "a particular impermanent heap of five aggregates" is reborn, I will simply affirm "a person" is reborn.

After death one can be reborn in one of six possible realms: as a god, a human being, a ghost, an *asura* (an anti-god), an animal or in a hell. These realms are obviously just temporary destinations, as one will stay in a certain realm only as long as the effect of karma lasts. The inferior destinies are the result of letting one's mind be darkened by the three poisons—greed (*raga, lobha*), aversion (*dvesha, dosa*) and delusion (*avidya, avijja*). Higher forms of rebirth—as that of a god or a privileged human being—are the result of cultivating the opposite states of mind: non-attachment, loving-kindness and wisdom.[19] The gods have attained their status by cultivating

---

17. In the *Milinda Panha* (5,5) we find two illustrations to explain rebirth without a self: the flame of an oil-lamp is lighted from another lamp without substantial transfer and the verse is learned by the pupil from his teacher also without substantial transfer (Pesala, *The Debate of King Milinda*, 23).

18. Gethin, *The Foundations of Buddhism*, 146. According to the distinguished Indian scholar Surendranath Dasgupta, when the Buddha was referring to his previous lives "he only meant that his past and his present belonged to one and the same lineage of momentary existences" (Dasgupta, *A History of Indian Philosophy*, 118).

19. Since these positive states of mind can also lead to enlightenment, to which I will refer later, I must specify that the higher forms of rebirth, as for instance that of a god, are attained as a result of cultivating non-attachment, loving-kindness and wisdom by a Buddhist who does not follow the Buddhist path completely, or by one who is not a Buddhist, but follows these precepts intuitively (for instance the follower of a theistic religion).

these positive states of mind, but their achievement lasts only for a limited time, and therefore one should not simply seek a better rebirth. Gods, as all other sentient beings, are only temporary products of rebirth. They too are ignorant, impermanent and suffer.

Of utmost importance for my whole project is to emphasize the fact that the fundamental doctrines of suffering, impermanence and not-Self leave no room in Buddhism for a creator God as Ultimate Reality.[20] *All* beings are the result of beginningless processes of rebirth. Although, as we have seen, Buddhism does not deny the existence of "gods" and of other supernatural beings, they are mere forms in which a particular heap of aggregates can be reborn, according to the mental states cultivated during a human existence. In Harvey's words, "Buddhism sees no need for a creator of the world, as it postulates no ultimate beginning to the world, and regards it sustained by natural laws."[21] Buddhism does not admit an Ultimate Reality in the form of a permanent and changeless God, for it is a form of delusion and attachment which would ultimately bring suffering and rebirth. All gods were once humans that gained great merits, but will nevertheless suffer rebirth as humans or worse when the store of merits that promoted them to a rebirth as a god is depleted. Despite their merits, they still have not achieved the right knowledge and liberation from illusion.

Since the series of rebirths extends infinitely into the past, the Buddha criticized the idea of a creator God as found in Hinduism, considering it the product of ignorance. According to the first *Sutra* of the *Digha Nikaya* (the *Brahmajala Sutra*), the Hindu creator god Brahma is merely the first product of an everlasting and cyclic manifestation of the world.[22] He was the first being to be manifested at the beginning of a new cycle and wished the company of other beings. When he noticed the manifestation of all other beings, Brahma thought he had created them and proclaimed himself the creator god. Therefore theistic Hinduism is nothing but a form of delusion followed by those who accept Brahma's own delusion. By extension this can be said against the Christian view of God as well. To believe that Buddhist arguments against the concept of a creator God are directed only against the Hindu versions of which the Buddha was aware and not against the God of Christianity "is simply wrong" for, according to Williams, "there can be no creator of everything."[23]

20. Collins, *Selfless Persons*, 5.

21. Harvey, *Introduction to Buddhism*, 36.

22. "Brahmajala Sutta: The Supreme Net," in Walshe, *The Long Discourses of the Buddha*, 75–76.

23. Paul Williams, "Aquinas Meets the Buddhists: Prolegomenon to an Authentically Thomas-ist Basis for Dialogue," in Fodor and Bauerschmidt, eds., *Aquinas in*

Since this is the condition of gods in Buddhism, to hold a firm belief in a personal form of Ultimate Reality is an illusion, a view that leads to attachment and thus will ultimately bring suffering and rebirth. To affirm belief in God as in Christianity is against the fundamental Buddhist teachings of impermanence and not-Self. Not only an Ultimate Reality as a personal God, but *any* kind of substantial Ultimate Reality is denied (such as the Brahman of Hinduism) for it would contradict impermanence.[24] If we are to define what Ultimate Reality is in early Buddhism, it is a *truth* one has to realize, as the facts of suffering, impermanence and not-Self. Since this *truth* is foundational in Buddhism, there cannot be any sort of substantial Ultimate Reality as the first cause or ground of existence.

## 2.3 THE MEANING OF ENLIGHTENMENT

The Third Noble Truth states a logical conclusion following the first and the second. Since the cause of suffering is craving, the cessation of craving will lead to the cessation of suffering. If craving ceases, ignorance is defeated and one becomes enlightened. The shortest definition of enlightenment would be that of "seeing things as they really are."[25] It is a valid definition in all traditions of Buddhism. The state in which the enlightened monk exists while alive, in early Buddhism, is called "nirvana with a remainder" (Sanskrit: *sopadhisheshanirvana*; Pali: *sa-upadisesanibbana*).[26] It means that one is "released from desire and suffering, but still has a psycho-physical name-and-form as the basis of continued life."[27] The word "nirvana" (Pali: *nibbana*) suggests that something has been "extinguished" or "blown out." It does not refer to the annihilation of a self, because there is no self at the core of human existence, but rather to the annihilation of the fires that fuel re-

---

*Dialogue*, 90. According to Williams, "Buddhists have no objection to the existence of the Hindu gods, although they deny completely the existence of God as spoken of in e.g. orthodox Christianity, understood as the omnipotent, omniscient, all-good, and primordially existent creator deity, who can be thought of as in some sense a person" (Williams, *Buddhist Thought*, 4). See also Williams, *Songs of Love*, 2.

24. Collins, *Selfless Persons*, 97.

25. Ibid., 92. Williams also uses this formula. For instance, he states: "From the beginning the Buddhist tradition has characterized enlightenment as "seeing things the way they really are" (*yathabhutadarshana*), a seeing which differs in some crucial way from a perception of the way things appear to be to the unenlightened person" (Paul Williams, "Non-conceptuality, critical reasoning and religious experience. Some Tibetan Buddhist discussions," in McGhee, ed., *Philosophy, Religion and the Spiritual Life*, 189–90).

26. Gethin, *The Foundations of Buddhism*, 76.

27. Collins, *Selfless Persons*, 206.

birth—greed, aversion and delusion (ignorance)—and with them, the cycle of existence as an unenlightened sentient being. When the forces of craving are blocked, karma is left without a fuel, suffering ceases, and one attains enlightenment. When this person dies, he or she attains "nirvana without a remainder" (Sanskrit: *nirupadhisheshanirvana;* Pali: *anupadisesanibbana*), also known as *parinirvana,*[28] which means that the impermanent aggregates that make up personhood do not regroup in the form of a new sentient being, because the driving force of craving which generated karmically determinative forces has vanished. In the words of Gethin, when the enlightened person dies "he or she will not be reborn into some new life, the physical and mental constituents of being will not come together in some new existence, there will be no new being or person."[29]

In order to draw a proper portrait of *parinirvana*, the Buddha used the illustration of the flame of an oil lamp which goes out when wick and oil are finished.[30] Following the way human nature has been defined, *parinirvana* cannot mean eternal communion with a personal god, or a pantheistic re-absorption into an impersonal Ultimate Reality (as the *atman*-Brahman reunion of which the Hindu Upanishads speak), because such a thing does not exist. Whether *parinirvana* means annihilation at death is a highly controversial issue.[31] When asked about the status of the enlightened person after death, the Buddha answered it does not belong to any of the four possible categories: existing, non-existing, both existing and non-existing, neither existing nor non-existing.[32] He gave such answers to discourage philosophical speculation, which would fuel attachment to views and hinder one's progress towards enlightenment. Since there is no permanent "something," one should not attempt to define *nirvana* in terms of the annihilation of "something." In the words of Harvey, *nirvana* "has nothing in it which could support the feeling of I-ness; for this can only arise with respect to the *khandhas.*"[33]

28. Gethin, *The Foundations of Buddhism,* 76.

29. Ibid.

30. This illustration is found in the *Majjhima Nikaya* 72, 19–20, in Nanamoli and Bodhi, *The Middle Length Discourses of the Buddha,* 593–94.

31. Collins mentions the position of several Western Buddhist scholars such as Oldenberg, Poussin, Burnouf and Stcherbatsky who hold an annihilationist view of *parinirvana* (Collins, *Selfless Persons,* 11–12).

32. *Majjhima Nikaya* 63,7, 536.

33. Harvey, *Introduction to Buddhism,* 52.

## 2.4 THE MEANING OF HUMAN PERFECTION IN EARLY BUDDHISM

Buddhist soteriology resembles in some ways that of the Upanishads. Both see the cause of suffering and bondage to be spiritual ignorance (*avidya*) and therefore both place great emphasis on knowing the ultimate nature of things.[34] But while the Upanishads require knowing the self (*atman*) and its ontological identity with Brahman, the impersonal Ultimate Reality, Buddhism requires knowing the ultimate truth that no such substantial ultimate reality exists. How one comes to realize it in practice is the content of the Fourth Noble Truth. The path one has to follow in order to end suffering and attain *nirvana* is called the Noble Eightfold Path as it consists of eight spiritual practices aimed at attaining perfection in ethical conduct, mental discipline and wisdom. Buddhist wisdom is the result of both a theoretical critical investigation of the world and also of experiential, direct knowledge of how it works, by means of meditation. I will not enter into details of Buddhist practice here, as it would take me beyond the purposes of this book. I would only add that Buddhist practice is primarily about training the mind to discern the true nature of things, or to use the already classic definition, to know "how things really are." It is thus not a matter of extreme asceticism, as in Jainism. As Williams states, the thirst for experiencing the world as permanent is eliminated "by mental transformation through meditation. . . . Liberation is all about the mind."[35]

For the purposes of my inquiry it is important to remember that the follower of early Buddhism must trust exclusively his or her own inner abilities, as no proper help is available from a personal god. Shortly before his death the Buddha advised his followers:

> You should live as islands unto yourselves, being your own refuge, with no one else as your refuge, with the Dhamma as an island, with the Dhamma as your refuge, with no other refuge.[36]

In early Buddhism escape from suffering is highly individualistic. One has to rely on inner strength to tame his or her own mind, i.e., to extinguish greed, aversion and delusion by cultivating non-attachment, loving-kindness and wisdom. The role of the teacher is to instruct one how to cultivate

---

34. The Upanishads shaped the course of most Indian religious traditions by stating the fundamental link between illusion (*maya*), ignorance (*avidya*), karma and reincarnation (*samsara*) and thus viewing true knowledge (*vidya*) as the condition for liberation.

35. Williams, *Buddhist Thought*, 45.

36. *Mahaparinibbana Sutra: The Great Passing*, in Walshe, *Digha Nikaya* 16, 2, 26, 245.

inner resources, as no grace is available or even conceivable. The formula of taking refuge, which one declares when entering the Buddhist community, does not contradict this individualistic approach. When the new convert to Buddhism says: "I take refuge in the Buddha, I take refuge in the *Dharma* (the teaching of the Buddha), and I take refuge in the *Sangha* (the community of Buddhist followers)," he or she does not appeal to external help or grace. Taking refuge in the Buddha is not a kind of devotion to the historical Gautama, it is not a formula for invoking *him*, but rather of expressing "reverence and gratitude" to all "previous and future Buddhas, and to the principle of enlightenment as supremely worth of attainment."[37] Taking refuge in the Buddha "can also be taken as a pointer to the faculty of wisdom developing within the practitioner."[38] In other words, it is the *teaching* of the Buddha and not the *person* of the Buddha that is essential for enlightenment.[39] The same is true about taking refuge in the Sangha. The Buddhist community is the perfect context in which the teaching is to be practiced, while taking refuge in the Dharma expresses determination to follow the path opened by the Buddha.

In early Buddhism, human perfection is a perfection of wisdom, achieved exclusively by one's own inner strength. It means becoming an enlightened being who is no longer affected by suffering and ignorance. This person is called an *arhat* (Pali: *arahat*). He or she has given up craving, has defeated suffering and ignorance, and thus attained freedom from rebirth.

## 2.5 THE NEW VISION OF MAHAYANA BUDDHISM

The element that truly characterizes Mahayana Buddhism is its emphasis on compassion, in the sense that true perfection cannot mean finding enlightenment just for oneself, while leaving all other beings behind in the world of endless rebirth.[40] The rise of this new motivation was not a sudden reformation of Buddhism; it evolved so slowly among the monks of early Buddhism that one cannot even trace its exact origin.[41]

37. Harvey, *Introduction to Buddhism*, 177.

38. Ibid.

39. According to Nathan Katz, "the only difference (between the *arhat* and the Buddha) is that of precedence, which may or may not be considered significant." In terms of spiritual knowledge and spiritual powers attained "there are no grounds for their conceptual separation" (Katz, *Buddhist Images of Human Perfection*, 96 and 117).

40. Gethin, *Foundations of Buddhism*, 228; Harvey, *Introduction to Buddhism*, 92.

41. According to Harvey, Mahayana Buddhism arose between 150 BC and AD 100 (Harvey, *Introduction to Buddhism*, 89). Williams rejects the view of several scholars, such as Etienne Lamotte and Akira Hirakawa, who argue for the lay origins of the

Once it became clearly established in India and in its various forms outside India, what all Mahayana Buddhists have in common is first of all a vision, that "of attaining full Buddhahood for the benefit of all sentient beings," so that all beings may escape suffering.[42] This is the core element that differentiates it from early Buddhism. The other two factors that triggered the rise of Mahayana Buddhism are a new status assigned to the Buddha[43] and the emergence of a new kind of Buddhist literature, said to have been "originally delivered by the Buddha himself" but "not taught until the time was ripe."[44]

In early Buddhism the Buddha was seen as a man who (re)discovered and embodied the Dharma and then made it known to his disciples. At the time of his death he left them with his teaching and nothing more. It is generally held that he did not appoint a leader or a committee to lead the Sangha after his death. Truth itself was the only help they needed to make the journey out of suffering. A new stand is clearly expressed in one of the most famous Mahayana sutras, the *Saddharmapundarika Sutra* (Sanskrit: *the Lotus of the True Law*), known by its shorter name as the *Lotus Sutra*. In this *Sutra*, unknown to early Buddhism,[45] the Buddha addresses not only his disciples, lay people or wandering mendicants who question his doctrine, but a huge audience, consisting of *arhats*, *bodhisattvas*, gods and other beings. They are presented two important new teachings: that of skilful means and that the Buddha did not abandon the world and is still around to help them.

The teaching of skilful means (*upayakaushalya*) is the object of a few very famous parables in the *Lotus Sutra* which depict how, through aeons of time, the Buddha used a large variety of teaching devices to adapt his teaching to the understanding of ignorant beings in order to help them progress towards true enlightenment, which is expressed as a new vision of

Mahayana, as a movement against monks" privileges (Lamotte) or as a development of *stupa* worship (Hirakawa) (Williams, *Mahayana Buddhism*, 22–24; and Williams and Tribe, *Buddhist Thought*, 105). A more realistic hypothesis, encouraged by the latest research on Mahayana origins, suggests that it "may have been the result of an austere . . . 'revivalist movement' that felt it was returning to the example of the Buddha himself" (Williams, *Mahayana Buddhism*, 31). A similar account is given by Gethin, who argues that the origins of Mahayana should be seen "in the activity of forest-dwelling ascetic monks attempting to return to the ideals of original Buddhism" (Gethin, *The Foundations of Buddhism*, 225).

42. Williams and Tribe, *Buddhist Thought*, 103.

43. Gethin, *Foundations of Buddhism*, 227.

44. Ibid., 225.

45. The *Lotus Sutra* was probably composed around AD 200 (Harvey, *Introduction to Buddhism*, 92).

perfection—that of reaching Buddhahood by all of them.[46] In the *Parable of the Burning House* (chapter 3) the Buddha is depicted as a father who wants to rescue his children from a house that has caught fire. He skilfully promises his stubborn children delightful toys in order to lure them out of the burning house. Each is promised a toy suited to do the trick, but in the end, when all are saved from danger, the only toy each gets is the best of them, the bullock cart. The story is an illustration of human ignorance, out of which the Buddha calls humans by using the most suited means (including *arhatship* for early Buddhism), in order to reveal finally the greatest path of all, that of becoming a Buddha oneself.

In the *Parable of the Magic City* (chapter 7), the Buddha is portrayed as a guide to a group of merchants who are tired of walking through the desert toward their destination and decide to go back. In an instant, he creates the illusion of a magic city where all find shelter and refreshment, but which vanishes the next morning when they are fit to continue the journey. The meaning of this story is that the Buddha taught *arhatship* as a limited achievement for those too ignorant ("tired") to see the true perfection of Buddhahood. In the *Parable of the Prodigal Son* (chapter 4), the way one is led from little spiritual achievements to the highest goal of Buddhahood is illustrated by the story of a prodigal son who is trained incognito by his wealthy father to rise from the condition of a beggar to that of heir of all his wealth. The *Parable of the Good Physician* (chapter 16) teaches that even the death of the Buddha was a clever teaching device for his followers. He faked his death to motivate them to follow the lesser path of *arhatship* with great ardour, until the highest path of the *bodhisattva* would be revealed. All these parables, as the *Lotus Sutra* itself,[47] teach that perfection cannot mean attaining liberation just for oneself while leaving all other sentient beings in suffering. True perfection is to become oneself a Buddha, and so to help countless other beings to escape suffering.[48]

---

46. Gethin, *Foundations of Buddhism*, 228.

47. The *Lotus Sutra* itself has become an object of veneration. Nichiren, a Japanese monk in the thirteenth century AD, came to preach that the *Lotus Sutra* is the only means for salvation in an era of religious decline and required chanting a formula of adoration of the *Sutra* (*Nam Myo ho renge kyo*). Two forms in which it survived to this day is the Nichiren Shoshu movement (for monks) and the Soka Gakkai organization (for lay people).

48. In other Mahayana sutras we can find even more dramatic ways of the Buddha using skilful means to help people towards enlightenment. For instance, Williams provides two examples from the *Upayakaushalya Sutra* in which the Buddha breaks the rules of normal conduct (Williams, *Mahayana Buddhism*, 152). The first tells the story of how the Buddha in a former life "had sexual intercourse in order to save a poor girl who threatened to die for love of him." The second example speaks of the Buddha

In order to attain Buddhahood there is a very long way to go, so one needs astronomical numbers of existences in which to grow in compassion and wisdom.[49] This long journey starts with the vow to become a *bodhisattva*, "one who is on the way of attaining perfect knowledge" and who aspires to attain full Buddhahood. He or she vows to be reborn no matter how many times it takes, no matter in which form and how much effort it would take to save all beings. In the *Bodhicaryavatara*, one of the major writings of Shantideva (the illustrious promoter of the *bodhisattva* path in the eighth century AD), the *bodhisattva* vows to become "the doctor" and "medicine" to heal all sick beings, to provide "drink and food" to eradicate hunger and thirst, and "an inexhaustible treasure" to eradicate poverty.[50] For having such a compassionate and wide vision, the followers of the new trend in Buddhism called it Mahayana ("the great vehicle"), in contrast with the traditional teaching, which they scornfully called Hinayana ("the inferior vehicle"). I will therefore make the distinction from here onwards between Mahayana Buddhism and early Buddhism, as the two major branches of Buddhism.

The *bodhisattva* path begins by a transformation of the way one sees the world and his or her role in it, and by the determination to help all other beings escape suffering by becoming oneself a Buddha.[51] This transformation is called the rising of the *bodhicitta* (the "awakening mind") and continues with the ten stages of *bodhisattva* practice, which consist in training one's mind and conduct.[52] I will mention here only two meditation patterns for cultivating compassion for all beings as a *bodhisattva* practice. The first is prescribed by Kamalashila (eighth century) and Atisha (eleventh century), the great promoters of Mahayana Buddhism in Tibet.[53] It says that since the *bodhisattva* has experienced innumerable existences in the past, due to rebirth, all other suffering beings must have once been his or her mother,

---

murdering a ferryman who planned to kill all the passengers on his ship. By acting so, the Buddha saved not only the passengers, but also the ferryman from the karmic consequences of his plan.

49. If we were to calculate the time span which was necessary for the Buddha to reach this stage, Conze reached the astronomical figure of about $3 \times 10^{51}$ years (Conze, *Buddhism*, 35). This is quite a long time, compared to the age of our universe, dated by scientists to have less than $14 \times 10^9$ years.

50. Williams, *Mahayana Buddhism*, 199.

51. Gethin, *Foundations of Buddhism*, 229.

52. For my present inquiry it is important to understand motivations and goals rather than details of Buddhist practice. As I did not enter into details of the practices associated with the Noble Eightfold Path, neither will I go into details of Buddhist practice here.

53. Williams, *Buddhist Thought*, 178.

father, and other caring beings and therefore one has a duty to repay them for their good deeds. The other meditation pattern to cultivate compassion is affirmed by Shantideva in the *Bodhicaryavatara* chapter 8, and follows the understanding that one's own suffering is like that of all other beings.[54] As Harvey argues, for Shantideva "indifference to the suffering of 'others' is as absurd as indifference to one's 'own' suffering" and as such "one should strive to prevent suffering in any being."[55]

Williams provides a careful examination of Shantideva's argument in his article "On Altruism and Rebirth."[56] Briefly paraphrased, Shantideva argues that one should realize that his or her own suffering is no more significant than the suffering of others. Since impermanence does not allow for the real preservation of the person who experiences suffering, there is no constant subject that experiences suffering from one moment to the next. Impermanence teaches that "myself" at this moment and "myself" at any later moment are not the same subject, nor is there personal continuity between "my" present existence as human, and "my" next existence as another sentient being.[57] Therefore why should I care more for removing "my" suffering than for that of "others"? In other words, since I constantly change, I have no reasons for caring more about "my" welfare in the future than for that of others. What will exist in the future is just suffering, not "my" suffering or "his" suffering. This should not lead to total passivity, but to act for removing all suffering, no matter "whose" it is.

Although this argument seems to follow from sound logical reasoning, it leads to a contradictory conclusion. Williams argues that since one cannot make sense of "free-floating" pains, or of "pains not anchored to subjects," but only of pains belonging to a subject, Shantideva's argument for removing all suffering becomes problematic.[58] If there is no difference between my pain and that of others, and there is no real "owner" of pain, there cannot be pain either, and therefore Shantideva has destroyed the *bodhisattva* path.

54. Ibid., 177.

55. Harvey, *Introduction to Buddhist Ethics*, 125; also in Collins, *Selfless Persons*, 194.

56. Williams, "On Altruism and Rebirth," in *Studies in the Philosophy of the Bodhicaryavatara*, 48–49.

57. Yet, in the *Milinda Panha*, which belongs to early Buddhism, we find that between myself now and myself at any later moment of time, or in a future existence, there is causal connectivity (chapter 2, 11–14). Instead of saying "I am not the same person," the right position is to say "I am neither the same, nor different," while between me and contemporary others there is no such causal link, so they are definitely "different."

58. Williams, "The Absence of Self and the Removal of Pain," in *Studies in the Philosophy of the Bodhicaryavatara*, 156. See also his "Response to Mark Siderits' Review," 433–34.

There really is no suffering that the *bodhisattva* could remove and thus his or her vow is irrational.[59]

One possible way to overcome this difficulty could be in seeing Shantideva's argumentation just as skilful means for justifying compassionate action. Even if there is logical consistency in Williams' deduction (dissolving the object who experiences pain leads to denying pain *per se*), one can argue that the point is not to establish *whose* pain it is. Otherwise one becomes attached to identifying a subject of pain and falls into the error of accepting the self. The selfless action required by Shantideva is intended to erase selfishness and, as such, to cultivate compassion and loving-kindness as attitudes of mind which work out one's perfection.

## 2.6 DEVOTION TO THE BUDDHA AMITABHA

The belief that Buddhas and *bodhisattvas* are ready to help one escape suffering gave rise to a variety of devotional traditions in Mahayana Buddhism. I will mention only one such being who generated a devotional cult, as he bears special importance for my study of Buddhist-Christian dialogue. This being attained the highest possible goal of perfection as the Buddha Amitabha (or Amida, in Japanese). To be able to help more effectively the ignorant beings of this decadent world to advance towards enlightenment, Amitabha manifested a "heavenly" domain where his followers can be reborn in order to attain enlightenment more easily, called a Pure Land.[60] This is not the equivalent of the temporary heavens of early Buddhism, where one collects rewards for earthly merits, but a platform for one's instruction and progress towards true enlightenment. Once reborn in Amitabha's Pure Land, called the Western Paradise (*Sukhavati*), one is able to hear the doctrine and follow it unhindered and thus attain enlightenment much more easily than in this present impure world.

In the *Sukhavativyuha Sutras*[61] we find that what one needs to do in order to be reborn in Amitabha's Pure Land is quite simple. According to the *Larger Sutra*, worshippers need to "earnestly desire it, have faith in Amitab-

---

59. Williams, "The Absence of Self and the Removal of Pain," 167–68. Williams argues that "without persons even conventionally there are no pains. Without pains there is no removal of *duhkha*. Without removal of *duhkha* there is no Buddhahood" (ibid., 174). Therefore Shantideva's argument for the removal of pain is not valid.

60. For this reason, the devotional form of Buddhism generated by Amitabha worship in Japan is called Pure Land Buddhism.

61. There are two sutras bearing this name, the *Larger* and the *Smaller Sukhavativyuha Sutra*. They have been composed at the end of the second century AD (Harvey, *Introduction to Buddhism*, 129).

ha, generate 'merit,' and dedicate this towards such a rebirth."[62] According to the *Smaller Sutra* there is a simpler condition to be met, that of "repeating and remembering Amitabha's name for several nights before death."[63] As we can see, in order to be reborn in Amitabha's Pure Land, one needs faith. According to Shandao, a Chinese worshipper of Amitabha in the seventh century, faith must be "sincere," "deep" and "accompanied by an overriding desire for rebirth in Amitabha's Pure Land of Sukhavati."[64] In practice, it has to be expressed in meditating and repeating his name (reciting the *nembutsu*), in reciting his sutras, worshipping his images, and making offerings. Enlightenment is achieved there much more easily than in this defiled world, for it would consist of "a paradise full of 'jewel-trees,' which would stimulate calm and contemplative states of mind, a realm where everything would be as beings wished, free from temptation and defilement."[65]

Honen Shonin (1133–1212) argued that in an age of utter depravation of religion (the age of *mappo*) only recourse to the Other Power of Amida can save us. In the situation in which effort in meditation and accumulation of wisdom is no longer a practical option to follow, enlightenment can be attained only by invoking Amida's name in the form of a short formula called the *nembutsu* (*namu amida butsu*—"Adoration to Amida Buddha"). For this revolutionary view of Buddhism, Honen was criticized by other Japanese Buddhists of seeking a selfish escape into Amida's Pure Land, and even of the "non-Buddhist search for heaven in another guise."[66] But although Pure Land Buddhism seems to be "contaminated" by theistic elements, one must be aware that Honen claimed to have started this tradition as a desperate solution for an age in which the traditional formulas no longer work. By no means is a Pure Land to be seen as a permanent paradise as in a theistic religion, where the saved one spends eternity in personal communion with God. Such a permanent paradise would be a realm of attachment to that god, which would only ensnare and alienate one from enlightenment.

Another important representative of the Amida devotional trend in Japan was Shinran Shonin (1173–1262), the founder of the Jodo Shin Shu ("True Pure Land") school. As a monk dedicated to his people, Shinran preached the "good news" of Amida's grace to peasants throughout Japan, thus relying on Amida's vow to save all sentient beings.[67] As his master Honen

---

62. Harvey, *Introduction to Buddhism*, 130.

63. Ibid., 130.

64. Williams, *Mahayana Buddhism*, 250.

65. Harvey, *Introduction to Buddhism*, 129.

66. Williams, *Mahayana Buddhism*, 257.

67. In his 18th vow, Amida states: "O Bhagavat, if, when I attain Buddhahood,

before him, Shinran pleaded for the attainment of *nirvana* by the exclusive means of Other Power (Japanese: *tariki*), instead of the traditional Buddhist way of using Own Power (Japanese: *jiriki*). Shinran was so pessimistic of the capacity of human nature to defeat its evil ways through Own Power that he developed an almost Calvinistic attitude to human resources for reaching enlightenment. True wisdom would then lie in recourse to Other Power (the help of Amida) instead of relying on Own Power. Although it seems to have departed from Buddhism and grounded a theistic tradition, Shin Buddhism is still a form of Buddhism. Shinran's view of faith (*shinjin*) is not a way of relating to a god as a bond of trust which becomes more and more stable, but is rather a self-abandonment to Amida and his vow, a negation of all efforts that can be counted as creating any sort of merit. In fact, this self-abandonment is the most efficient way of destroying greed, aversion and delusion, and thus constitutes enlightenment itself, attained by means of Other Power.

## 2.7 TRUE WISDOM. THE DOCTRINE OF EMPTINESS

Further developments of Mahayana thought on knowing how things really are were brought by a group of writings known as the *Prajnaparamita* ("Perfection of Wisdom") *sutras*, a group of new writings not known to early Buddhism. They provided the foundation for the doctrine of emptiness, which came about as the result of following the doctrine of not-Self (*anatman*) to its natural end, that of denying that there is *any* primary existent in *any* physical or mental aspect of the world. This is the stand taken by the Madhyamaka school of Mahayana Buddhism, and its founder Nagarjuna (end of the second century AD). In order to understand the key doctrine of emptiness I need to start from the Abhidharma philosophy of the schools of early Buddhism on the "elementary particles" of reality.

The Abhidharma texts are part of the canonical literature of early Buddhism, along with the Vinaya texts (on monastic rules) and the Sutras (the discourses of the Buddha and his disciples), which attempt to systematize the teachings of the Buddha, especially in matters of ontology. According to Abhidharma philosophy of early Buddhism, physical and mental events consist of a kind of fundamental building-blocks called *dharmas* (Pali:

---

sentient beings in the lands of the ten quarters who sincerely and joyfully entrust themselves to me, desire to be born in my land, and call my Name, even ten times, should not be born there, may I not attain perfect Enlightenment. Excluded, however, are those who commit the five gravest offenses and abuse the right Dharma" (trans. Müller from *The Larger Sukhavativyuha Sutra*).

*dhammas*) which are said to have "an inherent nature" and can "*exist* independently," i.e., can be defined without reference to other such elements.[68] For instance, the Theravada school lists 82 *dharmas*, out of which 81 are conditioned (and thus impermanent) and one is unconditioned (*nirvana*).[69] Following the early Buddhist Abhidharma, one must be aware that conditioned *dharmas* are impermanent, as they exist just for a very short time in the flux of causality.[70] *Dharmas* are generated by other *dharmas* and then cease to exist by becoming the source for those that succeed them. But since they really exist, even for a very short time, they are said to have an inherent nature (*svabhava*). Secondary existents, such as people, gods, material objects and thoughts, are combinations of *dharmas* and thus are called empty (*shunya*) of own existence. This is the Abhidharma view of *dharmas* in early Buddhism.

The *Prajnaparamita sutras* and the resulting Madhyamaka school went further in this reasoning by affirming that even *dharmas* do not have an inherent nature and that perfection of wisdom consists of seeing everything empty of inherent existence.[71] In the words of Gethin, "the idea that anything exists of and in itself is simply a trick that our minds and language play on us."[72] Therefore *dharmas* must be seen as having the nature of "dreams, magical illusions, echoes, reflected images, mirages . . . ."[73] In other words, to follow the doctrine of impermanence to its natural end takes us to see that "the ultimate truth is that dharmas too are empty of their own existence."[74] Otherwise the doctrines of impermanence and of not-Self would be compromised. That is to say, as one should see the human being merely as a product of the five aggregates, *dharmas* must also be seen as secondary existents, or products of interaction. While in the Abhidharma philosophy the property of being empty of inherent nature is applied only to the so-called secondary existents, the products of *dharmas*, we now see it applied to *dharmas* as well. Nothing exists in its own right or is causally independent. Not even *nirvana* is causally independent, since it exists on the basis of the world of *samsara*. Far from accepting that this position ruins the fundamentals of

68. Harvey, *Introduction to Buddhism*, 97.

69. Out of the 81 *dharmas* which are conditioned, 52 represent mental associates, 28 represent material form, and one stands separate as consciousness (Gethin, *Foundations of Buddhism*, 210). The Sarvastivada school lists 75 *dharmas*, while the Yogacara 100.

70. Gethin, *Foundations of Buddhism*, 210.

71. Paul Williams, "Indian Philosophy," in Grayling, ed., *Philosophy 2*, 828.

72. Gethin, *Foundations of Buddhism*, 237.

73. Ibid., 237.

74. Ibid., 245.

Buddhism, Nagarjuna argued that "'the emptiness of dharmas' (*dharma-shunyata*) is not a further teaching, but something required by the logic of 'the emptiness of persons' (*pudgala-shunyata*)."[75] One can thus redefine human nature in terms of a flux of empty *dharmas*. From a mere heap of five aggregates, as human nature is seen in the early *sutras*, we have reached the Abhidharma definition as a "linear series of momentary dharmas arising and ceasing in every moment,"[76] to end up with the view of being "just fluxes of empty '*dharmas*.'"[77]

Two misconceptions must be avoided in understanding the position of Madhyamaka. First, to say that everything is empty of inherent existence does not mean that nothing exists.[78] Entities such as people, objects, thoughts, gods, *dharmas* exist, but they do not have and do not rely on an enduring self-essence. They are just conventional existents, just temporary products in the flow of continuous becoming, fluxes of empty *dharmas*. The true nature of anything is that it is empty of intrinsic existence, because in one way or another it is always the result of causes and conditions. Second, emptiness (*shunyata*) is not a kind of Ultimate Reality that pervades all things. It is rather the fundamental quality or property that describes *how* all things really are, empty of inherent existence. Against all speculation that one can encounter in Buddhist-Christian dialogue, emptiness must not be taken as a kind of substantial Ultimate Reality in which everything finds its origin. In the words of Gethin, emptiness must also be seen as "empty of its own existence." Therefore "nirvana cannot be understood as some *thing*, some existent, which is other than the conditioned round of existence, samsara."[79] As Gethin further explains, one must avoid two equally wrong views. First, "emptiness is not a 'nothing,' it is not nihilism," and second, "it is not a 'something,' it is not some absolute reality; it is the absolute truth about the way things are but it is not *the* Absolute. For to think of emptiness in terms of either an Absolute or a Nothingness is precisely to turn emptiness into a view of either eternalism or annihilationism."[80] Instead of a substantial Ultimate Reality, emptiness is the ultimate truth one must follow for cutting grasping and reaching enlightenment. Knowing that everything is a product of the *dharmas* and that *dharmas* themselves lack an inherent

75. Ibid., 243.

76. Ibid., 219.

77. Harvey, *Introduction to Buddhism*, 121.

78. Following Nagarjuna, Gethin argues: "It is not that nothing exists, but that nothing exists as an individual essence possessed of its own inherent existence." (Gethin, *Foundations of Buddhism*, 239).

79. Ibid.

80. Ibid., 240.

nature will help one detach from the objects of craving and free his or her mind from ignorance.

## 2.8 THE BUDDHA-NATURE AND THE THREE BODIES OF THE BUDDHA

I need to mention two more Mahayana doctrines which deal with issues of ontology and thus are related to the doctrine of emptiness. Both doctrines, the Buddha-nature and the three bodies of the Buddha, make important contributions to a proper understanding of ultimate truth in Mahayana Buddhism and as such will be of help in assessing references made to them in Buddhist-Christian dialogue.

The Buddha-nature (*tathagatagarbha*) is defined as "the factor possessed by each sentient being which enables him or her to become a fully enlightened Buddha."[81] As Gethin observes, the (Mahayana) *Mahaparinirvana Sutra* "goes so far as to speak of it as our true self."[82] At first sight it would seem to reiterate belief in a substantial self (*atman*), so much rejected and quite "heretical" in Buddhism.[83] However, the factor all humans possess and which helps them attain enlightenment must not be a substantial self. What all sentient beings have in common is emptiness as a property, not as an enduring self. This property, the very absence of inherent existence, is the key element that enables one to find enlightenment.[84]

A form of Buddhism in which the *tathagatagarbha* doctrine is especially important is Zen.[85] The Japanese master Dogen (thirteenth century) brought to Japan and adapted the Chinese Buddhist tradition of Ch'an as Soto Zen. According to Dogen's reading of the *Mahaparinirvana Sutra*

81. Williams, *Buddhist Thought,* 160. This doctrine is first mentioned in the *Tathagatagarbha Sutra,* composed in the third century AD (ibid., 160–61).

82. Gethin, *Foundations of Buddhism,* 252.

83. However, in the same *Sutra* we find that this teaching is meant as skilful method to convert non-Buddhists, as they suspect the not-Self doctrine of involving nihilism (Williams, *Buddhist Thought,* 108).

84. However, this is not the standard interpretation of the Buddha-nature in Buddhism. Other traditions see the Buddha-nature as "a really existing, permanent element . . . which enables sentient beings to become Buddhas" (Williams, *Mahayana Buddhism,* 108). The two positions are expressed in Tibet as *rang stong* and *gzhan stong.* The first is that of the dGe lugs tradition (to which the Dalai Lama belongs), while the second is that of the Jo nang pa school, which takes the Buddha-nature doctrine literally, as being the "pure radiant nondual consciousness . . . of a fully enlightened Buddha" (ibid., 114).

85. There are two traditions of Zen—Soto and Rinzai Zen. In Soto Zen enlightenment is experienced in sitting meditation (*Zazen*). In Rinzai a series of formulas are used that defy logic and thus let one experience enlightenment.

"everything *is* the Buddha-nature."[86] Unlike the traditional view that every sentient being *has* the Buddha-nature, Dogen argues that all reality must be seen as being the Buddha-nature itself, but obviously not as a hidden substantial self. Thus it is wrong and useless to search for some secret, hidden, inner Buddha-nature, and instead one should see the world of phenomena in its continuous change as being the Buddha-nature itself. To *have* the Buddha-nature would lead to dualism and attachment (*I* should then discover *my* hidden Buddha-nature), while to see everything as being the Buddha-nature is the enlightening truth. Therefore, as Harvey emphasizes, the method of Zen meditation known as *zazen* (sitting-meditation)

> is not seen as a "method" to "attain" enlightenment, but is itself enlightenment, a way of simply exhibiting one's innate Buddha-nature. A person must sit in *zazen* with constant awareness, and with faith that he is already a Buddha. The process is one of self-forgetting in which the Buddha-nature gradually unfolds its infinite potential through one's life.[87]

In Zen enlightenment is reached under the direct guidance of a master as a sudden perception of one's Buddha-nature, for it is already there in every aspect of the world. As a result, one does not have to strive for enlightenment, one is *already* enlightened but does not realize it. In this context practice is not a way of *attaining* enlightenment, but of *manifesting* it.

Now let me turn to the other significant doctrine for my research, that of the three bodies (*Trikaya*) of the Buddha. As we have seen earlier, one of the elements that triggered the rise of Mahayana Buddhism was the refusal to accept that the Buddha disappeared forever at his physical death. The view of early Buddhism that he remained only in the form of his teaching grew into the doctrine of his three bodies (*Trikaya*).[88] It speaks of three levels of reality unfolding to us. The first and lowest is the "Transformation-body" (*Nirmana-kaya*), which is the physical body of the Buddha and of all other earthly Buddhas, "seen as teaching devices compassionately projected into the world to show people the path to Buddhahood."[89] A second level of reality is the "Enjoyment-body" (*Sambhoga-kaya*), which is "the product of the 'merit' of a Bodhisattva's training."[90] By the power of his mind a Buddha can use "his immeasurable store of 'merit'" accumulated during countless

86. Williams, *Mahayana Buddhism*, 120, emphasis mine.

87. Harvey, *Introduction to Buddhism*, 166.

88. The *Trikaya* doctrine was systematized by the Yogacara school of Mahayana Buddhism by around AD 300 (Harvey, *Introduction to Buddhism*, 125).

89. Ibid., 126.

90. Ibid.

lives and "conjure up a world for the benefit of others" as a heavenly realm "where it is easy to hear and practice the *Dharma*" and finally attain enlightenment.[91] The highest level of reality is the "Dharma-body" (*Dharma-kaya*), which has two aspects. Harvey describes them as the "Knowledge-body" (*Jnana-kaya*), "the inner nature shared by all Buddhas, their Buddha-ness (*buddhata*),"[92] and the "Self-existent-body" (*Svabhavika-kaya*), which is "the ultimate nature of reality, thusness, emptiness: the non-nature which is the very nature of *dharmas*."[93]

The first two bodies are the expression of compassion, as they are manifested by the Dharma-body for the benefit of sentient beings. A Buddha appears in his Pure Land preaching the doctrine to beings reborn there in his Enjoyment-body (*Sambhoga-kaya*), while the Transformation-body (*Nirmana-kaya*) is his earthly manifestation produced "for the benefit of those whose attainments are so weak that they are unable to reach a Pure Land."[94] One form taken by this body was that of the historical teacher *Siddhartha* Gautama, preaching in India two and a half thousand years ago. The "historical" details of his life, his striving to find enlightenment, his living among monks and his death, were nothing but skilful means for those too weak to understand the true nature of things, the wisdom of the Mahayana. Williams adds here an interesting application for my research. In Mahayana philosophy, Jesus Christ could also be seen as a Transformation Body of the Buddha:

> Mahayana Buddhists in the modern world commonly have no objection to seeing the historical Jesus Christ as a Transformation Body Buddha—a manifestation from an Enjoyment Body out of compassion in a form suitable to his particular time and place.[95]

---

91. Ibid, 126.

92. The Knowledge-body is "the omniscient knowledge, perfect wisdom, and spiritual qualities through which a *Bodhisattva* becomes a Buddha" (ibid., 127).

93. Ibid.

94. Williams, *Mahayana Buddhism*, 181.

95. Ibid., 181–82. Robert Thurman argues that the saving act of Jesus is an instance of using skilful means by a *bodhisattva*, according to the teaching of the "Parable of the Burning House" in the *Lotus Sutra*. Therefore Jesus' claims of uniqueness as expressed in the Gospels would be "God's little white lie" (Thurman, "Panel Discussion," in Lopez and Rockefeller, eds., *The Christ and the Bodhisattva*, 254).

## 2.9 HUMAN PERFECTION IN MAHAYANA BUDDHISM. PERFECTION IN WISDOM AND COMPASSION

Although Mahayana Buddhism is a sum of complex traditions and sub-traditions, each with so many subtleties that one can hardly make general affirmations that could apply to all of them, when it comes to defining the image of human perfection these traditions would probably all agree that it is the Buddha (or the Buddha of one's own tradition, as for example the Amida Buddha in Pure Land Buddhism). He is the perfect illustration of how perfect wisdom and compassion work together for the benefit of sentient beings.

We have seen that in Mahayana Buddhism the becoming of a Buddha is the result of following the path of the *bodhisattva*, by keeping the right balance between wisdom and compassion. However, one could spot a contradiction between the wisdom one should develop considering the doctrine of emptiness and the *bodhisattva*'s compassion for all suffering beings. How could a *bodhisattva* be wise and have compassion for all beings, when he or she knows that ultimately they are all empty of inherent existence? Would not this kind of compassion be ignorance? The answer lies in realizing that wisdom and compassion do not compete but complement each other. The *bodhisattva* is aware of both the suffering "beings" in the world of *samsara*, and of the fact that ultimately there is no "inherently existing being who is helped."[96] Wisdom holds in balance both aspects, both the ultimate truth of emptiness and the relative truth of suffering, so that the *bodhisattva* can act in both worlds without developing attachments to any of them. Compassion urges him or her to help sentient beings to escape suffering and thus to be involved in the world of ignorance, while wisdom keeps him or her from being affected by ignorance so as to provide the best help for the suffering being to be saved. According to Williams, "the Perfection of Wisdom literature repeatedly states that the bodhisattva takes such great vows without perceiving that there is any actual being who is saved, for all is really empty."[97]

The perfect harmony between wisdom and compassion generates a new vision of *nirvana* in Mahayana Buddhism. The criticism addressed to early Buddhism was that the *arhat* abandons not only greed, aversion and delusion, but also all other suffering beings in order to pursue his or her quest for perfection. In contrast, the *bodhisattva* is said to achieve a "non-abiding" *nirvana*, which has two dimensions: an "upward movement away

96. Williams, *Mahayana Buddhism*, 56.

97. Ibid., 138.

from samsara, away from greed, aversion, and delusion, and a downward movement returning out of compassion to the maelstrom of samsaric institutions and persons."[98] The enlightened being of Mahayana is capable of seeing and handling both sides of the story. He or she is capable of helping others only because of not being trapped by ignorance, least of all by the ignorance of seeking a selfish liberation. This leads us to the formula of human perfection in Mahayana Buddhism. It is becoming a *bodhisattva* and ultimately to attain full Buddhahood for the sake of all suffering beings, no matter how long it might take. It requires realizing the emptiness of all beings, and despite knowing that they ultimately are mere fluxes of empty *dharmas*, to see their suffering as very real from their subjective point of view and thus engage in helping them to escape from ignorance and rebirth. This is what the Buddha achieved, and all humans have the potential to become one and do what he did.

98. Ibid., 185.

# 3

# An Examination of Doctrinal Presuppositions in Orthodox Christianity as a Foundation for Assessing Buddhist-Christian Dialogue

## Human Perfection as Deification

DUMITRU STĂNILOAE (1903–1993) IS definitively the most important Romanian Orthodox theologian of all times.[1] Respected contemporary theologians have called him "le plus grand théologien orthodoxe" (Olivier Clément),[2] "the most influential and creative contemporary Orthodox theologian" (Jürgen Moltmann),[3] and "the greatest Orthodox theologian alive today,"[4] holding a position in twentieth century Orthodox theology "comparable to that of Karl Barth in Protestantism or Karl Rahner in Catholicism"[5] (Kallistos Ware). But despite his huge body of works, most of Stăniloae's theological thought is still very little known to the Western world.

---

1. All translations from his (yet untranslated) Romanian texts are mine unless otherwise specified.

2. Olivier Clément, "Le père Dumitru Stăniloae et le génie de l'orthodoxie Roumaine," in Ică, ed., *Persoană și Comuniune*, 82.

3. Jürgen Moltmann, "Geleitwort," in Stăniloae, *Orthodoxe Dogmatik*, 10.

4. Kallistos Ware, "Foreword," in Stăniloae, *Experience of God*, ix.

5. Ibid., xxiv.

Stăniloae studied theology at the Theological Faculty in Cernăuţi, where he graduated in 1922. He was awarded his PhD in theology in 1928,[6] and until 1930 he pursued post-doctoral studies in Patristics and Dogmatics in Munich, Berlin, Paris, Belgrade and Istanbul. Back home in Romania he served as Professor of Dogmatics (1929–1946) at the Orthodox Theological Academy of Sibiu, where he was also appointed as Rector (1936–1946). In 1946 he was forced to step down from rectorship by the newly installed communist regime and moved to the Orthodox Theological Institute of Bucharest, where he served until 1958 as Professor of Ascetics and Mystics. In 1958 he was arrested and imprisoned for his role in the rejuvenation of Orthodox life and spent five years in several infamous prisons. After his release in 1963, he went back to the Theological Institute of Bucharest, but got only a modest chair as a supervisor of PhD studies, which he held until his retirement in 1973. For the next 20 years, until his death in 1993, he continued to supervise PhD candidates of the Institute as consultant professor.[7] His published work is immense: 20 books, 1300 articles in theological periodicals, newspapers, reviews, forewords, interviews and 30 translations of Patristic and contemporary Orthodox authors.[8]

Stăniloae is a major theologian on the doctrine of the Holy Trinity and on the Christian view of the fulfilment of the human person through deification. Among the defining features of Stăniloae's theology I would mention the following four that bear special relevance for my book:

1. The starting point and perennial assessment tool for building up Orthodox Dogmatics is the Holy Trinity as the ultimate communion and love between God the Father, God the Son and God the Holy Spirit. The church itself is the image of the Holy Trinity on earth and human perfection as deification can be reached only in the context of the ecclesial community. His theology was thus called "a theology of personhood."[9]

6. His doctoral work is *Viaţa şi Activitatea Patriarhului Dosofteiu al Ierusalimului şi Legăturile lui cu Ţările Româneşti* [*The Life and Work of Dosoftei of Jerusalem and His Connections with Romanian Principalities*].

7. For a complete biography see Păcurariu, "Preotul Profesor şi Academician Dumitru Stăniloae," in Ică, ed., *Persoană şi Comuniune*, 1–15. For a short biography in English see Ware, "Foreword," in Stăniloae, *Experience of God*, x–xv.

8. The list of his works is itself a long article. See Gh. Anghelescu, "Părintele Prof. Acad. Dumitru Stăniloae. Bibliografie Sistematică" [Father Prof. Dumitru Stăniloae Systematic Bibliography], in Ică, ed., *Persoană şi Comuniune*, 16–67.

9. S. Frunză, "Pentru o metafizică a persoanei implicită în teologia Părintelui Dumitru Stăniloae" [Towards an implicit metaphysics of personhood in the theology of Father Dumitru Stăniloae], in Ică, ed., *Persoană şi Comuniune*, 94.

2. Theology must be imbedded in church life, as a living and daily experience of God, not as mere theoretical systematization of dogmas. According to Ion Bria, one of his many disciples, for Stăniloae "theology is a gift of God which is offered within the context of a personal experience with God and his acts in history."[10]

3. Stăniloae rejected the new Orthodox scholasticism he found in manuals of theology of the nineteenth century,[11] which affirmed dogmas as "abstract propositions,"[12] in favour of a more experiential theology, based on the Greek Fathers of the church.[13] Although he advocates for an apophatic experience of God, defining apophaticism as "the most intense experience of the relationship with God as person,"[14] Stăniloae does not get lost in mystical apophaticism, but argues for the right balance between the apophatic and the cataphatic approach. He rejects both the scholastic cataphaticism of the West and the radical apophaticism of Eastern theology for, as he says, "these two kinds of knowledge are neither contradictory nor mutually exclusive, rather they complete each other."[15]

4. Stăniloae was aware both of Western Catholic and Protestant theology and of Western existentialist philosophy as a result of his stay in Berlin, Paris and Munich. Although his theological resources are mainly the Greek Fathers and the Bible, he often proves to be aware of contemporary theological and philosophical debates in Western culture.

Unlike the Buddhist scholars that I have chosen to describe the Buddhist view of perfection in the previous chapter, who live in a Western culture and thus are well-acquainted with the essentials of Christianity, Stăniloae was to a lesser degree familiar with Buddhist philosophy. There are only a few references to Buddhism in Stăniloae's works, for Buddhism was not an issue in the writings of the Greek Fathers, and of minor importance

10. Ion Bria, "The Creative Vision of Dumitru Stăniloae," in Ică, ed., *Persoană și Comuniune*, 76.

11. This position is emphasized in his preface to Christos Androutsos" manual of Orthodox theology, translated by him from Greek as Hristu Andrutsos, *Dogmatica Bisericii Ortodoxe Răsăritene* [The Dogmatics of the Eastern Orthodox Church], v.

12. Stăniloae, *Teologia Dogmatică Ortodoxă*, vol. 1, 7.

13. In his writings Stăniloae relied especially on the Cappadocians, John Chrysostom, Dionysius, Maximus the Confessor, Leontius of Byzantium, John of Damascus, Symeon the New Theologian, and Gregory Palamas.

14. Stăniloae, *Experience of God*, 116–17.

15. Ibid., 96.

in Romania during Stăniloae's lifetime.[16] He was much more engaged in addressing pantheism, a position he encountered in his study of Western philosophy. Nevertheless, many of the critiques he addresses to pantheism will be equally valid for contrasting Orthodox fundamental themes with their possible equivalents in Buddhism.

Given the huge amount of theological writings produced by Stăniloae, I must limit myself to a short introduction to his view of human perfection as deification and refrain from assessing it in the overall context of the Orthodox tradition and its Patristic roots.[17] I am bound to setting up a guiding line for assessing Buddhist-Christian dialogue, and therefore I need to limit this introduction to key elements that are relevant for this book and completely overlook otherwise fundamental issues, such as the doctrine of uncreated energies, pneumatology and ecclesiology.

## 3.1 THE HOLY TRINITY. A PERMANENT AND CHANGELESS ULTIMATE REALITY

As we have seen in the previous chapter, Buddhism does not need to state a first cause for the existence of the world. It rejects both the Hindu gods and an impersonal essence such as Brahman as accounting for an Ultimate Reality. The series of rebirths extends infinitely into the past and there is nothing that could stand the test of impermanence. Buddhism holds instead to the ultimate *truth* of how things really are.

Orthodox Christianity starts from a different doctrinal foundation. Contrary to the Buddhist view of impermanence and inherent existence, it affirms a permanent, changeless and knowable Ultimate Reality. Stăniloae, as a true follower of the tradition of Orthodox Christianity, builds his whole theology on the personal Ultimate Reality represented by the Holy Trinity. He says:

> God's being subsists from eternity, thus without beginning, in three Persons: in the unbegotten Father, in the Son begotten of the Father and of the Holy Spirit proceeded from the Father towards the Son.[18]

Unlike in Buddhism, God is not a being that has reached a temporary status that anyone can achieve due to merits accumulated in previous

---

16. However, he quotes a Romanian author who refers to Buddhism, proving he knew its basic doctrines. See Stăniloae, *Poziția D-lui Lucian Blaga*, 36, 44.

17. A good resource is Bartoș, *Deification in Eastern Orthodox Theology*.

18. Stăniloae, *Sfânta Treime*, 37.

human lives. He is not the equivalent of the Hindu deities which are portrayed in Buddhist sutras as ignorant beings seeking enlightenment for themselves[19] and there is no supra-essence in which the Father, Son, and Holy Spirit would have their origin. This would be the case of the Hindu view of the triad we find in the *Puranas*—that of Brahma, Vishnu and Shiva (the creator, the preserver and the destroyer) as manifestations of the impersonal Brahman. The Persons of the Trinity are not functional projections of a hidden impersonal Ultimate Reality, but their relationship is the Ultimate Reality itself. In other words, God does not exist otherwise than as the communion of the three Persons.[20]

A common view that resurfaces quite often in Buddhist-Christian dialogue is that the Holy Trinity would be the equivalent of the Mahayana Buddhist doctrine of the three bodies of the Buddha (*Trikaya*).[21] In contrast to the Buddhist view, the Christian teaching is that God the Father is an eternal Person, not an everlasting Truth (emptiness), and the other two Persons are co-eternal with him, so he does not manifest the Son and the Spirit out of compassion for the lowliest of beings. Unlike in other theistic religions, Stăniloae emphasizes that God is personal, but not a uni-personal, solitary being, in need of other beings in order for his personal status to make sense. There is an intense movement in God himself, as a dynamic relationship between the three Persons of the Trinity. Following the Church Fathers, the Romanian theologian argues that in God there is not "only a power generating movement in creatures as a result of his fullness, but also a movement in himself, i.e., in his quality of being a Trinity."[22] A solitary God could not be called good and loving unless there were other beings towards which he could manifest such qualities. Since such a god would not have "a movement of love inside himself," he would need other personal beings to which he would reveal himself as good and loving. In other words, a uni-personal God would be imperfect without his creation.[23] But although

19. For instance, one of the most cherished Hindu gods, Indra, called Sakka in the Buddhist sutras, is depicted in the *Digha Nikaya* as visiting different religious teachers and seeking enlightenment for himself. However, instead of finding enlightenment, the teachers he visits become his worshippers. Finally he goes to the Buddha and only with him finds the answers to his metaphysical doubts (Walshe, trans., *The Long Discourses*, 328–32).

20. Stăniloae, *Sfánta Treime*, 38.

21. Three authors who hold this view and are referred to in this book are Masao Abe (section 7.3), John Cobb (section 8.5) and John Hick (section 1.4).

22. Stăniloae, *Chipul Nemuritor al lui Dumnezeu*, vol. 2, 7.

23. In Stăniloae's words, "a uni-personal god would then be neither a person nor God. He would lack perfection. His almightiness would not be united with goodness and love. Would this be almightiness, if he were a tyrant incapable of a loving

Christians speak of three Persons in the Trinity, Stăniloae warns that this does not mean tri-theism, since each Person is God only in union with the other two. Each Person of the Holy Trinity—Father, Son, and Holy Spirit—is God, "because he shares the same being with the other two."[24]

Instead of an "unchangeable substance" and of "continuous becoming," which for Stăniloae are both "a false eternity,"[25] for Stăniloae the basis of existence is the very communion inside the Trinity. No wonder then that he has been called an "ontological personalist" for his high view on the personal relationships in the Trinity as being the essence of Ultimate Reality.[26] Although believers usually speak of the love *of* God, love is first and best defined *in* God, in the movement of the Persons towards one another. In Stăniloae's words,

> Love is the movement between them, the total union between them and the lack of movement of one beyond the other two. It means that each is resting in the other two (the *perichoresis*), having everything in the other two and is in no need to search for anything beyond them.[27]

Thus the most appropriate way of speaking of God in Orthodox Christianity is as "the supreme unconfused unity of tri-personal communion."[28] Love has not simply appeared sometime in the history of religious thought, but defines the atemporal relationships between the Persons of the Holy Trinity, in which "one Person loves as a Father and another as a Son, while the third with each of the two enjoys the other, as the Holy Spirit."[29] They exist in and of themselves, and thus are not to be seen as a manifestation of an impersonal substance.[30]

---

relationship with other forms of existence?" (Stăniloae, *Sfânta Treime*, 26).

24. Stăniloae, *Chipul Nemuritor*, vol. 2, 12. He says elsewhere: "He is in an eminent way one and three, or rather he transcends the mode in which one and three exist in our experience. The three subjects are so interior in their unity as Being that knows no dispersal that they can in no way be separated so as to be counted as three entities having a certain discontinuity between them" (*Experience of God*, 265–66).

25. Stăniloae, *Experience of God*, 151.

26. Bartoş, *Deification in Eastern Orthodox Theology*, 100.

27. Stăniloae, *Chipul Nemuritor*, vol. 2, 11.

28. Stăniloae, *Sfânta Treime*, 23.

29. Stăniloae, *Chipul Nemuritor*, vol. 2, 10.

30. Orthodox theology does not leave room for us to think in terms of an impersonal side of the Trinity. Although Orthodox theologians refer to a "cataphatic" and an "apophatic" knowledge of God, as referring to what can be known and what cannot be known of God, apophatic theology is not a way of speculating on what may be "beyond" the Trinity. Apophaticism is not a way of abandoning the personal status of

## 3.2 THE HOLY TRINITY AND CREATION. IMAGE AND LIKENESS

Because God is self-sufficient, he can create the world without external constraints or by altering his nature. Stăniloae argues that only a self-sufficient God is *free* to create the world, and can do it without using pre-existing matter.[31] Creation *ex nihilo* is thus the only mode of creation compatible with the nature of God as personal, loving and omnipotent.[32] He does not create the world compelled by external constraints, but out of his love, power, and freedom, which are displayed to the highest degree in the creation of human beings. Stăniloae finds God's reason for creating humankind to be the extension of the movement of love inside the Trinity:

> By creation the Father wants to increase the number of subjects who could enjoy the eternal happiness of communion with Him. Not for his own happiness, since the communion with the other divine subjects leaves no gap in His happiness. He wants to have more sons. He wants more subjects to be their father. But divinity cannot increase or decrease. Therefore other subjects can come into being only by creation.[33]

In defining human nature Stăniloae starts from the account of creation in Genesis 1:26: "Then God said, 'Let us make humankind in our image, according to our likeness'" (NRSV). Following the Orthodox tradition he sees a significant difference between the meaning of "image" and that of "likeness."[34] The "image of God" would consist in the relational aspect of human beings, while "likeness with God" would be the very activation of one's personal relationship with God. In other words, the image is about *what* humans are, an expression of human personhood, while likeness concerns *how* humans should be, in communion with God and other people,

---

God in favour of affirming an impersonal divine essence in the form of Eckhart's *Gottheit* or Böhme's *Ungrund*, a kind of primordial matrix in which originates the God of traditional Christianity.

31. A more thorough examination of the concept of *ex nihilo* creation in the works of Stăniloae can be found in Bartoş, *Deification in Eastern Orthodox Theology*, 100–102.

32. Stăniloae, *Ascetică şi Mistică Creştină*, 28–29; "Sfânta Treime: Creatoarea, Mântuitoarea," 19.

33. Stăniloae, *Iisus Hristos*, 79. See also "Fiul şi Cuvântul lui Dumnezeu," 168; "Sfânta Treime: Creatoarea, Mântuitoarea," 17– 21, *Trăirea lui Dumnezeu în Ortodoxie*, 208, *Chipul Nemuritor*, vol. 1, 24.

34. He follows the thought of Irenaeus, Gregory of Nyssa, John of Damascus and Gregory Palamas in articulating this argument. See Stăniloae, "Starea Primordială a Omului," 323–57.

following the harmony existing between the persons of the Trinity. Image is a gift, while likeness is a process and a perfected state of communion with God and other humans.[35] As a potential that has to be developed into actuality, likeness is to be worked out by one's moral choices, in dialogue with God and one's neighbours. The ultimate goal of human existence is that this dialogue may be perfected in eternity. In Stăniloae's words, "being created as a partner in a communicating dialogue with God, (the human being) is created for eternal life."[36]

As a direct consequence of one's call to live in communion with God, eternal life is not an illusion, a projection of unfulfilled desires (as in Freudian psychology) or an attachment to the doctrine of a self. Eternal life is the ultimate fulfilment of the way humans have been created, of the very plan God has intended for humankind, that of making human beings his partners in an everlasting dialogue of love. Therefore the thirst for eternal personal existence cannot be taken as the product of ignorance or as a source of attachment to false views, as in Buddhism. On the contrary, personhood is the very ground of human's drive, and eternal communion is its fulfilment. Since human beings are created by an infinite personal God, their thirst for eternal communion with him is not a product of illusion, of a wrong way of seeing how things really are, for communion is the very fulfilment of human nature. As Stăniloae boldly affirms,

> we have been created for eternity inasmuch as we gasp, like suffocating beings, after eternity, after the absolute. We wish to love and to be loved more and more, striving after a love which is absolute and endless.[37]

The Orthodox view on human nature leads to an interesting contrast on the nature of consciousness in Christianity and in Buddhism. On the one hand, in Buddhism we have seen that consciousness (*vijnana*) is the fifth aggregate of human nature, which generates the illusion of personhood. It is merely the effect produced by a sensory or mental object, being as impermanent as its source and generating attachments to false views. Enlightenment consists of breaking the bondage of these attachments, and becoming free from enjoying personal existence. On the other hand, in all mainstream Christian traditions consciousness is a key element for developing a personal relationship with God and with other humans. It does not fuel ignorance and suffering *per se*, for it gives meaning to the human subject, as "the

---

35. Stăniloae says: "[T]he divine image in man is an image of the Trinity and reveals itself in human communion" ("Image, Likeness, and Deification," 77).

36. Stăniloae, *Chipul Nemuritor*, vol. 1, 19.

37. Stăniloae, *Experience of God*, 5.

highest level of existence,"[38] and as such is the condition for having eternal communion with God.

An important aspect to be emphasized here is that immortality is not an intrinsic property of human nature given by a divine essence inside it, but the gift of God.[39] The human being is called into existence from nothingness and is sustained in existence by God, as is the whole universe, for nothing outside him can exist by own resources.[40] Since there is no essence inside human beings that could survive death by its own nature (like the *atman* in Hinduism), humans must be held in existence by the power and will of God. Human existence is not the result of blind chance, as in naturalism, or of the manifestation of an impersonal essence, as in pantheism. Stăniloae is very critical of the pantheist worldview according to which the human being is "a mere particle in a continuous tumbling of individualities which appear and disappear from and intvo this unconscious essence."[41] Immortality is given to human beings by grace and can be defined only in relationship with God. Therefore human fulfilment is not found in the loss of personhood, but in a perfect communion with God, the perfect and transcendent personal being. In other words, personhood is a condition for fulfilling God's plan for his created beings, which is becoming and remaining partners in dialogue with him. In the words of Stăniloae, "man strains towards an infinite personal reality higher than himself, a reality from which he can nourish himself infinitely."[42] Therefore the human condition is paradoxical: created *ex nihilo*, but meant for eternal life; of no self-sustained essence, but still capable of communion with God. Or to quote Stăniloae again, "[b]y himself the human being is nothing, and for this very reason his existence is given and sustained exclusively by the power of God."[43]

---

38. Stăniloae, *Studii de Teologie Dogmatică*, 225. See also *Experience of God*, 6.

39. Such is the nature of the self (*atman*) in Hinduism, which reincarnates until it finds its rest in Brahman. Stăniloae strongly opposes any suggestion of a divine self in man, as a kind of *atman*. He opposes the view of the Russian theologian and philosopher Sergey Bulgakov, who held that "the self or the subject in man is not created" and has "a divine essence" (Stăniloae, *Iisus Hristos*, 68). He says against Bulgakov: "The thesis that the subject in the human being is an uncreated spark of the divine essence is a fantasy which renders incomprehensible the human fall into sin and its need of salvation" (Stăniloae, *Iisus Hristos*, 118).

40. Stăniloae, *Iisus Hristos*, 96.

41. Stăniloae, "Sfânta Treime: Creatoarea, Mântuitoarea," 21.

42. Stăniloae, *Experience of God*, 8.

43. Stăniloae, "Sfânta Treime: Creatoarea, Mântuitoarea," 20.

## 3.3 THE PROBLEM OF SIN AND THE MEANING OF SALVATION

An essential condition for the human being as image of God to attain likeness with God is free will.[44] Only so can love be meaningful. But this opens the possibility for rejecting communion with God and attempting to define the meaning of life in isolation from him. The use of free will against God, the one who designed it to make one's love for him possible, is the basic understanding of sin. It is the tragedy that has thoroughly affected humanity. Stăniloae defines it as "human closure against God," "willingness to no longer take him into account" and also as "closure against fellow humans."[45] As a result, the presence of evil in the world is neither the action of a co-eternal being opposing God, as in the dualist religions, nor of ignorance in knowing the ultimate nature of reality, but of the misuse of free will. In terms of how sin has affected human nature, Stăniloae follows the Eastern Fathers arguing that likeness has been lost, but the image has been preserved, although tainted by sin. In other words, human beings have lost their relationship with God but nevertheless have retained the personal status given at creation.

As a consequence of the different perspectives on human nature, suffering is seen as having a different source and meaning in the two traditions. On the one hand, in Buddhism, the omnipresence of suffering is the First Noble Truth discovered by the Buddha. Its source is craving for permanence, i.e., not only for the immediate gratification given by the things of this world, but in an ultimate sense for the permanence of personhood. It will last as long as personal existence lasts. On the other hand, in Christianity permanent personal existence is the very purpose for which humans are created. Therefore suffering must have a different source. It is the result of refusing the relationship they have been created for. In the words of Stăniloae:

> Since human beings were created for communion and were created as such because God himself exists in communion, we can understand why refusing communion produces in their very being a state of abnormality, of discontentment, of suffering.[46]

---

44. As Stăniloae argues, unlike the rest of God's creation, we are "subjects who can respond to his will of living in eternal communion with him" (Stăniloae, *Studii de Teologie Dogmatică Ortodoxă*, 264).

45. Stăniloae, *Teologia Dogmatică Ortodoxă*, vol. 2, 61.

46. Stăniloae, *Iisus Hristos*, 267.

Therefore, according to the Orthodox Christian perspective, suffering is not the result of being unaware of an inner structure and of impermanence, but of a broken relationship with God, of no longer being connected to the source of true meaning. In other words, problems arise not because one does not understand how things really are (impermanent and lacking a true self), but because one refuses communion with the God who created humans as communion-oriented beings.

And there is yet another aspect of the nature of suffering in Christianity. Suffering is meaningful even in the life of those who do have a relationship with God. Stăniloae argues that suffering is the force which "melts away the glaciers"[47] of egoism and brings "complete self-surrender to God."[48] Suffering is allowed by God not to destroy us, but to draw us closer to him and to produce an "increased openness towards the pains of our neighbours."[49] It is thus an efficient way of reducing egoism and of producing an increased thirst for communion, both with God "as our supreme Thou" and with our neighbors "as our equals."[50] Therefore, for the Christian, suffering must not lead to redefining the world as being marked by impermanence and devaluing personhood *per se*, but to refocusing on the real source of meaning, which is God. If he did not exist, Buddhist teaching would probably be the best human response to suffering. The Buddha was consistent in his findings as long as he searched for meaning away from a personal Ultimate Reality, by looking inside himself and observing psycho-physical mechanisms in introspective meditation. For an Orthodox Christian, as Stăniloae argues, if the personal God were not the Ultimate Reality, the world would have no meaning and human beings would truly appear and disappear in a meaningless everlasting cycle. In this case "everything would be a meaningless development, purposeless, devoid of explanation, devoid of any light of meaning, a mere blind movement."[51]

As one can expect, there is a similar contrast in how the two religious traditions define the meaning of salvation and the way it is achieved. All major Christian traditions agree that there is no way of mending the broken relationship with God by the use of own resources. Since sin does not mean losing precious information that could revive the human being and bring it back to the fountain of knowledge, but a broken relationship with the personal God, coming back into communion with him needs *his* special

---

47. Ibid., 250.

48. Ibid., 248.

49. Ibid., 250.

50. Ibid.

51. Stăniloae, *Trăirea lui Dumnezeu în Ortodoxie*, 207.

intervention. Stăniloae emphasizes the core Christian belief of God the Son becoming man for human salvation:

> Christian Dogmatics presents us with the saving and eternal life-giving work of the divine Person of Christ became man, as well as our free relationship with Him. It is by his merits that we can receive eternal life. On this Person and on the relationship with Him depends our salvation, human escape from insufficiency and mortality.[52]

This quotation is a succinct introduction to what salvation means in Orthodox Christianity, and to the contrast it presents to Buddhism. Stăniloae argues that the broken relationship with God cannot be repaired by observing the inner mechanisms that rule the human being and by following a "well-established technique."[53] Since "without his initiative God cannot be known,"[54] there is no human-initiated technique that could accomplish salvation for us. Salvation means being brought into a relationship by the supreme Personal being who called humans into existence. Stăniloae defines it as communion with Jesus Christ, against a mere conformation to a certain doctrine. He says:

> [Salvation] is not achieved by knowing something or by doing something, but by being a partner in a relationship with Jesus Christ. From this relationship with Christ come both the knowing and the doing.[55]

Another essential aspect in Orthodox theology is that salvation is not achieved as a perfected individual in isolation, but by becoming a member of a perfected community. This is the meaning of the Kingdom of God, the state of perfect communion with God and with other perfected human beings. In Stăniloae's words, it is "the union between humans and God, as well as the love between them, out of the power of their union with God."[56]

---

52. Stăniloae, *Teologia Dogmatică Ortodoxă*, vol. 2, 73–74. ("Merits" in this context has obviously a different meaning from that in Buddhism.) Stăniloae does not admit any compromise on the issue of being saved by "Own Power" vs. "Other Power." He says: "Jesus Christ saves as the *irreplaceable Person* that could save us, since his quality of being a divine person who made himself accessible as a human being is the only fountain of power which liberates us from sin and its effects, among which the most serious is death" (Stăniloae, *Teologia Dogmatică Ortodoxă*, vol. 2, 73).

53. Stăniloae, *Ascetică și Mistică Creștină*, 18; "Desăvîrșirea noastră în Hristos," part 1, 82, 88.

54. Stăniloae, *Ascetică și Mistică Creștină*, 19.

55. Stăniloae, *Iisus Hristos*, 198.

56. Stăniloae, *Chipul Evanghelic*, 87.

Therefore Buddhism and Christianity define not only different means for achieving salvation, but also different meanings of what salvation itself consists of. On the one hand, in Orthodox terms salvation is the elevation of the human being from a state of separation from God, due to sin, to a state of perfect communion with him and with other human beings. Stăniloae emphasizes that salvation means being saved from isolation into communion, and therefore personhood must be "a permanent aspect of being," not an object of attachment that needs to be discarded.[57] On the other hand, in Buddhism, enlightenment involves forsaking the bond of personal existence in favour of "knowing how things really are." However, the way of pure knowledge is not a legitimate way to salvation in Orthodox Christianity. It is not enough to have a theoretical knowledge of all Christian Dogmatics and of the laws that rule the world. What saves is the personal relationship with God.

## 3.4 JESUS CHRIST—"TRULY GOD AND TRULY MAN." THE DOCTRINE OF THE KENOSIS

In Jesus Christ we face a different direction of becoming from what is commonly accepted in the story of the Buddha. Instead of acquiring merits and growing from ignorance to enlightenment over countless lives, in Jesus God the Son descended from the unhindered trinitarian communion to the limitations of a human nature. In the words of Stăniloae, "from being the most distant, God made himself our closest subject."[58] While the Buddha is for Theravada Buddhists the discoverer of the ultimate truth, for Christians Jesus Christ is the embodiment of truth in human form. In other words, in one tradition truth is a predicate describing how things really are, while in the other tradition truth is a person who reveals himself to us. As Stăniloae points out, in Jesus God communicates as a human subject with the people he created as potential partners in dialogue, by making himself "a Thou of every one of us."[59]

As we have seen in the contrast depicted between the Trinity and the Buddhist *Trikaya*, God the Son is not an inferior aspect of the Godhead, or a compassionate manifestation of God the Father. As a Person of the Holy Trinity, the Son possesses the full divine nature in an unaltered state. He never ceases to be God the Son, even in his incarnation as man. Following the tradition of the Orthodox Church, Stăniloae builds his view of the

---

57. Stăniloae, *Teologia Dogmatică Ortodoxă*, vol. 2, 74.

58. Stăniloae, *Iisus Hristos*, 107.

59. Stăniloae, *Poziţia D-lui Lucian Blaga*, 79.

two natures in Christ forming one person on the formula of Chalcedon, which affirms that the two natures of Christ, divine and human, are recognized "without confusion, without change, without division, and without separation."[60] Only if Christ was both truly God and truly man could he have achieved the salvation of humankind. On the one hand, Christ had to be divine because salvation is the elevation of human beings to communion *with God*. If he were not "one of the Trinity," according to the Patristic formula, "our union with him is the union with a man subjected to definitive death as are all other humans."[61] On the other hand, he had to be human to elevate a true *human nature* to communion with God. His human nature was not a mere garment or mask he could easily discard, for he remains forever united with it "and through it he communicates to them (to human beings) the power of his human nature, which leads to eternal life."[62] The communication of divine life to humankind through Christ's human nature is an important theme in the Orthodox tradition called the renewal of human nature from the inside, a theme to which I will refer in the next section.

To what extent the divine nature was limited by the incarnation is expressed by the doctrine of the *kenosis* of God the Son.[63] This topic is of special importance for my research, for it is seen by the Kyoto philosophers as an important contact point between the two religious traditions. Stăniloae provides us with excellent insights into the doctrine of the *kenosis* in a whole chapter dedicated to it in his christological treatise *Iisus Hristos sau Restaurarea Omului* [*Jesus Christ or the Restoration of Humankind*]. He rejects a popular Protestant view of the nineteenth century, according to which God the Son gave up or set aside for the period of his earthly mission his divine attributes of almightiness, omnipresence and omniscience.[64] Stăniloae argues that the *kenosis* does not involve a giving up of divine attributes, but

---

60. Stăniloae's commentary on the union of the two natures in Christ can be found in his *Teologia Dogmatică Ortodoxă*, vol. 2, 35–39.

61. Stăniloae, "Sfânta Treime: Creatoarea, Mântuitoarea," 23–24. See also D. Radu, "Coordonate și permanențe în opera păr. prof. D. Stăniloae" [Coordinates and permanent features in Father Prof. D. Stăniloae's works], in Ică, ed., *Persoană și Comuniune*, 152.

62. Stăniloae, *Trăirea lui Dumnezeu în Ortodoxie*, 74.

63. The concept of *kenosis* was introduced by the apostle Paul in the hymn we find in Philippians 2:5–8: "Let the same mind be in you that was in Christ Jesus, who, though he was in the form of God, did not regard equality with God as something to be exploited, but *emptied himself* (ἑαυτὸν ἐκένωσεν), taking the form of a slave, being born in human likeness. And being found in human form, he humbled himself and became obedient to the point of death—even death on a cross" (NRSV, emphasis mine).

64. Stăniloae, *Iisus Hristos*, 128–29, 135, and *Teologia Dogmatică Ortodoxă*, vol. 2, 47.

instead that the divine nature accepted the limitation of communicating it-self through the means of a human nature in order to elevate this human na-ture to total dependence on God. The whole life of Jesus—from his humble birth in a stable, to his youth as a carpenter and his ministry as teacher, to his passion on the cross—must be seen as the result of that initial act of God the Son limiting himself to the possibilities of a human nature. The miracles he performed, his teachings and his sinless life were the result of a human nature becoming transparent for the divine nature to manifest itself through it. Everything that Jesus Christ did was the result of his two natures coop-erating in harmony. In Stăniloae's words, "all his deeds are theandric, divine and human."[65] In Christ the divine nature did not push aside the human nature, for the divine initiative was not meant to crush the human nature, but to perfect it in order to make it fit to express the divine in new ways. In the words of Stăniloae, as Jesus "grew 'in wisdom and stature,' the vessel of his human consciousness became more and more capable of capturing and transmitting the light of divine knowledge."[66]

As we have seen earlier in this section, Jesus Christ had to be fully hu-man to be the saviour of humankind. Through the *kenosis*, God the Son gave just as much power to the human nature of Jesus as it needed in order to make it capable to achieve human salvation.[67] As Stăniloae emphasized, the *kenosis* was a limitation of the divine nature in *expressing* itself according to the measure of growth of the human nature of Jesus. Therefore Jesus Christ is not the equivalent of the *Nirmanakaya* (the third body of the Buddha), as a manifestation of the ultimate truth for the sake of ignorant beings. In him one meets the Personal ultimate truth itself, expressing itself through the (growing) capacity of a human nature, so that humankind could be healed of sin from the inside. Commenting on the words of Maximus the Confes-sor, Stăniloae says that

> the *kenosis* does not involve the fall of God from his divinity, but an act of his goodness and a way of manifesting his power in order to strengthen the human nature from the inside. . . . Therefore the divine nature remained unchanged during the *kenosis*.[68]

---

65. Stăniloae, *Iisus Hristos*, 139.

66. Ibid., 144.

67. Stăniloae, *Teologia Dogmatică Ortodoxă*, vol. 2, 49.

68. Ibid., 50.

## 3.5 THE SAVING WORK OF CHRIST IN HIS INCARNATION, DEATH ON THE CROSS, RESURRECTION AND ASCENSION

As we have seen, in Buddhism enlightenment means seeing things as they really are, while in Orthodox Christianity salvation is found in a relationship with God. This relationship is initiated by God, "who reaches to us making himself human, and thereby coming to us in the closest way possible."[69] All Christian traditions agree that the human sinful nature cannot be mended by the use of own resources and all insist on the importance of Jesus Christ's death on the cross for achieving human salvation. But Stăniloae, as a true representative of the Orthodox tradition, rejects the view that salvation is achieved by Jesus Christ's death on the cross *alone*.[70] Salvation is by Jesus Christ's incarnation, death on the cross, resurrection and ascension. All are important, not just the cross. Therefore I will give a short account of how these events contribute to human salvation, as it will reveal important facts for my assessment of Buddhist-Christian dialogue.

First of all, the incarnation, death on the cross, resurrection and ascension must be historical events in order for the Christian doctrine of salvation to be meaningful. If Jesus did not exist as a historical figure Christian teaching would be worthless. As we have seen in the previous chapter, this is not the case with the Buddha. Even if it could somehow be proved that he did not really exist as the historical Siddhartha Gautama, Buddhists would still be able to reach enlightenment since it is the Buddha's teaching that saves, not his historical deeds. In the case of Christ we face a different situation. The historical events of his life are essential for human salvation, starting with his humble birth in a stable. As Stăniloae emphasizes, his incarnation was the start of a sinless human life of unconditional surrender to the Father, by which "he assumes the nature of the descendants of Adam in order to renew it from the inside."[71] Another way of formulating this teaching in Orthodox theology is that of Christ "recapitulating humankind" in his earthly life.[72] This is a process of undertaking all the lost battles of humanity against sin and of proving that a human nature fully reliant on God's resources is capable of staying sinless and attaining likeness with God. This view finds its origin in Maximus' formula of "Christ re-establishing

---

69. Stăniloae, *Teologia Dogmatică Ortodoxă*, vol. 3, 170–71.

70. Stăniloae's whole book *Iisus Hristos* is dedicated to this topic. See especially, 94–98.

71. Stăniloae, *Teologia Dogmatică Ortodoxă*, vol. 2, 57.

72. Stăniloae, *Experience of God*, 76.

human nature in conformity with itself,"[73] i.e., in conformity with its goal established at creation.

The climax of Jesus' submission to the Father's will was reached in his crucifixion under Pontius Pilate. To understand it properly, Stăniloae invites us to consider it in the religious background of first century AD Judaism, which placed great importance on sacrifices as the means of relating to God. Old Testament sacrifices were constant reminders that the sinner who brought the sacrifices deserves the death penalty for his or her sins, and that the innocent animal is his or her substitute in death. When it comes to interpreting the sacrifice of Christ on the cross in the light of Old Testament sacrifices, Stăniloae rejects the Protestant view that the death of Christ on the cross has effects only in the way God sees the sinner in Christ, *as if* he were sinless. This view provides a limited account of what really brings about human salvation. Since Old Testament sacrifices were lessons that taught self-sacrifice as total surrender to God, the principle they emphasized was that "not the blood itself is what God requires, but the suffering and self-annulling of man as a spiritual being, manifested through death."[74] Given this exemplary role of Old Testament sacrifices, Stăniloae emphasizes that Christ's death on the cross should not be taken as just a juridical atonement before the Father.[75] He reacts against the limitations of this Protestant view, which could give the impression that he rejects the importance of the atonement altogether. But he does not. Instead he speaks of the "ontological necessity indicated by the divine being and grounded in the divine will at creation" that has been met by the death of Christ.[76] Therefore his death is both an atoning and an exemplary sacrifice, as it is directed both towards the Father and towards humankind, as if he stretched his hands on the cross in both directions.[77] Both aspects of his sacrifice are important, both "to give satisfaction to the moral order which originates in the divine will" and "to restore by this act the human being in its essence."[78] As Stăniloae notes, Christ suffered from "hunger, thirst, fatigue, fear of death, the tor-

73. Stăniloae, *Theology and the Church*, 189.

74. Stăniloae, *Iisus Hristos*, 247, *Trăirea lui Dumnezeu în Ortodoxie*, 59.

75. He reacts against the limitations of the theory of Anselm of Canterbury, which sees human sin as an offence to the honour of God, and thus the sacrifice of his Son as a satisfaction brought to his honour (Stăniloae, *Iisus Hristos*, 92–93).

76. Stăniloae, *Iisus Hristos*, 327.

77. Stăniloae argues that we should see the death of Christ both as a "power oriented directly towards humankind," and also "under its aspect of being oriented towards God, i.e., as an atoning sacrifice" (*Trăirea lui Dumnezeu în Ortodoxie*, 64; also *Iisus Hristos*, 253).

78. Stăniloae, *Iisus Hristos*, 97.

ment of death and death itself," not because he was a sinner, but in order to "strengthen the human will" and so to perfect it for its role of transmitting divine power to all believers who are fighting against sin.[79]

Without rejecting the atoning aspect of Christ's death on the cross, Stăniloae speaks a lot more about what it achieves in the human nature. The sacrifice of Christ is a true and complete self-giving of a human being to the Father, that of the only human being that remained sinless until death and made of his death the form of ultimate surrender to the Father's will. More than solving a juridical puzzle in God, Christ's death brings a real change in the human being, a real cleansing of sin and a real sanctification. His sacrifice is the source of power for the renewal of human nature from the inside, as a result of conquering death from the inside. As Stăniloae says, "[i]n this consists the truth of the saying of some Holy Fathers that Jesus surrendered himself to death that he may defeat it on its own ground."[80] Christ defeated death for humans' sake so that they could live a sinless life by the power that the humanity of Christ transmits to them all. In Stăniloae's words, Christ conquered death as a man "so that humans could also conquer death in union with Him, made man."[81] Because Jesus died as a sinless man, his death fulfils God's justice *and* renews human nature from the inside.

If one were to assess from a Buddhist point of view Jesus' display of love through the means of ultimate suffering, there could hardly be found a way to account for it. A possible way of making sense of Jesus' suffering, in a Mahayana Buddhist context, would be to interpret it as skilful means to evoke selflessness in his followers in order to help them to be cured of greed. The meaning that Jesus gave to his suffering, that of carrying another person's sins and being put to death for his sins, in order to be forgiven by God, would for a Buddhist lead only to ignorance and attachments for at least two reasons. First, there is no God who could "forgive" sins, and second, "sins" would be just wrong views that can be corrected by following the right instructions. Atoning for sins would be the equivalent of one person suffering for another's ignorance and in this way taking away his or her karma. It cannot work in Buddhism, but it does make sense according to the Orthodox Christian view on Christ's redemptive suffering. Stăniloae emphasizes that Christ's suffering was "a substitutive suffering on behalf of humankind, for the destruction of sin."[82] Therefore it cannot be taken as a mere teaching device that would encourage one to be less selfish. As Stăniloae says, Christ's

79. Stăniloae, *Trăirea lui Dumnezeu în Ortodoxie*, 80.

80. Ibid., 314.

81. Stăniloae, *Chipul Evanghelic*, 56.

82. Stăniloae, *Iisus Hristos*, 299.

suffering was not "just a play."[83] He speaks very clearly of the atoning aspect of Christ's sacrifice on humans' behalf:

> Without being an actual sinner, by the fact that he chose to be born as a human and take over the entire responsibility of humankind, all sins were crowded upon himself, not as a result of being committed by him, but of the choice he assumed.[84]

An apparent equivalent of the Christian concept of atonement could be seen as the Mahayana Buddhist teaching of transfer of merits. This is the practice at the end of a ceremony of "bestowing of whatever merit may have been attained to the benefit of other sentient beings."[85] However, at a closer look, the equivalence between the Buddhist concept of transfer of merits and Christ's atonement does not work. Karma cannot be taken upon by another (as Christ takes away human sins), for this would break the continuity of the mental causal flow that makes up a person. One possible way of escaping this difficulty would be by arguing, as Williams does, that in the context of persons lacking inherent existence, "karma does lose its rigidity,"[86] and what really matters is the *bodhisattva*'s own intention. However, if it can be argued that karma "loses its rigidity," then the one who gives away his or her merits, the one who receives these merits, and merits themselves also lose their conceptual rigidity and therefore transfer of merits becomes only skilful means for the "giver" to lose his or her attachments for the "merits" one allegedly possesses.

A different view of the concept of transfer of merits is that of Maximus the Confessor in the Orthodox tradition, who said that "Christ won the battle against sin, not for himself, but on our behalf, for he became human for our sake, and transferred to our benefit all he won."[87] Christ operates a true transfer of merits which works in two directions. On the one hand, humans' sins are transferred onto him, as "the Lamb of God who takes away the sin of the world" (John 1:29, NRSV). On the other hand, his sinless human nature is the instrument through which the power for defeating a sinful nature is gradually transferred to humans. Stăniloae argues that the death of one person as a sacrifice for the other can make sense only if the person has true value. Although he referred to a pantheistic worldview as

83. Ibid., 291. Or to adapt this in Buddhist terms, it was not just displaying "skilful means."

84. Stăniloae, *Iisus Hristos*, 291.

85. Williams, *Mahayana Buddhism*, 203.

86. Ibid.

87. Stăniloae, *Chipul Evanghelic*, 35, his translation from Maximus the Confessor, *Against Talasius*, Romanian translation of the *Filokalia*, 64.

the context where "death as sacrifice cannot have any meaning,"[88] his words apply to Buddhism as well.

As mentioned in the beginning of this section, Christ's work of salvation is not limited to his sacrifice on the cross. The New Testament Gospels tell us that Jesus was crucified on a Friday, died on the cross and was buried. But on the following Sunday and for the next forty days he was seen alive and met his disciples in a resurrected body.[89] The Christian tradition speaks of the resurrection of Jesus as of fundamental importance for faith. For Stăniloae it is not just the confirmation of Jesus' sinless earthly life or of his sacrifice for sins being accepted by the Father. He sees in the resurrection God's willingness to continue his dialogue with humankind.[90] What was started by the incarnation was continued in the crucifixion and perfected in the resurrection. The three aspects of Christ's saving work are thus closely linked. In Stăniloae's words,

> [i]f the incarnation is the fruit of God's love for mankind with whom he unites himself definitively and indissolubly, and if in the passion this love goes further still, then its purpose and result are seen in the resurrection which brings to perfection God's union with us for all eternity.[91]

Since Jesus was resurrected and ascended to heaven in a physical human body, we find in it a confirmation of the value of human nature and of God's willingness to continue to transform it. Jesus' resurrected body is the bridge over which God is transmitting to believers the power for being transformed into his likeness. As such he perfects the healing of the human nature "from the inside" during a process that continues through the work of the Holy Spirit and the sacraments of the church throughout our life.

88. Stăniloae, *Chipul Nemuritor*, vol. 2, 146.

89. According to Stăniloae, the resurrection could not have been made up by the apostles. He argues that "a human mind could not have invented it" and that its reality "was certified by the witness of those who died testifying for it" (Stăniloae, *Chipul Evanghelic*, 86).

90. Stăniloae, *Iisus Hristos*, 353.

91. Stăniloae, *Theology and the Church*, 198–99.

## 3.6 THE ACTUALIZATION OF SALVATION IN THE LIFE OF THE BELIEVER AS A MEMBER OF THE CHRISTIAN COMMUNITY

The salvific work of Christ in his incarnation, death on the cross, resurrection and ascension is continued by the descent of the Holy Spirit at Pentecost. This event is seen as the birth of the church, the body of Christ, the community of those who have responded to the initiative of God for their salvation. Although it is a very important theme in the theology of Stăniloae, my research will not pursue an analysis of his ecclesiology.[92] For the goal of this book it will be sufficient to emphasize the personalist and communal aspect of salvation in Orthodox theology.

According to Stăniloae and the tradition of the Orthodox Church, the process of renewing one's nature starts at baptism and continues for all the rest of his or her life. Baptism is the spiritual death of the person who lives in separation from God, and the birth of a new believer who starts growing in a personal relationship with him. This dying to sins and being born again to a new life in Christ is re-actualized whenever sins are committed, confessed and repented of. Stăniloae argues that whenever a Christian commits a sin and repents, he or she experiences again the spiritual death and the resurrection in communion with Christ.[93] Repentance has two facets. On the one hand, it means being sorry for living an egoistic life of isolation from God and neighbours, and for particular sins which are the effects of such a life.[94] On the other hand, it is a strong desire to change and no longer manifest such egoism. Repentance makes sense only in a personal relationship in which one is sorry about his deeds against another person.[95] It is a turning point which re-establishes the natural order of God's creation in one's life.

The power for human regeneration is transmitted by Christ through the Eucharist. Partaking in the Eucharist brings about a real shattering of human sinful nature, for it is the influx of "power for liberating our nature from the weakness produced by sin."[96] In this process the Christian is assisted by the power of the Holy Spirit dwelling in him or her, which completes the picture of being saved out of egoistic isolation and elevated

---

92. For an academic assessment of Stăniloae's ecclesiology see Dănuț Mănăstireanu, *A Perichoretic Model of the Church*. A more recent work on this topic is Radu Bordeianu, *Dumitru Stăniloae: Ecumenical Ecclesiology*.

93. Stăniloae, *Iisus Hristos*, 96.

94. Stăniloae, *Chipul Nemuritor*, vol. 2, 156–57.

95. Stăniloae, *Iisus Hristos*, 95.

96. Stăniloae, *Teologia Dogmatică Ortodoxă*, vol. 2, 231.

into communion with the Holy Trinity. Here is how Stăniloae formulates this process:

> By communicating with him (Christ) through his human na-
> ture, we communicate with One of the Trinity, and together with
> him, we communicate with the Father, while we have inside us
> the Holy Spirit. Through the Son of God who made himself for
> all eternity one of us, the Holy Trinity gathers us all . . . inside
> her interpersonal communion.[97]

A regenerated human being in Christ cannot be imagined without having renewed relationships with his or her neighbours. God's love for us must generate "perfect love between us as brothers, through the power of the love of the one who created us as his brothers, and made himself man and our perfect brother."[98] Christian salvation means being saved through a relationship with God into communion with God, but also into a new human community, which is the church. This community is called the body of Christ, and is the result of uniting "humanity with God through his incarnation in a manner which is most intimate and at the same time indissoluble, inseparable and definitive."[99] The church is thus the image of the Holy Trinity on earth, a community of love which transforms and heals our fallen world.

## 3.7 HUMAN PERFECTION AS DEIFICATION IN ORTHODOX THEOLOGY

As we have seen earlier, Christ had to be truly human in order to elevate a true human nature to genuine communion with the Holy Trinity. It is in this perfected human nature of Jesus manifested through complete submission to the Father's will in all aspects of his life, from birth to crucifixion, that we find represented the Orthodox ideal of human perfection as deification. Stăniloae says:

> In Christ human nature reaches its perfection through deifica-
> tion, as a result of his descent to humanity, by his incarnation.[100]

97. Stăniloae, *Chipul Nemuritor*, vol. 1, 36–37.

98. Stăniloae, *Studii de Teologie Dogmatică Ortodoxă*, 160.

99. Stăniloae, *Theology and the Church*, 187–88.

100. In fact Stăniloae uses a different term here. He is not satisfied with "incarnation" as it could suggest taking a mere human body, as a mask for the divine nature.
Therefore he uses "înomenire," which would translate as "in-humanization," thus emphasizing that we speak of a full human nature in Christ.

> By cleaving to him, all who want can grow infinitely in their
> deification, i.e. in the perfection of their human nature.[101]

Since the perfection of human nature is achieved by "cleaving to him," one must be aware that in Christ we find more than the perfect *human example* for one to follow. Jesus is not just the perfect example for one to imitate by the use of own resources, as the perfect illustration of the holy life. If this were all he achieved, it would not even have been necessary for him to exist. A perfect story would have been enough. There are at least two main reasons for rejecting such a possibility. First, human perfection is worked out in a direct and constant personal relationship with him. In order to grow towards perfection, the Christian must rely on Christ's daily help, not on his mere historical example. Second, unlike in Mahayana Buddhism, which defines perfection as attaining Buddhahood, the exact stage of perfection the Buddha himself has attained, in Christianity one cannot become a Christ. He is the only one who can be said to have been both "truly man" and "truly God." What one has to imitate in Christ is the submission of his *human nature* to God, its total dependence on the divine nature. The Orthodox Christian's goal is thus to reach the perfection the *human nature* has achieved in Christ.

In Buddhism we cannot speak of human perfection as total submission to and dependence on God. This would be a major barrier towards reaching enlightenment. A Buddhist needs to eliminate dependence on personal relationships, for they represent a form of craving and reflect one's lack of detachment from illusion. This is consistent with the doctrinal foundations of Buddhism, and reflects a difference that one could have expected in matters of the value of relationships. While the Buddha demanded an acknowledgement of the all-present impermanence, Jesus Christ perfected a human nature by emphasizing the ultimate value of personhood, and the fact that it can work perfectly only in full harmony with God. Therefore the Orthodox view of perfection requires the strongest bond with God, the most intimate relationship with him.

The best image of a restored and deified humanity was shown by Christ in his resurrected body. It had new features added to those displayed before the crucifixion, a "new structure, belonging to a transcendent sphere,"[102] but nevertheless could still display the features of a physical body and was in continuity with the pre-resurrection body. He could be touched, eat human food and show the scars of the crucifixion. According to Stăniloae, "in the

101. Stăniloae, *Chipul Evanghelic*, 115.

102. Stăniloae, *Iisus Hristos*, 352.

risen Christ we have continuously the real image of what we will become."[103] The resurrection of believers in such a renewed physical body is consistent with God's goal in creating us. The physical body is God's creation; it has nothing intrinsically bad in its nature and is not itself a source of ignorance, or a burden one must get rid of. The body has become corrupted by sin and needs restoration, not annihilation. Stăniloae argues that since "the body is not the cause of sin and diminishing of spiritual life, its destruction (at physical death) can only be a condition for its renewal, for its elevation in a form in which it will no longer bear the stigmata of sin."[104]

Although Western theologians occasionally express theological worries about the appropriateness of the term "deification,"[105] this concept is a key feature of Orthodox Christianity. One must be aware that deification does not mean divinization, i.e., the process by which an individual is declared to have become a god (as for instance Julius Cesar was declared a god by Augustus). Stăniloae insists that deification has nothing to do with an ontological shift of the human nature. Although it advances in perfection, it can never attain the nature of God. He says:

> The human being will reflect more and more of God, but will never become what God is. This distinguishes likeness from identification, or the quality of attaining deification through grace from attaining a divine nature.[106]

The term "deification" has its origin in a famous saying of several Church Fathers: "God made himself man so that man might become God."[107] According to Bartoş, the author of an extensive study on the meaning of dei-

---

103. Stăniloae, *Teologia Dogmatică Ortodoxă*, vol. 2, 78–79. Stăniloae argues that another glimpse of what restored humanity will look like was offered by Christ at his Transfiguration (Stăniloae, *Chipul Evanghelic*, 116).

104. Stăniloae, *Iisus Hristos*, 341.

105. Bartoş gives several examples in his *Deification in Eastern Orthodox Theology*, 7.

106. Stăniloae, *Trăirea lui Dumnezeu în Ortodoxie*, 182, *Ascetică şi Mistică Creştină*, 340.

107. The original statement belongs to St. Athanasius the Great (296–373), Archbishop of Alexandria, in his debate with Arius: "For He was made man that we might be made God" (Athanasius the Great, *On the Incarnation of the Word*, 54, 3). This formula, in its context, is not a heresy, as it does not refer to attaining God's essence. The quotation continues: "and He manifested Himself by a body that we might receive the idea of the unseen Father; and He endured the insolence of men that we might inherit immortality." Other Fathers of the church who used this term are Irenaeus, in *Adversus Haereses* 10, 5–9 (PG 37, 465) and Gregory of Nyssa, in *Oratio Catechetica Magna* 25 (PG 45, 65D). An in-depth study of the concept of deification as used by the Greek Church Fathers is Russell, *The Doctrine of Deification in Greek Patristic Thought*.

fication in Orthodox theology in general, and in the theology of Stăniloae in particular, the Church Fathers borrowed this term from Neoplatonism in order to express one's unity with God in the philosophical language of their time.[108] It does not refer to an ontological upgrading of the human nature. The human being advances towards likeness with God through his resources, which means that deification is by grace, and not by nature. The human being will always remain dependent on God for his existence and will never go beyond the status of a created being. As Stăniloae says, "we are called to become an absolute by grace through our participation in the one who is personal Absolute by nature."[109] A perfected humanity is a sinless, holy humanity, but nevertheless remains a *humanity*. It does not reach divine status.

In terms of my earlier discussion on humankind as being created in the image and likeness of God, we can understand deification as the equivalent of restoring likeness with God, a process that was interrupted by sin. In the words of Stăniloae, "in deification is the image fulfilled, as a maximum likeness with God."[110] The process of deification has thus the same meaning as attaining likeness with God. It is the way in which one's personal status finds its fulfillment in a perfected relationship with God. In other words, the "image" as a human potential attains "likeness" with God as an actuality.

According to Stăniloae, there are two stages in human deification. The first is what I have referred to so far, a process of restoration of the human nature in this life according to the image we have in the human nature of Christ. The second stage of deification refers to "the progress made by the human being beyond the limits of his natural powers, beyond the margins of his nature, in the exclusive region of supernatural and superhuman."[111] This second stage refers to a never-ending growth in perfection, beyond the limits of this life, in the Kingdom of God.[112] Since human perfection is defined in the context of a relationship with God, the infinite Person, and this relationship continues in eternity in the Kingdom of God, deification cannot be seen as a static achievement to which nothing can be added. Deification is not an ultimate knowledge that one could attain, but an unlimited growth in fellowship with God. Nevertheless, it is a growth which does not lead to attaining divine attributes. Once a Christian goes beyond

---

108. Bartoş, *Deification in Eastern Orthodox Theology*, 15.

109. Stăniloae, *Experience of God*, 28.

110. Stăniloae, *Teologia Dogmatică Ortodoxă*, vol. 1, 272.

111. Stăniloae, *Ascetică şi Mistică Creştină*, 338. See also *Trăirea lui Dumnezeu în Ortodoxie*, 179–83.

112. Stăniloae, *Ascetică şi Mistică Creştină*, 338.

the barriers of this sinful life and is resurrected in the Kingdom of God, he or she does not attain a divine ontological status. God will still be infinite and the resurrected humans will still be finite beings. Eternal life is eternal communion with him and with all other beings who have joined the process of deification. It is an unending process of growing in knowledge and love in which "our knowledge of God makes us seek to know him even more; and our love for him stimulates us to an even greater love."[113]

## 3.8 DEIFICATION AND BUDDHAHOOD AS TWO VIEWS OF HUMAN PERFECTION

In order to summarize this and the previous chapter, let me briefly recapitulate the Four Noble Truths of Buddhism, and then contrast them with what might be formulated as their Christian counterpart. As we have seen, the First Noble Truth states that an honest examination of human existence would render it as sheer suffering. The cause of suffering is defined by the Second Noble Truth as ignorance, or not seeing how things really are. It is manifested as craving for the (impermanent) things of this world, and especially for experiencing a (permanent) personal status. The Third Noble Truth gives the solution for ceasing suffering as giving up greed, aversion and ignorance, the three poisons that darken human mind and fuel karma. In essence, in order to escape suffering one needs to give up the thirst for enjoying personhood. Lastly, the Fourth Noble Truth provides the practice one must follow to reach enlightenment, which requires perfection in morality, meditation and wisdom. The *arhat*, the one who has attained enlightenment according to early Buddhism, is one in whom ignorance and the fuel of karma has ceased, and therefore he or she is no longer a prisoner of the vicious rebirth cycle. To this so-called selfish perspective of perfection, Mahayana Buddhism brought a correction, insisting that one should become a Buddha himself or herself and as such to strive for the liberation of all other sentient beings. Buddhahood is the state of perfect mastery of wisdom and compassion that would lead to the eradication of all suffering.

In contrast, if I were to define the "four noble truths" of Orthodox Christianity, the first could be stated as an existing permanent and changeless Ultimate Reality, which is the Holy Trinity. It is the supremely personal and relational Ultimate Reality found in the communion between the God the Father, God the Son and the Holy Spirit. A second "noble truth" of Orthodox Christianity could be defined as considering human beings to be created by God in his "image" and "likeness." This means that humans are

113. Stăniloae, *Experience of God*, 103.

given a personal status for enjoying his love in eternal communion with him. However, this communion has been lost, due to sin, which is an orientation of the person upon herself. As a result, the "third noble truth" would state that salvation cannot be earned by self-effort. It is achieved only in Christ, by his incarnation, sacrifice on the cross, resurrection and ascension, followed by the human response by faith and participation in the sacraments of the church. God redeems the world through the suffering of Christ, and allows suffering in one's life in order to bring humans closer to communion with him. Last, the "fourth noble truth" would state that the image of human perfection as deification is the perfection of a relationship with God, following the status reached by the human nature of Christ. It is a process in which persons are perfected in a community and as a community.

As we could have expected, different views of how Ultimate Reality and human nature are defined result in different views of the barriers which prevent one from achieving perfection. On the one hand, in Buddhism beings must be taken out of a vicious cycle of rebirth by giving up craving for permanence, including craving for a permanent form of personal existence. This is the major barrier to achieving perfection in wisdom. Beings are mere ephemeral constructs that must realize how things really are. On the other hand, in all mainstream Christian traditions the barrier towards achieving perfection has a different nature. Personhood is God's design to enable a human being have personal communion with him and thus the barrier to achieving perfection in this relationship is sin, defined as an egoistic isolation from God and neighbours. Since the human being is to experience the fullness of a permanent relationship with God, deification is the perfection of personhood.

Towards accomplishing such different goals, different means are used. Since in Buddhism one must realize how things really are, we speak of Own Power[114] and its use in meditation and introspection. But in Christianity the only resource for salvation is in the Other Power found in Christ, in his incarnation, death on the cross, resurrection and ascension. Therefore Christianity requires complete openness towards God and his provision in Jesus Christ. His perfected human nature is the goal which one is called to attain and also the source of power for human renewal and deification. It is the means through which he communicates the power for transformation, starting at baptism and continuing with the Holy Communion and the work of the Holy Spirit in the believer in everyday life. In other words, the human nature of Christ is both the goal and the resource for reaching perfection. The Christian is not left alone in an individualistic struggle for attaining

114. Pure Land Buddhism is an exception to this general affirmation.

perfection, with just a great example to follow, and there is no way in which one could attain perfection without Christ.

The two views on human perfection—that of the Mahayana Buddhist tradition, and that of Orthodox Christianity—are obviously very different. On the one hand, Buddhahood is becoming a Buddha and teaching other beings to escape suffering and ignorance by giving up the thirst for personal existence. On the other hand, deification is reaching the perfection of the human nature of Christ, by attaining the most intimate communion with a personal God. Concluding with an emphasis on differences between the two traditions is not an attempt of establishing which one is wrong. Buddhism will always be wrong when seen from the Christian premises of a permanent God, and conversely, Christianity will always be wrong when considered in the light of emptiness as ultimate truth. Since the two religious traditions started from fundamentally different premises, they have naturally developed different views of human perfection. Each has the appropriate means for reaching its goal, and it seems that there is no way in which one could use any resources from the other. Even if I have occasionally pointed out how different a certain doctrine in one religious tradition looks when seen from the perspective of the other religious tradition, this is part of understanding them better, not a criticism addressed to that tradition *per se*. The aim of this comparison is to understand the two religious traditions on their own terms, and on this basis to pursue an honest assessment of contemporary Buddhist-Christian dialogue and then to formulate an Orthodox contribution to comparative theology.

# 4

# A Revisiting of Pluralism in Light of the Doctrinal Foundations of Orthodox Christianity and Mahayana Buddhism and Its Impact on Buddhist and Christian Dual Belonging

IN LIGHT OF WHAT we have seen to be the ideal of human perfection in Mahayana Buddhism and in Orthodox Christianity, I can engage in a further assessment of pluralism as we find it represented in contemporary Buddhist-Christian dialogue. After we have seen Hick's pluralist approach in section 1.4, in this chapter I will continue the assessment of pluralism by referring to the work of two other Christian authors involved in Buddhist-Christian dialogue and to the related issue of Buddhist and Christian dual belonging.

## 4.1 PERRY SCHMIDT-LEUKEL'S VIEW OF A SYNCRETISTIC TRANSFORMATION OF BUDDHISM AND CHRISTIANITY

Perry Schmidt-Leukel (b. 1954) starts from a working assumption similar to that of Hick: World religions are all related to an Ultimate Reality that transcends their particularities.[1] Coming closer to my area of special interest, that of Buddhist-Christian dialogue, he affirms that from a historical

---

1. Schmidt-Leukel, *Transformation by Integration*, 41.

and phenomenological point of view God and emptiness act as "functional equivalents."[2] Beyond what Buddhists and Christians describe as Ultimate Reality there would be a higher ground "which is the ultimate source of salvation or liberation" and which makes the two religious traditions converge.[3]

While Hick found that the doctrine of the Trinity and that of the *dharmakaya* are natural products of the religious mind, Schmidt-Leukel states their equivalence on two of his own criteria. In his view "any functional equivalent to God can be seen as genuine" 1) "if it does not entail idolatry"; and 2) "if it is intrinsically linked to the evocation of selfless love."[4] His conclusion is that "*dharmakaya* complies exceptionally well" with the two criteria and thus "Christians can and should regard it as a genuine equivalent" of God.[5] However, his argumentation is unconvincing. The first criterion is too loose, as Schmidt-Leukel does not explain what he means by idolatry. If he has in mind anything that could take the place of God, *dharmakaya* does not comply, for it *does* hinder the worship of God. (In Buddhism a personal god is just an impermanent manifestation in the flux of rebirths.) If he means worshipping another god (a pagan god), *dharmakaya* does comply, but it equally hinders the worship of the Christian God. Neither does the second criterion work, for Schmidt-Leukel does not show how *dharmakaya* can evoke *agape*, i.e., how an interpersonal bond can be fuelled by emptiness. To be true to the Buddhist view, *dharmakaya* must equally evoke compassion *and* detachment.

Schmidt-Leukel's belief in the ultimate equivalence between the Christian God and the Buddhist *dharmakaya* leads him to argue for a syncretistic transformation of the two religious traditions. In his view, Christianity "has always been syncretistic," and thus Christians should not fear to further transform it "through the intake of elements/insights from non-Christian traditions."[6] Buddhism and Christianity could be reciprocally transformed

2. Ibid., 141.

3. Ibid., and Perry Schmidt-Leukel, "Buddha and Christ as Mediators of the Transcendent: A Christian Perspective," in Schmidt-Leukel, ed., *Buddhism and Christianity in Dialogue*, 170.

4. Schmidt-Leukel, *Transformation by Integration*, 141.

5. Ibid. In his debate with Paul Williams, Schmidt-Leukel argued that *nirvana* and God "can be interpreted as expressing and mediating *different salvific experiences with the same ultimate reality* which shines through both of them" (Schmidt-Leukel, "Light and Darkness," in May, ed., *Converging Ways?*, 87).

6. Schmidt-Leukel, *Transformation by Integration*, 6–7. Schmidt-Leukel's uncritical openness towards other religious traditions leads him to discard traditional Christian doctrines. For instance, he came to reject not only that Christ would be the only way to God, but also that he had to die for our sins and for our salvation (*Transformation by Integration*, 156–57). Along with "numerous Christian theologians," he affirms that the

by teaching each other detachment and involvement.[7] Christians should learn detachment from Buddhists, while Buddhists should learn involvement from Christians. However, his project is hardly realistic. Although Buddhism also speaks of involvement as an expression of compassion (*karuna*), and Christianity also speaks of detachment, as giving away things that hinder the manifestation of love (such as treasures on earth), this is not what Schmidt-Leukel refers to. What he exhorts is that Christians should learn to meditate, and thus learn of *shunyata*, while Buddhists should get involved in curing the wounds of our world.[8] But since the doctrinal foundation for this project is lacking, this exchange cannot really work. As we have seen in the previous two chapters, Buddhist detachment and Christian involvement are defined in different doctrinal settings, so neither can be easily adapted by the other tradition. Buddhist detachment is the mark of wisdom, of attaining the right way of seeing things, while Christian involvement is the reflection of a loving relationship with God, which flows into relationships with other people. Christians cannot learn Buddhist detachment without also accepting its ground as emptiness, while Buddhists cannot learn Christian involvement without also accepting the enduring nature of relationships.

The basic issue that generates tensions when one tries to adapt the teachings of Christianity to those of Buddhism, and vice-versa, is the impossibility of formulating a common transcendent reality for both Buddhism and Christianity. Neither Buddhism nor Christianity could admit a higher Ultimate Reality as demanded by Schmidt-Leukel (and Hick). Buddhism rejects any form of Ultimate Reality that cannot be analyzed away and negated by the doctrine of emptiness, while Christianity cannot accept a view of Ultimate Reality other than that of the Holy Trinity.

## 4.2 THE CHRISTIAN PLURALIST "PARTICULARISM" OF MARK HEIM

Mark Heim belongs to the group of "particularist" pluralists according to Knitter's classification.[9] While most pluralists see religions as different paths

---

"theological construct that God would require the bloody sacrifice of Jesus so as to be able to forgive our sins is as bizarre as it is repulsive" (Perry Schmidt-Leukel, "Response to John Makransky," in Schmidt-Leukel, ed., *Buddhism and Christianity in Dialogue*, 201).

7. Schmidt-Leukel, *Transformation by Integration*, 122.

8. Ibid.

9. See section 1.4.

to the same Ultimate Reality, Heim seems to propose a more realistic and respectful variant of pluralism by recognizing diverse religions as different paths to *different* summits. He does not attempt to rally all religions behind a common ground, or a common goal to which all should conform, but rather argues that religions should be allowed to be genuinely different. To emphasize this view he coined the term *salvations*, in the plural.[10] A true religious pluralism would consider many possible salvations and acknowledge the "distinctness of various religious ends."[11] Since this is the conclusion I have reached in my study on human perfection, Heim's view seems to me to be the most respectful so far towards both Buddhism and Christianity.

However, one begins to doubt its appropriateness when Heim assumes that his view of different salvations is not only coherent with, but also a consequence of the Christian doctrine of the Trinity.[12] Since the Persons in the Trinity are really different and their relationships so complex, the possibility opens for "a variety of distinct relations with God" to exist. This variety would then be the basis for admitting "truly different religious ends."[13] As a result, Jesus Christ would not be the only and exhaustive way in which God saves a believer, for the Holy Spirit can and does open alternative ways, appropriate for each culture and religious tradition.[14]

Starting from a fair understanding of the Orthodox view of the Trinity,[15] Heim proposes that it would have several equivalents in other world religions.[16] Since my assessment of his pluralism must focus on his

10. Heim, *Salvations*, 129–57.

11. Ibid., 7. A similar stand is that of the Shin Buddhist Kenneth Tanaka, who argues that each religion can lead its members to the ultimate goal its tradition claims (see Tanaka, "Buddhist Pluralism: Can Buddhism Accept Other Religions as Equal Ways?" in Schmidt-Leukel, ed., *Buddhist Attitudes to Other Religions*, 69–75.

12. Heim, *Depth of the Riches*, 127. A similar position is expressed by Gavin D'Costa in his "Christ, the Trinity and Religious Plurality" in D'Costa, ed., *Christian Uniqueness Reconsidered*, 18–20.

13. Heim, *Depth of the Riches*, 179.

14. Ibid., 134.

15. See his analysis of the thought of the Orthodox theologian Ioannis Zizioulas in *Depth of the Riches*, 168–77.

16. For instance, he argues that a link can be established between God and the followers of pantheistic religions through what he calls the "impersonal dimension of God" (ibid., 179). In his attempt to link Christianity with pantheistic Hinduism, he sees God's act of sustaining his creation as equivalent with the manifestation of Brahman in Hinduism. From the point of view of Hindu Advaita Vedanta, he justly affirms that Brahman is "the one unshakeable reality, (which) sustains all things by pervading all things, by identity with all things" (*Depth of the Riches*, 190). However, this is not the equivalent of creation *ex nihilo*, for Brahman *is* all things, while in Christianity God *sustains* all things by his power and grace.

view of the relationship between Christianity and Buddhism, I would only mention his thought that Buddhist emptiness is "an accurate, if limited, description of God's relation with the world."[17] Emptiness would translate as "making space for the other" and as "a feature of the inner-trinitarian relations of the divine persons."[18] As a result, Christianity would need the Buddhist insight on emptiness, for it "fills out the apophatic side of the Trinity's impersonal dimension . . . in a way Christianity alone never has or could."[19]

If we recall the Orthodox doctrine of the Trinity, one can easily realize that Heim's speculative thought cannot be upheld if one wants to remain consistent with Orthodox theology. According to Stăniloae, "through apophatic knowledge we gain a kind of direct experience of his (God's) mystical presence"[20] and therefore apophaticism is not a way of abandoning the personal status of God in favour of his alleged "impersonal" dimension. For Stăniloae apophatic and cataphatic knowledge of God "are neither contradictory nor mutually exclusive, but rather complete each other."[21] As a mystical experience of God, apophaticism prevents Christians from limiting God to the possibilities of rational knowledge and to the descriptive possibilities of language, while the doctrine of emptiness is a way of rejecting Being *per se*.[22] As we have seen in chapter 3, Orthodox theology does not leave room for us to think in terms of an impersonal side of the Trinity. On the one hand, Heim's speculation of an "impersonal note of the divine" as "the fire in the presence of which everything mortal is consumed" derives from a way of representing God's attitude against sin that we find in the Old Testament.[23] As such it speaks about God's judgement of sin and has a juridical meaning, and cannot be taken as fueling ontological speculations on the nature of God. On the other hand, Heim's way of illustrating an impersonal side of the Trinity as "an electrical charge or field, generated

---

17. Ibid., 187.

18. Ibid.

19. Ibid., 183.

20. Stăniloae, *Experience of God*, 95.

21. Ibid., 96.

22. In his criticism of the Russian Orthodox theologian Vladimir Lossky, Stăniloae argues that there is more to apophatic theology than becoming conscious of the impossibility of knowing the divine mystery (Stăniloae, *Ascetică și Mistică Creștină*, 212). The Romanian theologian opposes Lossky's total incognoscibility of God which leads to overstressing apophaticism, while lessening the importance of realizing the vision of divine light and the direct knowledge of God (ibid., 218). Positive and negative theology are complementary, and negative theology can only be done "alternately with positive theology" (ibid., 228).

23. Ibid., 185.

by the constant interchange of the three divine persons with each other"[24] is far from a fair representation of the Orthodox view. There is no room for such an impersonal "interchange," since such an approach could lead to viewing the Persons of the Trinity as the manifestation of that impersonal "field," and thus advocate for a pantheistic Ultimate Reality resembling the *Gottheit* of Eckhart.

Although Heim's view of different salvations seemed to be a promising path in interfaith dialogue, it appears to be a form of Christian inclusivism rather than of genuine pluralism. When compared with Christian salvation as communion with the trinitarian God, other salvations are categorized as "penultimate at best."[25] Ultimately it is (the Christian) God who allows one to pursue his or her religious tradition and makes sure that he or she finds the best fulfilment through it.[26] Different salvations would thus still be "relations with God" and "depend on Christ," for it is Christ who clears "the path to these ends as well as to salvation."[27] Such affirmations could hardly be accepted by a Buddhist or by any other religionist.[28] Since Heim's proposal of "pluralism" is a paternalistic way of "knowing better" what one's non-Christian religious tradition really aims at, it cannot make sense for Buddhists. In fact, his proposal cannot work for either Buddhists or Christians. He hardly does justice to either Christians or Buddhists when he says that a Christian could admit that the Buddha "attained salvation" in the Christian sense, while a Buddhist could admit that Jesus finally "transcended attach-

24. Ibid., 186.

25. Heim, *Depth of the Riches*, 128. In his view, "the 'finality of Christ' and the 'independent validity of other ways' are not mutually exclusive" (Heim, *Salvations*, 3).

26. Heim, *Depth of the Riches*, 263. We have encountered a similar view on the Buddhist side expressed by the Dalai Lama: Christians can reach a personal afterlife in the *Tushita* heavens, but it is only for a limited period (Dalai Lama, "Religious Harmony," 169). True liberation is found only in *nirvana*.

27. Heim, *Depth of the Riches*, 286. The same approach can be pursued from the Buddhist side. For instance, John Makransky says that Christ can be seen "as a remarkable *rupakaya* manifestation of Buddhahood itself, a powerful means through which followers of Christ have indeed communed with and learned to embody liberating qualities of *dharmakaya*" (John Makransky, "Buddha and Christ as Mediators of the Transcendent: A Buddhist Perspective," in Schmidt-Leukel, ed., *Buddhism and Christianity in Dialogue*, 199).

28. Heim finds another source for supporting his view of multiple salvations in Dante's *Divine Comedy*. Those who did not accept the Christian revelation (as well as those who did not know of it at all), but still lived virtuous lives (for instance Muslims such as Saladin and Averroes) would attain a state of immortality in the absence of God resembling Dante's limbo (*Depth of the Riches*, 106). But this solution cannot work from either a Christian or a Muslim point of view. The Christian would argue that the problem of sin can be mediated only by Christ, while the Muslim would be insulted for having his or her heroes (especially Saladin) banned from Allah's heaven.

ment to God and humans, the very conditions of relation, and entered true enlightenment."[29] We must simply remember that the Orthodox Christian sense of salvation is one's perfected communion with the Trinity, while true enlightenment for a Buddhist requires a strong rejection of such a communion. Therefore Heim's project cannot work. On the one hand, although it seemed to provide a way for Christians to understand the salvation of those who follow other religions, the price for doing so is the corruption of major Christian doctrines. To acknowledge an impersonal side of the Trinity is not only useless, but a challenge to the Orthodox view of Ultimate Reality itself. On the other hand, it is of limited use, if any, for Buddhists as well. What other genuine salvations, or rather "enlightenments," could a Buddhist acknowledge besides that of knowing how things really are? If Heim's pluralism cannot work in Buddhist-Christian dialogue, it could hardly provide a genuine formula for any other pairing in interfaith dialogue.

## 4.3 BUDDHIST AND CHRISTIAN DUAL BELONGING

Since pluralism opens the gate for one's belonging to more than one religious tradition, a closely related issue to religious pluralism is that of dual belonging. In her study of six cases of Buddhist and Christian dual belonging, Rose Drew describes dual belongers as people who "practise within both traditions, belong to a Buddhist and a Christian community, identify themselves as fully Buddhist and fully Christian and have made a formal commitment to both traditions (usually through baptism and the taking of the three refuges)."[30] In light of my study of human perfection we can reflect on whether dual belongers can really be representative of both traditions and pursue both ideals of perfection[31] and whether they can provide viable solutions to what appear to be conflicting truth claims.

If we examine the religious beliefs of the dual belongers studied by Drew, we will soon realize that all of them have adopted views that are inconsistent with those of traditional Christianity. Ruben Habito, a Roman

---

29. Heim, *Depth of the Riches*, 285.

30. Drew, *Buddhist and Christian?*, 3–4.

31. Although most Christians who are engaged in interfaith dialogue are either Catholic or Protestant, their view of perfection is not incompatible with deification. The Catholic and the Protestant views of perfection are expressed by the term "sanctification," which is compatible with the Orthodox view of deification, since it too speaks of conformity with the perfected humanity of Jesus Christ. In the *Catechism of the Catholic Church* we find several synonyms of deification, such as being "partakers of the divine nature" (460, 1129, 1996, 2009), being "divinized" (398, 1988), and made "sharers in the divine nature" (51, 1212).

Catholic and former Jesuit, can no longer believe in a creator God that sustains the universe, and instead speaks of an "Unknowable Mystery" to which we should all surrender.[32] John Keenan, an Episcopal priest, took the three Buddhist refuges and argues in a truly Mahayana fashion that God is "not a noun, but a verb."[33] Sallie King, a Christian Quaker, took the three refuges with Thich Nhat Hanh, and reached the conclusion that God is not "a being with a will."[34] Don Cupitt, a former Anglican priest, argues that God and *nirvana* do not describe an objective reality, but represent in a symbolic way what is spiritually required of us. In other words, God and *nirvana* would be functional equivalents to something that cannot be expressed by words.[35] For Maria Reis Habito, a Roman Catholic, *nirvana* and the Kingdom of God point to the same reality.[36] As we can see, for all of them the price of dual belonging is that of adopting doctrinal views that are far from those of traditional Christianity. Catherine Cornille concluded that multiple religious belonging is open for those "who no longer feel compelled to accept every single aspect of the tradition without question" and thus "come to adopt a more piecemeal approach to doctrine, symbols and practices governed by personal judgment and taste."[37] As a result, she is very skeptical about the real possibility and consistency of dual belonging.[38] In the next two sections I will verify the soundness of her skepticism by assessing the thought of two important participants in Buddhist-Christian dialogue who call themselves dual belongers: Paul Knitter and Thich Nhat Hanh.

## 4.3.1 Knitter's Crossing of the Rubicon

Paul Knitter affirms a pluralistic approach he calls the "Mutuality Model," which would mean more than simply acknowledging the existing plurality of religions. In his view one should seek their relationship, or their openness to learning from each other.[39] In other words, what is needed today

---

32. Drew, *Buddhist and Christian?*, 25.

33. Ibid., 57.

34. Ibid.

35. Ibid., 43.

36. Ibid., 129.

37. Catherine Cornille, "The Dynamics of Multiple Belonging," in Cornille, ed., *Many Mansions?*, 3.

38. For Cornille, religious double belonging is similar to adultery, while adherence to a tradition is likened to complete faithfulness in marriage (Cornille, "Double Religious Belonging," 48).

39. Knitter, *Introducing Theologies of Religions*, 110.

in interfaith dialogue is a "crossing of the Rubicon," which is a move by which all religions are called to explore a "new terrain full of new possibilities as well as new uncertainties."[40] Knitter sees three possible bridges for the religions to cross into this new terrain: (1) the "philosophical-historical bridge," which searches for an Ultimate Reality behind all religions which would unite them; (2) the "religious-mystical bridge," which sees the meeting point of religions in the mystical experiences of their adherents, and (3) the "ethical-practical bridge," which seeks to formulate a common ethics and the pursuit of common concerns for the welfare of our world.

In 2002, when Knitter wrote his book *Introducing Theologies of Religions,* he opted for the third bridge (the "Ethical-practical bridge"). Liberation theology led him to cultivate a special concern for social justice, the eradication of poverty, violence, and other such social plagues.[41] From this perspective, the true reference point to indicate whether a religion is true or false is not whether it believes in one God, or in Jesus as Saviour, but rather whether it brings peace and justice in the world. Although the concern for peace and justice should concern any human, religious or not, Knitter's approach led him to views that are no longer consistent with Catholic faith.

The development of Paul Knitter's theological thought could itself constitute the topic of an entire research thesis. After graduating from the Pontifical Gregorian University in 1966, he taught at the Catholic Theological Union in Chicago and served as a priest until 1975. After leaving the priesthood he taught undergraduates at Xavier University in Cincinnati for about thirty years, but over time doubts arose in his mind on key Christian doctrines, and he slowly distanced himself from traditional Catholic doctrines.[42] He came to reject the personhood of God[43] and admitted he could no longer accept the foundational "stone beliefs" of Christianity such as the atonement through Jesus' sacrifice, his physical resurrection, his second return, that he is the only Son of God, and his dual nature—divine and

---

40. Ibid., 112.

41. Ibid., 137. Knitter was a member of the Board of Directors for CRISPAZ (Christians for Peace in El Salvador) from 1986 until 2004. He explores liberation theology in his books *One Earth, Many Religions* and *Jesus and the Other Names.* A similar social stand is seen in the liberation theology of Aloysius Pieris, who argues that Jesus brings to the religions of Asia "the covenant between YHWH and the nonpersons of the world" (Pieris, *Fire and Water,* 150).

42. Knitter, *Without Buddha,* ix–xiii.

43. He came to express the view that God is not a Person, but rather "a personal energy" or "a creative, sustaining vitality that is one with my vitality" (ibid., 135).

human.[44] Such beliefs no longer "make sense" for him, and he assures his readers that it is the same for many other Christians.[45]

In his recent book, *Without Buddha I Could not be a Christian*, he states that a relational God must be understood as an empty God, for he exists only "*in and out of* relationships" and therefore "an appropriate symbol for God" is "Emptiness or InterBeing."[46] In his words, "God is neither a noun nor an adjective. God is a verb!"[47] We have already encountered this definition of Ultimate Reality as a way of expressing how things really are. But it was in Buddhism, not in Christian Dogmatics. This shift in the way of seeing God was the key aspect that transformed Knitter's understanding of traditional Christian doctrines. It led him to affirm that "Son of God" should rather be interpreted as "the awakened One," for this would be a "more engaging and challenging way of understanding the divinity of Jesus' instead of the "two natures in one person."[48] But in light of what we have seen expressed by Stăniloae in chapter 3, such a view would obviously destroy the concept of human perfection as deification. Knitter's interpretation of Jesus' physical resurrection would have the same effect. He argues it should be seen as only one of many "symbolic stories" that "need not to be taken literally," for its truth "lies not in its historical facticity but in its empowering meaning."[49] However, as we have seen explained by Stăniloae, the resurrection is foundational for the Christian faith, as it represents the very image of fulfilled perfection. Once he rejected the personhood of God, the natural result was that Knitter rejected an ideal of human perfection in a personal form as well.[50]

---

44. Ibid., 92–93.

45. Ibid., 93.

46. Ibid., 18–19. He borrowed the term "Interbeing" from Nhat Hanh, who uses it as a translation of *shunyata* (ibid.,12). He is equally happy with a synonym coined by the Tibetan nun Pema Chödrön as "Groundlessness" (ibid.).

47. Ibid., 19.

48. Ibid., 114. In contradiction to Stăniloae's view of the relationship between the two natures in Christ, for Knitter Jesus' divinity "was something he *became*" (ibid.). In saying that Jesus' divinity is the realization of "the *full potential of human nature*" (ibid., 116), he claims to be consistent with Rahner, his former teacher. However, Rahner did not reject the doctrine of the two natures in Christ, or of his divine nature as *different* from his human nature. Rahner always maintains the incarnation of a real divine Son of God (*Foundations of Christian Faith*, 212).

49. Knitter, *Without Buddha*, 102.

50. Following a "new" and "fuller light" on a passage in John 12:24, in which Jesus speaks of the grain which needs to die in order to bear fruit, he came to realize that our destiny consists in "a life after death that is no longer life lived as individuals" (ibid., 89).

These are several brief remarks on the development of Knitter's theological thought. Nevertheless, they serve to affirm that Cobb's warning of the possibility of crossing into the other tradition and then not being able to come back is justified.[51] Although Knitter often speaks in his book of his "passing over and back from Buddhism to Christianity," it seems that his journey was just one way.[52] In 2008, 42 years after being ordained as a Catholic priest, he took refuge in the Buddha, in the *dharma* and the *sangha*, and pronounced the *Bodhisattva* vows. As a "Buddhist Christian," as he now calls himself,[53] he says that his "relationship with Buddha has clarified and deepened" his "commitment to Christ,"[54] that "double-belonging" is not only possible, but "necessary" and that he "can be a Christian only by also being a Buddhist."[55] Since such claims are hardly realistic in light of the traditional views of human perfection, in chapter 9 I will attempt to show that a better method for clarifying and deepening one's own tradition through dialogue with the others is that of comparative theology.

51. Cobb warns that once one crosses the bridge to experience Buddhism from within, he or she is "shut off from the Christian world," for "Buddhism can be understood only by rejecting Western modes of thought and experience" (Cobb, *Beyond Dialogue*, 65, 98). A similar warning is expressed by Cornille, when she says that "[t] here is often no 'coming back' from a deep identification with another religious tradition'" (Catherine Cornille, "The Dynamics of Multiple Belonging," in Cornille, ed., *Many Mansions?*, 4).

52. Knitter, *Without Buddha*, 17, 21, 40, 81, 82, etc. D'Costa has warned that "the Rubicon is a deeper and more treacherous river than initially recognized" (D'Costa, "Preface," in D'Costa, ed., *Christian Uniqueness Reconsidered*, xxii). This warning should be seriously considered by those who venture into its waters in search for a deeper spiritual experience, or a cross-fertilization of traditions.

53. Ibid., 216.

54. Ibid., 130.

55. Ibid., 216. Another notorious example of Christian and Buddhist dual religious belonging is the German Jesuit Hugo M. Enomiya-Lassalle (1898–1990). He went to Japan in 1929 as a missionary, but there he discovered Zen and became interested in finding ways to use it for renewing and deepening the Christian faith. In 1974 he had the experience of awakening (*kensho*) and became a Zen master, teaching Zen meditation to Catholics both in Japan and in Europe as a means for inner purification and sanctification. His interest was similar to that of William Johnston and Thomas Merton—the renewal of Christian mysticism with Buddhist resources. Enomiya-Lassalle did not encourage syncretism, but saw Zen as a method for contemplating Christ, not as a practice indebted to Buddhist philosophy. For a detailed account of his spiritual journey, see Ursula Baatz, *Hugo M. Enomiya-Lassalle*.

## 4.3.2 Thich Nhat Hanh's Dual Spiritual Citizenship

A famous Buddhist advocate of dual belonging is the Vietnamese Zen monk Thich Nhat Hanh (b. 1926). The element that has made him a very popular author in the West is his apparent total openness towards both Buddhism and Christianity, expressed by his claim to be a follower of both the Buddha and the Christ as his "spiritual ancestors."[56] Not only does he not see any contradiction in claiming such a dual religious citizenship, but he even claims it makes him feel stronger, for it gives him "more than one root."[57] In his view, the road is open for any of us to become "a Buddha or Lord Jesus,"[58] and a true follower of one of the two religions should consider himself or herself a follower of the other religion as well.[59]

Nhat Hanh's pluralist approach originates in the Kantian assumption of a distinction between *phenomena* and *noumena* and of a "ground of being" beyond the personal God.[60] Since there is a more fundamental Ultimate Reality than the personal God, one should not discuss "whether God is a person or not," for it would be "just a waste of time."[61] In his comment on the Nicene Creed, Nhat Hanh argues that the true nature of God the Father would be *nirvana*, which in his use is an equivalent for emptiness.[62] Since we have encountered and criticized this thought in the previous section on Knitter, there is no need to repeat why his proposal cannot be accepted by traditional Christians. When he calls for a reciprocal transformation of Buddhism and Christianity, affirming that "both traditions can learn a lot from each other,"[63] we find that the "reciprocal" transformation of the two traditions consists only of the transformation of Christianity, which should be enriched by the "insight of interbeing and of non-duality" provided by Buddhism.[64]

In fact, although I have included Nhat Hanh among the dual belongers, he hardly is one. He should rather be seen as a Buddhist inclusivist

56. Nhat Hanh, *Living Buddha*, 100.

57. Ibid.

58. Ibid., 47.

59. Ibid., 197.

60. Nhat Hanh, *Going Home*, 11.

61. Ibid., 56.

62. Ibid., 137. His particular way of saying that we should discover the Buddha nature inside us is by exhorting that we should not "look for nirvana elsewhere or in the future. Because you are it" (ibid., 10).

63. Ibid., 98.

64. Ibid. "Interbeing" expresses the interdepence of all reality. It is another way of affirmaing the Buddhist doctrine of dependent co-arising.

who faithfully follows his Zen tradition, while using skilful means for conveying the Buddhist message in a Christian context. Therefore Kiblinger's verdict on Nhat Hanh's thought is justified when she says that "he privileges Buddhist ideas, ignores crucial differences, and interprets Christian teachings and practices very inadequately."[65] His paternalistic way of teaching Christians what their practice really means completely disregards the basics of Christianity and as such does not provide a real basis for dialogue.

## 4.4 PLURALISM, DUAL BELONGING AND SPIRITUAL PRACTICE

As we have seen in the previous sections, pluralism is a subtle way of rejecting at least one of the traditions in dialogue, usually one's Christian tradition, and eventually of grounding a new tradition which would benefit from the wisdom of both. The major difficulty of religious pluralism is that its adherents relativize all particular traditions, but fail to grasp their own limitations and be critical of their own assumptions. Whenever pluralists state a more fundamental Ultimate Reality, a higher ground from where one would have a bird's eye view of all others, they fail to realize that it must itself fall under the spell of relativism, and as such a true pluralism is not tenable. Stating a common goal of all religions always destroys (at least) the particular traditions of Christianity and favours heretical views on it. As a result, when McGrath argues that the Christianity advocated by pluralists "would not be recognizable as such to most of its adherents,"[66] he would probably be expressing Stăniloae's stand as well. Similar comments could come from the Buddhist side. As for a pluralism advocated by particularists such as Heim, it can rather be seen as a form of Christian inclusivism.

---

65. Kristin Beise Kiblinger, "Buddhist Stances Towards Others: Types, Examples, Considerations," in Schmidt-Leukel, ed., *Buddhist Attitudes*, 38. As examples of such "inadequate" interpretations, Nhat Hanh argues that the Eucharist is a way of becoming fully aware of "the body of reality in us" (*Living Buddha*, 32), or language meant to wake us up to mindfulness (*Going Home*, 106–7). The rite of baptism is for him "a way of recognizing that every human being . . . is capable of manifesting these qualities (the ten attributes of the Buddha)" (*Living Buddha*, 44). He admitted to being scandalized by the picture of Jesus on the cross, and argues that Jesus should rather be portrayed in other ways "like sitting in the lotus position or doing walking meditation" (*Going Home*, 46).

66. McGrath, "The Christian Church's Response to Pluralism," 489. He argues that "the pluralist agenda forces its advocates to adopt heretical views of Christ in order to meet its needs" (488).

Knitter uses an interesting analogy to explain the need for a pluralistic approach in interfaith dialogue.[67] If we look at the universe with our naked eye we will see only a tiny fraction of the multitude of stars and galaxies. To see more we need a telescope. This is what each religion does—it uses a telescope to have a better look at a particular realm of reality. But telescopes reduce the whole to a little portion of the sky. If we borrow another one's telescope we will see another portion of it, and so on. The more telescopes we use, the more we understand what is out there. Likewise, diverse religious traditions build together a wider perspective on reality. Although this is a nice story, my study has shown that it does not apply to Buddhist-Christian dialogue. When followers of diverse religious traditions attempt to help each other to see more of the universe, the usual result is that they ignore or forget what they have originally seen with their own telescope, at which point the whole process really ceases to be truly pluralistic. Knitter fails to see that pluralism is itself a telescope and thus has its own limitations. His pluralist telescope made him ignore the particularities which make each religious tradition unique and even irreconcilable with other traditions. And finally, his conversion to Buddhism shows that he did not remain faithful to his own agenda of using supplementary telescopes for broadening his view of reality, for he came to ignore what he had first seen with his "Christian telescope."

Cobb appears to be right when he reminds us that dialogue is not possible if one sacrifices all that identifies him or her as a partner in dialogue.[68] The pluralist agenda leaves no room for a respectful dialogue between genuine Buddhist and Christian traditions, and rather encourages a dialogue of their unorthodox variants. Therefore pluralism and its tolerance to all religious traditions is in fact a way of rejecting all in their particularities, which makes it hostile to all. As such, it appears that Knitter's illustration of the telescopes starts from the premise that world religions *must* form a whole and that *none of them*, taken by itself, can give a full account of Ultimate Reality. However, one could hardly have a bird's eye view on world religions from which to formulate a higher vision of religious unity. As a result, I agree with Netland when he says that "a genuinely pluralistic model that is coherent and does not privilege any particular religious perspective" is very hard to formulate.[69] The pluralist proposals we have seen so far cannot uphold an honest representation of *both* Buddhism *and* Christianity.

67. Knitter, *Introducing Theologies of Religions,* 11.
68. Cobb, *Beyond Dialogue,* 45.
69. Netland, *Encountering Religious Pluralism,* 213.

These comments are valid for the phenomenon of dual belonging as well, since its doctrinal foundation is religious pluralism. An intriguing aspect is that only Westerners who were brought up in a Christian background become dual belongers. Among the six cases studied by Drew in her book, there is no Buddhist that would claim dual belonging. In fact, except Nhat Hanh, I am not aware of any other Buddhist who claims to be a follower of Christ as well, which indicates that only Christians feel that their tradition is unsatisfactory and look for renewal in Buddhism. One can see this lack of satisfaction manifested among Christians when they adopt spiritual practices from Eastern religions. I will refer here only to the issue of adopting Buddhist (especially Zen) meditation by Christians, and I will analyze this issue in light of the weaknesses of religious pluralism.

The most vocal Christian tradition against borrowing forms of spiritual practice from the Eastern religions is the Roman Catholic Church.[70] Joseph Cardinal Ratzinger's "Letter to the Bishops of the Catholic Church on Some Aspects of Christian Meditation" warns against the attempt "to fuse Christian meditation with that which is non-Christian" which occurs in "the present diffusion of eastern methods of meditation in the Christian world and in ecclesial communities."[71] He warns against Buddhist methods which promote an equivalence between God and *dharmakaya*, for it would mean "abandoning not only meditation on the salvific works accomplished in history by the God of the Old and New Covenant, but also the very idea of the One and Triune God" in favour of an impersonal Ultimate Reality.[72] Another important Catholic theologian, Hans Urs von Balthasar, called the use of Eastern techniques a betrayal of Christian faith, for "the Eastern meditation methods cannot be isolated from a precise worldview."[73] In his view, one cannot extract spiritual practices from the soil that generated them without also importing their whole worldview.

The rejection of borrowing spiritual practices across very different religious traditions comes not only from Christian theologians. Klaus

70. According to the *Dominus Iesus* declaration, the Catholic Church rejects "the eclecticism of those who, in theological research, uncritically absorb ideas from a variety of philosophical and theological contexts without regard for consistency, systematic connection, or compatibility with Christian truth" (paragraph 4).

71. Cardinal Joseph Ratzinger warns in his homily "Pro Eligendo Romano Pontifice" against the new "dictatorship of relativism" and implicitly against the idea of Japanese Catholics getting involved in Zen meditation.

72. "Letter to the Bishops of the Catholic Church on Some Aspects of Christian Meditation."

73. Von Balthasar, "Meditation als Verrat [Meditation as Betrayal]," 261. In his view, "true Christians can never truly learn Zen meditation, for they are too heavily impregnated by the personal grace and love of Christ" (266).

Zernickow, a Zen teacher in Berlin, argues that Zen meditation for Christians would be a "vegetarian meat dish."[74] He is very critical of any syncretistic blending of Christianity and Zen, following the warnings of various Zen masters about the incompatibility between Zen and Pure Land Buddhism. Since Zen is devoted entirely to the use of Own Power (*jiriki*), it is hardly possible that a tradition which advocates the indispensability of faith and grace could be of any help, if not in fact destructive. Therefore in his view the so-called "Christian Zen" is "depriving Zen of its life, mutilating it and abusing it for internal Church innovation."[75] On the one hand, a follower of Zen must see everything the church teaches on grace and faith as the proof of a "profound spiritual blindness" and as such to reject it. On the other hand, a Christian who wants to find full enlightenment must acknowledge that Zen is "fundamentally opposed" to the Christian faith.[76] Although this is an example of intolerance on the Buddhist side, it is nevertheless consistent with Zen doctrine. As a result, it is hardly possible to reconcile Zen meditation with Christian practice or to justify other practices witnessed by Knitter in his encounters with people he calls "Asian Christians," such as a "Buddhist Mass" or an "Indian Eucharist."[77]

A real tasting of Buddhism by Christians and of Christianity by Buddhists is hardly possible, as long as they want to remain faithful to their tradition. A Christian cannot simply try out Buddhism on its own terms and then return to Christianity, as he or she must completely accept its foundations (impermanence and no creator God) in order to be able to have a true experience of Buddhism. Once done so, he or she no longer can be considered faithful to a Christian tradition. Likewise, for the Buddhist, it is hardly possible to taste Christianity by trusting a self-existing God and still remain a Buddhist. A mere experiencing of rituals, forms and gestures is not a real "crossing of the Rubicon." A real crossing always involves leaving one's identity on the other shore. Therefore Aloysius Pieris' requirement of "*a communicatio in sacris* with Buddhists,"[78] seen as a "self-effacing baptismal entry into the Buddhist tradition" is hardly realistic.[79]

---

74. Zernickow, "Christliches Zen." Paradoxically, the previous article in the same magazine praises the initiative of the Jesuit Hugo M. Enomiya-Lassalle in grounding a Zen meditation centre for Christians in Tokyo. According to this author, Christians who practice Zen meditation would be able to recover a "forgotten dimension" of Christian contemplation and find inner peace (Riesenhuber, "Zen unter Christen in Japan").

75. Zernickow, "Christliches Zen," 30.

76. Ibid., 31.

77. Knitter, *Without Buddha*, 166.

78. Pieris, *Love Meets Wisdom*, 120.

79. Ibid., 123. In Pieris' view, this would be a way of following Jesus' example: "Like

In the next part of this book I will pursue a more profound study of four scholars who laid the foundations of contemporary Buddhist-Christian dialogue. They are three Japanese Zen Buddhist scholars (Kitaro Nishida, Keiji Nishitani and Masao Abe) and an American Process theologian (John Cobb). They will offer help to get beyond the present impasse to which the classic theologies of religions lead and offer precious hints for applying the method of comparative theology to Buddhist-Christian dialogue.

---

our Lord and Master who humbly let himself be initiated by a recognized Guru in Israel, John the Baptizer, so too should we plunge into the Jordan of Buddhist spirituality in the presence of an authoritative guide" (ibid.). However, this example is irrelevant for Buddhist-Christian dialogue since both John the Baptist and Jesus belonged to the same Judaic tradition.

# PART 2

# A Critical Assessment of the Founding Fathers of Contemporary Buddhist-Christian Dialogue as a Lead towards Comparative Theology

Modern scholarly dialogue between Buddhists and Christians started only as late as the beginning of the twentieth century and was initiated by a group of philosophers centred at the University of Kyoto who attempted a creative adaptation of Western philosophy (especially existentialism and nihilism) to the Japanese context, or more precisely, to bring the concepts of Zen and Pure Land Buddhism into the domain of modern philosophy. As a result, my research has to start there, with the Kyoto School of Philosophy and its most important representatives. But first of all I need to present the historical context in which their philosophical views have developed.

The year 1868 marks for Japan the end of nearly 250 years of feudal isolation from the Western world, and the start of the Meiji Restoration (1868–1912), a period of heavy industrialization by adopting Western economic models and technology. Along with Western technology, information, jurisprudence and fashion came Western philosophy and Christianity, a religion which had been eradicated from the land of the shoguns during the first half of the seventeenth century. The influx of new philosophical ideas was initially welcomed, but as soon as Japan became the super-power of East Asia at the beginning of the twentieth century, especially during the Early Showa Period (1926–1945), Western philosophy came to be seen as a threat to traditional Japanese values and culture. As a result, in parallel with the need to build up a strong economy and army in order to protect its identity and not allow itself to become a colony of Western powers, Japan felt the need to revitalize its own traditional values. This is the historical context in which the Kyoto School emerged.

Most of the Kyoto philosophers are followers of either Zen or Pure Land Buddhism and, unlike their Western counterparts, they could never really separate philosophy from religion.[1] As Jan Van Bragt, the former president of the Nanzan Institute for Religion and Culture in Nagoya,[2] affirms, the philosophy of the Kyoto School is "through and through religious,"[3] having as characteristics "a thoroughgoing loyalty to its own traditions, a committed openness to Western traditions, and a deliberate attempt to bring about a synthesis of East and West."[4] The goal of reconciling philosophy and religion generates uneasiness *per se* since from the point of view of Western philosophy, Zen Buddhism (and religion in general) can hardly offer a valid epistemological base. Western philosophy demands the steady use of reason and logic, while Zen Buddhism explores a domain beyond them. Nevertheless, despite these contradictions in philosophical methodology, the efforts of the Kyoto philosophers have generated a genuine dialogue between the *religious* traditions of Buddhism and Christianity, for they have investigated not only Western existentialism and nihilism, but also fundamental themes of Christian theology and so opened the way for what is today modern Buddhist-Christian dialogue.[5]

In this part of my book I will assess the work of three of its most important representatives—Nishida, Nishitani and Abe—in light of what we have seen in Part I to be the view of human perfection in the traditions of Mahayana Buddhism and Orthodox Christianity. But first of all I must acknowledge at least two important limitations of my work. One stems from the need to study their work in translation, with much of their work being still untranslated and inaccessible in English. However, James Heisig, another ex-president of the Nanzan Institute, assures us that reading them

1. Kitaro Nishida, Shin'ichi Hisamatsu, Keiji Nishitani, and Shizuteru Ueda are Zen Buddhists, while Hajime Tanabe and Yoshinori Takeuchi are Shin Buddhists.

2. The aim of this institute is to create a space for studying the relationship between modern culture, Christianity and the religions of the Far East.

3. Jan Van Bragt, "Translator's Introduction," in Nishitani, *Religion and Nothingness*, xxxiii.

4. Ibid., xxviii.

5. In the words of Frederick Franck, the Kyoto School provided "the solid ground on which the dialogue between Mahayana Buddhism and the other world religions became possible" (Frederick Franck, "Prologue," in Franck, ed., *Buddha Eye*, 3).

in translation would not cause misunderstanding.[6] As for their works that are found so far only in Japanese, I must assume that they would not bring significant changes to what we have in translation. Another limitation concerns how much of their writings to consider, since they lived on average more than 80 years and each left us with a huge amount of writings, not to mention the further difficulty of following the development of their thought over time. As one can expect, I could not investigate their philosophy in depth, so I must limit myself to picking up recurrent themes for Buddhist-Christian dialogue in their thinking and focus on an assessment of their understanding of Christianity.

The first modern Japanese philosopher and the acknowledged founder of the Kyoto School was Kitaro Nishida (1875–1945), the first who conducted a serious study of the Western classics and tried to assess them through the lens of Zen Buddhism. Nishida was also the first Japanese scholar who really engaged Zen Buddhism in dialogue with Christianity and started a methodology among Kyoto philosophers that I will call a Zen hermeneutics of Christianity. The next important figure of the Kyoto School was Hajime Tanabe (1885–1962), a friend of Nishida and a follower of Shin Buddhism. In 1930 Tanabe started to criticize the religious turn taken by Nishida's philosophy as an attempt to break the academic boundaries between religion and philosophy and to "systematize the religious awareness" by the use of philosophy.[7] The ideological conflict that arose between them lasted until Nishida's death in 1945, and pushed them both to refine their thinking, thus giving way to new developments in Japanese philosophy.[8]

Tanabe is a less important figure for Buddhist-Christian dialogue, as he was less interested in this topic in comparison to Nishida and his disciple Nishitani. Therefore I will turn to assessing the third chronologically important figure of the Kyoto School, Keiji Nishitani (1900–1990), the one who continued to explore the line of thought initiated by Nishida and brought new insights into Buddhist-Christian dialogue through his attempt to counteract the phenomenon of nihilism, which was seen by him as threatening the very foundation of Western civilization. He argued that the traditional

6. James Heisig argues that "for the goal of the Kyoto philosophers—a grafting of Japanese thought on world philosophy—to be fulfilled, they *must* be read in translation (not only in the original)" (Heisig, *Philosophers of Nothingness*, 20).

7. Yusa, *Zen & Philosophy*, 231. The tension between Nishida and Tanabe arose in 1930 when Nishida published his *System of the Self-awareness of the Universal*, to which Tanabe responded with the critical article "Requesting Professor Nishida's elucidation" (ibid.).

8. Michiko Yusa, Nishida's biographer, argues that their split gave to the Kyoto School two lines of thought—Nishidan and Tanabean philosophy (ibid., 232).

Christian view of God as personal and trinitarian is of no help in overcoming nihilism and that a valid solution would be provided by adopting the standpoint of emptiness, as formulated in Zen Buddhism.

The third important figure of the Kyoto School I chose to include in my research is Masao Abe (1916–2006), who is significantly different from Nishida and Nishitani. Although a disciple of Nishitani, he was less interested in teaching philosophy, and much more involved as a teacher and promoter of Zen Buddhism throughout the Western world. Unlike his predecessors at Kyoto, he was less concerned with bridging the gap between Western and Eastern *philosophy* and more interested in the religious aspects that Buddhism and Christianity can share. As a result, he started a dialogue with important Christian theologians such as Moltmann, Rahner, Pannenberg and Küng. He was the first to argue that Buddhist-Christian dialogue should go beyond the stage of mutual understanding and enter the stage of mutual transformation so that they could both meet the challenge of modern nihilism. In his view, Buddhism could improve its vision of time and history, and find a better ground for ethics and social justice, while Christianity would benefit from this dialogue by adopting a more realistic view of God as suprapersonal. His views will provide an important lead towards applying the method of comparative theology in Buddhist-Christian dialogue.

The fourth representative of Buddhist-Christian dialogue whose work I will assess in this part of my book is John B. Cobb Jr., an American theologian with close links to the Kyoto School. Hans Küng considers him and Masao Abe to be the founders of a scholarly Buddhist-Christian Dialogue, an affirmation we will see is well justified.[9] Cobb and Abe met at an international conference organized by the University of Hawaii and started a long and fruitful interfaith dialogue which lasted until Abe's death in 2006. Their efforts contributed to founding the Society for Buddhist-Christian Studies and its journal (*Buddhist-Christian Studies*) in 1981 at the University of Hawaii. In 1984 they started the International Buddhist-Christian Theological Encounter (informally known as the Cobb-Abe group).

John Cobb approaches Buddhist-Christian dialogue as a Process theologian. He also proposes a mutual transformation of Buddhism and Christianity, and invites us to recognize the complementarity of the two religious traditions and their capacity to fulfil different needs for the same person. In his view, Buddhists can learn from Christianity to develop a better sense of history and social action and a way of seeing the Amida Buddha as personal and ethical. What Christians can learn from Buddhism is a new vision of

---

9. Hans Küng, "God's Self-Renunciation and Buddhist Emptiness: A Christian Response to Masao Abe," in Ives, ed., *Divine Emptiness*, 208.

God as emptiness, and the replacement of the traditional view of the Kingdom of God with what he calls a "Christianized Nirvana." Cobb's views will provide another entry for applying comparative theology in my research.

Given the vast domain of research that is today Buddhist-Christian dialogue, the many authors involved in it both in the West and the East, and the huge amount of literature they have produced, it would probably be hard to find a general consensus that Nishida, Nishitani, Abe and Cobb are *the* founding fathers of Buddhist-Christian dialogue. However, no serious study of this topic can ignore them, and none of the many authors who contribute today to this topic can pretend not to have been influenced by them. Therefore, although I limit this part of my book to these four authors, this limitation still enables me to explore much of the essence of Buddhist-Christian dialogue and to lead me to apply the method of comparative theology to this vast domain of research.

# 5

# Kitaro Nishida (1870–1945)

## The First Modern Japanese Philosopher Encounters Christianity

Nishida is universally recognized as the founder of the Kyoto School and the first true modern Japanese philosopher. He graduated in 1894 from Tokyo University with a degree in philosophy and served as a high-school teacher until 1909. Besides Western philosophy, the other important influence on his life was Zen Buddhism, which he practiced in the Rinzai tradition from 1896 until 1906.[1] The tension between the methods of Zen and modern Western philosophy, one providing a direct insight on the nature of reality, and the other confined to reason and logic, was the fuel that made him seek a way of reconciling them by expressing Zen concepts in an acceptable modern philosophical language. This endeavour moulded him into a world-class philosopher and also challenged him to start a new line of philosophical thought, the result of which was the Kyoto School. In the words of Yoshinori Takeuchi, one of his many students, "in him Japan had the philosophical genius who was the first to know how to build a system permeated with the spirit of Buddhist meditation by fully employing Western methods of thinking."[2] In 1910 he was made assistant professor of philosophy at the

1. Yusa, *Zen & Philosophy*, 80–81. Yusa sees a direct link between Nishida's start of Zen practice and the birth of his first daughter, on March 25, 1896. In a letter to a friend, he expressed his sorrow for having chosen family life (ibid., 48–49). According to Fritz Buri, he eventually attained enlightenment (Buri, *The Buddha-Christ*, 39).

2. Yoshinori Takeuchi, "The Philosophy of Nishida," in Franck, ed., *Buddha Eye*, 181. Yusa affirms that Nishida's philosophy is grounded on "the solid understanding of the worldview espoused by Zen Buddhism" (Yusa, *Zen & Philosophy*, 73).

Kyoto Imperial University, and in 1913 full professor.[3] He retired in 1928, but continued to give lectures and work out his philosophical ideas. Shortly before his death in 1945, he published his major essay *The Logic of Place of Nothingness and the Religious Worldview*, in which he speaks openly of Zen as the true reference point of his philosophy.

Given his ambitious goal of establishing the rational foundations for the "certain characteristic truth" of Zen,[4] Nishida had to coin new terms as he was advancing in uncharted philosophical territory. This was no easy achievement, and the natural hardships are reflected in the difficult style of his writings and lectures.[5] An important clue for understanding Nishida is given by D.T. Suzuki, his life-long friend and best known promoter of Zen in the Western world, who said that understanding Nishida is difficult "unless one is passably acquainted with Zen experience."[6] This advice will prove to be of great help since, according to David Dilworth, "it was only in the last years of his career that Nishida made explicit use of his own religious heritage to illustrate his views."[7]

## 5.1 STAGES OF DEVELOPMENT IN NISHIDA'S PHILOSOPHY

The philosophy of Nishida developed in several stages.[8] The first culminated with the essay *An Inquiry into the Good* (1911), which set him apart as an original philosopher. The defining aspect of this stage is the appropriation of the concept of "pure experience" from William James' philosophy of

3. Ibid.,137.

4. Matao Noda, one of Nishida's students, recalls him expressing such an aim (Heisig, *Philosophers of Nothingness*, 288).

5. Even Shizuteru Ueda, one of his disciples, confesses that he did not understand Nishida at times (ibid., 33), while Heisig, the former director of the Nanzan Institute in Kyoto, himself one of the best scholars on the Kyoto School, admits of Nishida's last and most important essay ("The Logic of Place of Nothingness and the Religious Worldview") that large sections of it "are in effect unintelligible" (Heisig, *Philosophers of Nothingness*, 99).

6. D. T. Suzuki, "How to Read Nishida," in Nishida, *A Study of Good*, iii. This is the first English edition of Nishida's book, which was eventually retranslated in 1990 by Masao Abe and Christopher Ives as *An Inquiry into the Good*.

7. David Dilworth, "Introduction: Nishida's Critique of the Religious Consciousness," in Nishida, *Last Writings*, 2. According to Yusa, Nishida started to express the religious sources of his philosophical system only as late as 1929 (Yusa, *Zen & Philosophy*, 229).

8. I will follow Yoshinori Takeuchi in presenting this development ("The Philosophy of Nishida," in Franck, ed., *Buddha Eye*, 179–202).

radical empiricism. Nishida sets forth the meaning of pure experience as the stage of knowing something before judging or categorizing it. He calls it "pure" because it is not affected by the subject-object dichotomy and lacks "the least addition of deliberative discrimination."[9] Pure experience has a very close meaning to what the founder of Buddhism called "sensation," the second aggregate that constitutes human nature. Interestingly, James ascribes to the "prereflective stage of experience" the name "sensation," while the "subsequent mental operations performed upon sensation" are called "perception,"[10] the name of the third aggregate in Buddhism.

Nishida follows James on the nature of pure experience as being the "primary stuff of reality"[11] but criticizes him for not grasping "the unifying power at work at the foundation of all experiences,"[12] i.e., for not seeing the absolute truth behind them. Unlike the empiricists, who view experience as gathered from the outside by an "observer," Nishida claims that pure experience is to be viewed from the inside, as "active and constructive" and as building up the observer and what we currently call "self-awareness."[13] Therefore experience should not be defined in a dualistic way, as if an individual self becomes conscious of the external world, but rather as reality becoming aware of itself. In his *Inquiry into the Good*, Nishida uses a familiar Buddhist way of formulating his view of the individual, saying that "it is not that the individual possesses feeling and the will, but rather that feeling and the will create the individual."[14] We can recognize here the theme of

9. Nishida, *An Inquiry into the Good*, 3. The influence of James is obvious. In his *Essays in Radical Empiricism*, James says: "There is no thought-stuff different from thing-stuff, I said; but the same identical piece of 'pure experience' (which was the name I gave to the materia prima of everything) can stand alternately for a 'fact of consciousness' or for a physical reality, according as it is taken in one context or in another'" (James, *Essays in Radical Empiricism*, 56). Heisig confirms that Nishida imported his notion of pure experience from James's *Essays* (Heisig, *Philosophers of Nothingness*, 45). James's philosophy of radical empiricism comes very close to Buddhist doctrines, and Nishida acknowledged it (Yusa, *Zen & Philosophy*, 125). According to Yusa, Nishida studied the *Essays* in 1905 (ibid., 96).

10. Miranda Shaw, "William James and Yogacara Philosophy," 227. Shaw explains that in James' philosophy experience is "an encompassing category that envelops experiencer and content, or subject and object, in a single category through which a definite dividing line cannot be drawn" (227). Although James did have a basic knowledge of Buddhism, it is not clear whether his views were informed by Buddhism or just confirmed by it. For an analysis of their similarities, see Shaw's article, 223–44.

11. Yusa, *Zen & Philosophy*, 108.

12. Ibid., 109.

13. Masao Abe's commentary in his "Introduction" to Kitaro Nishida, *An Inquiry into the Good*, xviii.

14. Nishida, *An Inquiry into the Good*, 50.

the five aggregates, with the fifth aggregate of consciousness as responsible for producing self-awareness. In accordance with the Buddhist perspective, which argues that the human being is a construct, an interdependent heap of aggregates becoming aware of its status, Nishida says that "it is not that experience exists because there is an individual, but that an individual exists because there is experience."[15] In other words, it is not the individual having the experience, but rather the experience having, or building up, the individual from sensation, perception, mental activity and consciousness. Now we can better understand why pure experience is beyond subject-object dualism. It builds up the so-called "subject" from the experiences themselves, so there is no room left for an objective observer of experiences.

The second stage of Nishida's philosophical thinking was shaped under the influence of Bergson and Neo-Kantianism while he was a professor at Kyoto University. He refocused from the empiricism of James to the logic of Neo-Kantianism. The Kantian notion of the "unknowable things-in-themselves" made him curious to mine the resources of mysticism and to look for a definition of the self in the principle defined by Jakob Böhme as *Ungrund*, a kind of primordial matrix in which originates the God of traditional Christianity. This drive probably stimulated him to explore more thoroughly the resources of Zen for his philosophical goals and also helped him shape his view of the Christian doctrine of God. At the end of this stage he turned to religion for finding an Absolute principle for his philosophy, and ultimately found it in the nothingness (*mu*) of Zen.[16]

In the third stage of his philosophical career, after 1927, Nishida departed from the Idealism of the Neo-Kantians and followed more closely the influence of Zen Buddhism, exchanging his interest in Böhme's *Ungrund* for the nothingness of Zen as the ultimate truth on which to continue to build his philosophy. In this stage his primary objective was to define the individual against subject-object duality, according to his earlier views on non-dualism inherited from James, but also in accordance with the Buddhist concept of emptiness. Given his earlier conviction that pure experience does not belong to the individual but rather builds up the individual, he reached the conclusion that the true ground of the individual is nothingness, which itself is not a substantial reality. By adding the qualifier "Absolute" to the ultimate reality of nothingness, Nishida emphasizes that it does not refer at all to a hidden "something" as the Hindu Brahman, or the One of Neo-Platonism. Absolute Nothingness is "the universal of universals,"[17] not as a

---

15. Ibid., xxx.

16. Heisig, *Philosophers of Nothingness*, 61.

17. Ibid., 63.

subject, but always as a predicate, the equivalent of *shunyata-shunyata* (the emptiness of emptiness as declared by Nagarjuna), which leaves no room for any kind of substantial Ultimate Reality.

The completion of Nishida's philosophy came in the form of his "logic of the *basho* (place)."[18] In his words, the concept of *basho* is "the universal by which the knowledge of judgment (or knowledge obtained by judgment) is established."[19] In other words, it is the ground on which philosophical (or religious) concepts are built and the perspective from which one judges existing concepts and doctrines. For instance, if we take an event, we need to know the place where it happened in order to understand it, or if we are to refer to a color, we implicitly locate it in opposition to other colors, in the context of the spectrum the eye can discern. If a Christian were to state the *basho* of Christianity, it would be God's being, the Holy Trinity, as we have seen in chapter 3. In Mahayana Buddhism the ground of everything is *shunyata*, emptiness. Nishida adopted this concept in stating his "place of Absolute Nothingness"(*zettai-mu no basho*) as the ground zero of his philosophy.[20] From this standpoint things are seen as they really are, empty of inherent existence and, as a result, "we achieve an existential awareness through self-negation in this radical sense."[21] In Nishida's view, we become "truly self-conscious"[22] when we realize our eternal nothingness by having the direct experience of not-Self (*anatman*).[23] This line of thought reaches its final form in his masterpiece essay *The Logic of the Place of Nothingness and the Religious Worldview*, called by its translator "the *fons et origo* of the Kyoto School."[24]

18. According to Takeuchi, Nishida developed his idea of the "locus of Nothingness" from Plato's concept of the *topos* (Yoshinori Takeuchi, "The Philosophy of Nishida," in Franck, ed., *Buddha Eye*, 185). In his *Timaeus*, Plato says that "all existence must of necessity be in some place (*topos*) and occupy a space (*chora*)" (*Timaeus* 52b). However, it seems that the concept of *topos* is prevalent in Aristotle, while Plato preferred to put emphasis on *chora* as the experiential view of the *topos*, which expresses one's personal connection to it. The influence from Plato is confirmed by Yusa, who argues that Nishida never uses the term *topos*, but rather Plato's *chora*, as equivalent of his *basho* (Yusa, *Zen & Philosophy*, 204 and 376, n.1).

19. Yusa, *Zen & Philosophy*, 208.

20. According to Yusa Nishida started to develop the concept of *basho* in essays published in 1924 and 1925 (Yusa, *Zen & Philosophy*, 202–3).

21. Nishida, *Last Writings*, 67.

22. Ibid., 67.

23. In Heisig's words, the dualistically defined self ("the imperial I, standing in judgment over the phenomenal world of form and matter") has to awaken to "a true I aware of itself as an instance of the self-awareness of reality" (Heisig, *Philosophers of Nothingness*, 74).

24. David Dilworth, "Introduction," in Nishida, *Last Writings*, 6.

## 5.2 NISHIDA'S VIEW OF GOD

In his early essay *On Religion* (1909), the reader may be surprised by the way Nishida defines God's personal being vs. human beings, almost as a Christian theologian. In his words,

> we are not to infer the divine personality from our knowledge of human personality; rather, the situation is the other way around—it is the divine personality that makes us persons possible. That the divine consciousness is endowed with self-knowledge, free-will, and love makes it possible for human beings to partake of the qualities that are essential to making us "persons."[25]

Although such thoughts look promising for Buddhist-Christian dialogue, one must be aware that the "divine personality" Nishida is speaking of here is not the God of Christianity. Nishida rejected from the very start of his philosophical career a view of God as "wholly transcendent creator," and instead calls God "the unifying power of consciousness that permeates the entire universe."[26] This God is the "unifier of pure experience," a mere principle that permeates the world, not a person who created it and keeps it in existence. It is only to such a universal principle that Nishida can apply divine attributes such as "eternity, omnipresence, omniscience, and omnipotence."[27] In fact, he rejected the Christian view of God in all stages of his philosophical career. Under the influence of neo-Kantianism he adopted a view of God as a suprapersonal reality, which he best found expressed by the German mystics, especially Eckhart, as the *Gottheit*. And in the final stage of development of his philosophy he declared that his view of God is no longer consistent with Eckhart's *Gottheit* but must be formulated as the emptiness of the *Prajnaparamita* Sutras, for "God is the identity of absolute contradiction that includes absolute negation within itself."[28]

As one could have anticipated for a Zen practitioner, God cannot be "a transcendent entity apart from the universe who controls the world—including people—from the outside."[29] It must rather be "a fundamental

---

25. Yusa, *Zen & Philosophy*, 99.

26. Ibid.

27. Ibid.

28. Nishida, *Last Writings*, 75. Nishida seems to follow a Madhyamaka view of the absolute, as he says that "the schools of the *Prajnaparamita* thought can be truly said to have taken the paradox of God to its ultimate conclusion" (ibid., 70).

29. Nishida, *An Inquiry into the Good*, 155.

spiritual principle at the base of reality."[30] By no means should one imagine God as personal, or in his words, as "something like a great human who stands outside the universe and controls it,"[31] for such a view "not only conflicts with our reason but also falls short of the most profound religiosity."[32] The "God" that performs "the infinite activity of unifying the universe" is Absolute Nothingness,[33] and only as such can be called omnipresent. Since a personal God is defined in relationships, i.e., in opposition to other beings, his identity depends on other personal beings and thus cannot be a true Absolute. In other words, God cannot be called both personal and the Absolute. As Nishida affirms, "if there were something outside it (the absolute), negating and opposing it, it would not be the absolute."[34] This means that the Absolute must be beyond any opposition (and thus not relative to the things it would oppose), and must transcend subject-object dualism. According to the ultimate standpoint of emptiness, the true absolute is "absolute being only if it is opposed to absolutely nothing."[35] As such it can only be an all-encompassing Truth, the truth that everything is empty of inherent existence.

## 5.3 NISHIDA AND SOME TRADITIONAL CHRISTIAN DOCTRINES

The reader of Nishida's "intellectual biography" will be surprised to discover that the founder of the Kyoto School had a high esteem of Jesus.[36] He used to read the Bible and said he found comfort in it, holding it in higher esteem than for instance, the *Analects* of Confucius.[37] Considering that most of the 5,000 books in his library were about Buddhism, Asian philosophy and Christianity, one can imagine that he was well aware not only of Zen philosophy but also of Christian doctrines.[38] To what extent he had an orthodox understanding of Christian doctrines, however, is quite another issue.

We have seen that as a philosopher whose guiding principle is the Absolute Nothingness of Zen, Nishida strongly opposes the Christian view

30. Ibid., 80.
31. Ibid.
32. Ibid., 155.
33. Ibid., 82.
34. Nishida, *Last Writings*, 69.
35. Ibid., 68.
36. Yusa, *Zen & Philosophy*, 54, 67, 71.
37. Ibid., 54.
38. Heisig, in *Philosophers of Nothingness*, 32.

of God. Since the true absolute is Absolute Nothingness, he argues that Ultimate Reality "must express itself by negating itself"[39] and its true nature would be "absolute self-negation within itself."[40] He is obviously referring to the fact that the doctrine of emptiness requires that Ultimate Reality must be seen instead as an all-pervading truth, as a predicative truth that stands on negating any substantial absolute. Nishida finds a confirmation of his views in St. Paul's hymn in Philippians 2:6–7,[41] which is a favourite connection point for Nishida and several other Kyoto philosophers to Christian theology. Since the "absolute" can only be Absolute Nothingness,[42] this principle must apply to the Christian God as well, and therefore, in Nishida's understanding the doctrine of the *kenosis* means that "God must always, in St. Paul's words empty himself."[43]

As such we find Nishida developing a revolutionary understanding of the doctrine of the *kenosis*. Instead of Stăniloae's view of God the Son limiting himself to the abilities of a human nature, Nishida argues for the *necessity* in God to empty himself of his very nature, for "a God who does not empty himself through his own self-negation, is not the true absolute."[44]

---

39. Nishida, *Last Writings*, 68.

40. Ibid., 69.

41. Since this text is very important for the next two Kyoto philosophers as well, I will quote it in full:
Let the same mind be in you that was in Christ Jesus,
who, though he was in the form of God,
did not regard equality with God
as something to be exploited,
but emptied himself,
taking the form of a slave,
being born in human likeness.
And being found in human form,
he humbled himself
and became obedient to the point of death—
even death on a cross.
Therefore God also highly exalted him
and gave him the name
that is above every name,
so that at the name of Jesus
every knee should bend,
in heaven and on earth and under the earth,
and every tongue should confess
that Jesus Christ is Lord,
to the glory of God the Father. (Philippians 2:5–11, NRSV)

42. Nishida, *Last Writings*, 69.

43. Ibid., 70.

44. Ibid., 118

David Dilworth, Nishida's translator, affirms that the motivation behind stating such a view is a "doctrinal presupposition" which demands that Nishida's interpretation of Christian doctrines must be in conformity with "the existential signification of Buddhist discourse."[45] A view of the *kenosis* consistent with Zen Buddhism compels Nishida to ignore the context of St. Paul's words in Philippians. In Orthodox theology, as we have seen it expressed by Stăniloae in section 3.4, the *kenosis* refers to a *temporary* limitation of God the Son to the means of expression of a human nature. Dilworth explains that, in order to justify his Zen view of the *kenosis*, Nishida had "to suppress the 'And God shall exalt Him' conclusion to Philippians 2."[46] We will find the same pattern reiterated by Nishitani and Abe as a popular way in which the Kyoto philosophers, starting with Nishida, have formulated a contact point between Christian theology and the doctrine of emptiness.

Although Nishida has a high esteem for the figure of Jesus Christ, it is his moral example that counts, not his redeeming work. He says: "People believe in the divinity of Jesus Christ because his life exhibits the deepest truth of human life."[47] A "divinity" like that of Christ is to be treasured in any other human religious founder. As one might expect, his death on the cross and resurrection, are "Christian myths," and "salvation through Christ" is to be understood "in terms of Christian legends."[48] As Waldenfels observes, "the meaning of the historical figure of Jesus, the crucified Christ and the like do not make any sense to him."[49] Not only is Nishida's Christology at odds with the Orthodox view, but so are other interpretations of his of Christian doctrines, such as those of creation, faith, sin and repentance. For instance, Nishida's Zen hermeneutics of Christianity cannot admit an Orthodox view of creation, and therefore one must be aware that his meaning of creation is an "own self-transforming process in the form of a movement from the created to the creating."[50] We must remember here his earlier view of pure experience which builds up the individual and self-awareness. The "created" (for Nishida—the impermanent constituents of the world) become the "creating" self-aware beings without the need of "divine" intervention. The world continues to manifest itself due to its impermanence and is generating by itself higher forms of consciousness and self-awareness. The Zen view of "creation" is that of a perpetual transformation of impermanent

45. Ibid., 45.

46. Ibid., 44–45.

47. Nishida, *An Inquiry into the Good*, 155.

48. Ibid., 270.

49. Waldenfels, *Absolute Nothingness*, 46.

50. Nishida, *Last Writings*, 71.

combinations. This is what Nishida means by the world expressing "itself within itself."[51] It is also the context in which one must consider Nishida's view of God creating beings from his "internal nature,"[52] not out of his will, and of the universe as "not a creation of God but a manifestation of God."[53] Nishida's "God" that creates the world is Absolute Nothingness manifesting itself as the beings who become aware of their real status.

Unlike Orthodox Christianity, which demands that one should realize his or her eternal dependence on God for subsisting, Nishida argues that we become "truly self-conscious" when we realize our "eternal death" and "eternal nothingness."[54] In other words, it is by rejecting permanent relationships that true meaning is found. This is consistent with the way the human being is transformed in its encounter with the Absolute. According to Stăniloae and the Orthodox tradition, the Absolute (as the Holy Trinity) relates to humans and holds them in existence by the means of their relationship with him. But in Zen, as in Nishida's thought, the encounter with Absolute Nothingness makes the human being "pass over into nothing."[55] As he says, "Once he dies, a person is eternally dead" and "enters into eternal nothingness."[56] In such circumstances there is no room for a personal resurrection.

Nishida's Zen hermeneutics of Christianity lead him to formulate unorthodox views of the meaning of sin and repentance. Under the probable influence of Neo-Platonism he argues that the "fall" or "original sin" is not a loss of a relationship, but rather humankind "becoming self-conscious" as a result of "God's self-differentiation."[57] Since to sin means to become aware of ourselves, "sin" is a condition "for the spiritual advancement of humanity" and a necessity for one to "truly know the love of God."[58] From this perspective follows his view of repentance, as perfecting "things done in the past."[59] According to Nishida's interpretation of the *Parable of the Prodigal Son* in Luke 15, when the prodigal son returned home he "made the sins and the anguish of his past into the most beautiful and sacred events of his life."[60]

---

51. Ibid., 71.
52. Nishida, *An Inquiry into the Good*, 163.
53. Ibid., 158.
54. Nishida, *Last Writings*, 67.
55. Ibid., 68.
56. Ibid., 87.
57. Yusa, *Zen & Philosophy*, 100.
58. Nishida, *An Inquiry into the Good*, 172.
59. Ibid., 172.
60. Ibid.

This interpretation follows his understanding of "home" not as the restoration of a relationship, but as a realization of one's true nature, to which the "sins" of the past have contributed. This is at odds with the Orthodox Christian view, which defines repentance as a reorientation of the person towards its true source of meaning, who is God. In his last essay, Nishida clarifies his view of repentance by distinguishing between moral repentance and "genuinely religious remorse."[61] While the Orthodox meaning of repentance does not allow one to separate the two aspects, for repentance is the attitude of the sinner of being sorry for his sins committed against God and neighbours, for Nishida the two aspects are distinct. The first, moral repentance for the moral evil one has done, is a legitimate attitude for one to express towards his or her neighbour. But "religious repentance" has a totally different meaning, for it involves discovering one's true nature, that of emptiness, and as such it is a "shame concerning the very existence of the self."[62] It is a repentance for not having seen things as they really are and it leads to seeing "the true self," human nature as emptiness. Since this is the foundation of Nishida's philosophy, one can understand why faith in the Christian sense is useless, as it nurtures ignorance and prevents humans from knowing their true nature. The same is true about reciting the *nembutsu* in order to be reborn in Amida's Pure Land, which also "diverges from a true religious spirit."[63] As a result, faith does not operate in a personal relationship with God, but is rather "the unifying power"[64] that connects one with the "unifying reality" which is Absolute Nothingness.

## 5.4 TWO VIEWS ON NEGATING THE SELF FOR ATTAINING PERFECTION

As one can expect, personhood plays very different roles in Nishida's philosophy and in Orthodox Christianity. Since for Nishida Ultimate Reality is the Absolute Nothingness of Zen, not the Holy Trinity, the human encounter with the Absolute cannot lead to the fulfilment of personhood in a relationship in God. This is the perspective from which he interprets the story of the sacrifice of Isaac in Genesis 22. Instead of seeing in it a real test in which Abraham had to express his total surrender to God, Nishida interprets it as God's requirement for "the negation of the person itself."[65] However, as we

61. Nishida, *Last Writings*, 77.
62. Ibid.
63. Nishida, *An Inquiry into the Good*, 150.
64. Ibid., 167.
65. Nishida, *Last Writings*, 74.

have seen in chapter 3, the Orthodox Christian view is that God does not require the "negation of the person" but its fulfilment in a relationship with him. What God asks to be negated is the self-centredness of persons, called sin, not the quality of being a person *per se*. In other words, the human predicament is the person's orientation, not personhood itself.

Another biblical instance from which Nishida concludes that relative beings "must pass over into nothing"[66] when they face the absolute is taken from the words of Isaiah: "Woe to me! For I am undone; because I am a man of unclean lips; for my eyes have seen the King, the Lord of hosts."[67] From here Nishida concludes that the way in which "the living self relates to the divine" can be "only through dying."[68] From the standpoint of Zen Nishida is right: the absolute which opposes the human being is the absolute truth of emptiness, and human beings are mere impermanent clusters of change that must indeed "pass over into nothing."[69] According to the Zen hermeneutics of Isaiah's words, it means that once the true nature of things is seen as nothingness, one should adjust to this view and no longer cling to personal existence. From an Orthodox perspective, however, God is not a reality that annihilates the human being, but one who requires the perfection of personhood. Therefore the death of which Isaiah was afraid is generated by the awareness of sin and does not refer to a sudden realization of emptiness. Nishida's assumption that "the living self relates to the divine only through dying" is not a tenable conclusion for the Orthodox Christian, since the human being is made for eternal life and not for annihilation. Therefore, from a Christian perspective, what makes the individual "unique and ir-repeatable" is not entering into "eternal nothingness" as Nishida argues, but its entry into an eternal relationship with God.[70]

We find here different views of what self-negation means. Although negating the self is required for both Buddhists and Christians,[71] it bears a very different meaning. In Buddhism negating the self (*anatman*) requires realizing what we really are, that there is no self to cling to, while in Christianity it means negating egoism, i.e., correcting a wrong attitude towards others, and is realized in communion with God and other people. On the one hand, in Buddhism by facing the absolute the self becomes aware of its

66. Ibid., 68.

67. Isaiah 6:5, quoted in ibid.

68. Ibid.

69. Ibid.

70. Ibid., 77.

71. Many would agree with Nishida that "in any religion it is the effort of self-nega-tion that is necessary" (Nishida, *Last Writings*, 80), but this has very different meanings in world religions.

own eternal death and nothingness (the absolute devours the self, giving eternal death), while on the other hand in Christianity the encounter with God gives eternal life, as he is himself the source of life. Therefore we face very different views on the meaning of religion. For Nishida,

> The question of religion lies not in what the self *should be* as a consciously active being, but in the question of what the self *is*: not in how the self should *act*, but in the self's very *is and is not*.[72]

This is a different view from the Orthodox meaning of religion. Since personal identity is defined precisely in relationships (with God and other human beings), religious life stands precisely in what one "should be" in these relationships, and in how we "should act" one towards the other. It is not a matter of discovering one's nature in meditation by the use of Own Power, and of seeing how things really are, but rather of relating correctly to God and one's neighbours.

As we have seen in chapter 2, in Buddhism the way that leads to perfection does not treasure personhood and communion with God. Being consistent with the *basho* of Absolute Nothingness, Nishida says that the self must realize that "it is born to die eternally,"[73] which means that one must realize his or her "eternal nothingness."[74] This realization corresponds to the experience of enlightenment (*kensho*), the state of seeing one's true nature as empty of inherent existence. In Nishida's view, once "a person is eternally dead" he or she "never returns."[75] Although he finds that "rebirth in Christ"[76] and the Zen experience of *kensho* ("seeing one's true nature") are the same,[77] this can hardly be the case. In Orthodox Christianity "rebirth in Christ" brings a renewed relationship with God and other people, which finds its perfect fulfilment in an eternal communion with God. For Nishida the concept of "eternal life" bears a significant difference of meaning, as it is a name given for the paradoxical realization of the oneness of the two poles of Buddhist thought, *samsara* and *nirvana* (coming the point where they are "realized as one").[78]

---

72. Ibid., 76.
73. Ibid., 8.
74. Ibid., 87.
75. Ibid.
76. Yusa, *Zen & Philosophy*, 84.
77. Nishida, *An Inquiry into the Good*, 143.
78. Nishida, *Last Writings*, 87.

As we can see, Nishida proposes a view of perfection and eternal life that is very different from that of Orthodox Christianity. His view of perfection is that of Zen, in which "kensho, seeing one's nature, means to penetrate to the roots of one's own self."[79] Personal fulfilment in interpersonal relationships, as in Orthodox Christianity, is counterproductive. As Heisig rightly observes, Nishida is

> not opting for any sort of personalism that sees the interpersonal encounter as the prototype of all reality. For Nishida, the option for radical personalism in any form is excluded precisely because the fulfillment of the I is located in the transformation to non-I.[80]

What matters for Nishida is not engaging in relationships that can only complicate the realization of enlightenment, but escaping the illusion of duality and implicitly that of personhood in the Christian sense.[81] What is needed is "seeing into one's own nature and thus becoming the Buddha-nature."[82] In this context the perfection of love cannot mean a perfection of an I-you relationship.[83] In the words of Heisig, personal relationships become no more than "a depersonalized I encountering a deobjectified other, a seeing without a seer or seen."[84] As a result, the Christian *agape* means for Nishida "the self-awareness of absolute nothingness."[85] As for social responsibility, Heisig concludes that Nishida's definition of love points "away from responsibility to the concrete demands of history."[86] Contrary to the demand to love one's neighbour as oneself as the means for social well-being, Nishida's view of personhood points towards another path of action. In Heisig's words,

---

79. Ibid., 108.

80. Heisig, *Philosophers of Nothingness*, 81.

81. In the words of Heisig, "[t]he eternal now that breaks through time in the encounter of an I and a you never becomes for Nishida an Eternal Thou" (*Philosophers of Nothingness*, 82).

82. Nishida, *Last Writings*, 90.

83. Heisig, *Philosophers of Nothingness*, 84. In Heisig's commentary, "the I-you is no more than a stage in self-awareness, the stage in which one awakens to the fact of social existence" (ibid.).

84. Ibid.

85. Ibid., 85.

86. Ibid. This statement is consistent with the general attitude promoted by Zen towards social evil. In the words of Heisig, "moral responsibility towards concrete evil in history has long been the Achilles' heel for Zen" (ibid., 71).

the non-I that emerges from the self-awareness of absolute nothingness looks for all the world to be a highly cultivated form of ataraxia, a self-transcendence of which the highest good consists of its inability to be moved by either good or evil.[87]

In his last essay, in the concluding thoughts on the nature and future of Christianity, Nishida looks back to the dark episodes of Christian history and concludes that "such a religion must negate itself."[88] He sees the wrongdoings performed in the name of religion as originating in its very nature due to its belief in a personal God as Ultimate Reality. In his words, because Christianity has taken "God as the transcendent Lord . . . it fused with secular institutions" and thus "the successors of Peter also became the successors of Caesar."[89] Instead of repentance for the wrongdoings of the past and return to its essence, Nishida argues for a transformation of Christianity that would make it a variant of Zen Buddhism. This is the logical result of a Zen hermeneutics of Christianity. As a result, if we were to accept Nishida's proposal we would no longer be able to speak of a dialogue between genuine religious traditions, but rather of a Christianity that has lost its identity and thus can no longer engage in dialogue with Buddhism. In the next two chapters I will turn to the other two important representatives of the Kyoto School, Nishitani and Abe, and see in what ways they have managed to overcome these difficult issues.

87. Ibid., 86.
88. Nishida, *Last Writings*, 120.
89. Ibid.

# 6

## Keiji Nishitani (1900–1990)

### Defeating Western Nihilism with the Resources of Zen Buddhism

NISHITANI STUDIED UNDER BOTH Nishida and Tanabe, and graduated from Kyoto University in 1924 with a degree in philosophy. He was appointed lecturer in 1932, associate professor in 1935 and finally full professor in 1943, serving as such at Kyoto University until his retirement in 1963. Between 1937 and 1939 he studied in Freiburg under Martin Heidegger, who was lecturing at that time on Nietzsche's nihilism.[1] His academic career was interrupted in 1946 following the defeat of Japan in the war, when he was banned from the university for his support of the militarist government during the war, until 1952 when he was reinstated. From 1963 to 1971 he taught at Otani University in Kyoto. Among other responsibilities, he served as President of the Eastern Buddhist Society of Japan and as editor of its journal (*The Eastern Buddhist*).

Nishitani's interest in Western philosophy began earlier than his study under Nishida at Kyoto University. In his youth he felt attracted "by Nietzsche and Dostoyevsky, Emerson and Carlyle, and by the Bible and St. Francis of Assisi."[2] His other great interest in Western literature was the German mystics, especially Eckhart. Their writings aroused in him a "Great Doubt" concerning "the very existence of the self"[3] and triggered his commitment to study and practice Zen Buddhism in search for answers. Like his teacher Nishida, Nishitani was not only a philosopher but also a seri-

1. Heisig, *Philosophers of Nothingness*, 184.
2. Nishitani, *Religion and Nothingness*, xxxiv–xxxv.
3. Ibid., xxxv.

ous practitioner of Rinzai Zen for 24 years, starting in 1937. Zen eventually cleared up his doubts on the existence of the self and became the reference point in formulating his philosophy, the means by which he finally understood what his master Nishida meant by "direct experience."[4]

The point of major interest of his scholarly attention is the phenomenon of nihilism,[5] as occurring both in the West and in Japan, as a result of secularization and of abandoning traditional ethics and religion, a trend which was seen by him as threatening the very foundation of civilization. As he retrospectively affirmed: "The fundamental problem of my life. . . has always been, to put it simply, the overcoming of nihilism through nihilism."[6] As a phenomenon that finds its roots in "the mutual aversion of religion and science,"[7] nihilism started in the West, where the rationalist Greek and Christian traditions generated the modern scientific method and worldview but then were "devoured by their own progeny."[8] This led to the modern nihilism expressed by Nietzsche and Sartre. In Nishitani's thought, if Western culture wants to survive it should find itself "a more enduring foundation" than Christianity, one that would be "unassailable even by scientific and philosophical skepticism."[9] In Japan nihilism flourished as a result of importing Western technology and social models, which led to a situation in which Buddhist and Confucian structures "lost power, leaving a total void and vacuum" on Japanese soil.[10]

In his search for a way of overcoming nihilism, Nishitani studied the Western existentialist philosophers and praised them for their efforts, but found them incapable of providing a satisfactory solution. For instance, he was critical of Sartre because he "locates subjectivity at the standpoint of the Cartesian ego," and thus does not even consider "the Great Death" of Zen.[11] Sartre's nothingness would act as a principle that "shuts the ego up within

4. Heisig, *Philosophers of Nothingness*, 184. He says: "If I have frequently had occasion to deal with the standpoints of Buddhism, and particularly Zen Buddhism, the fundamental reason is that this original countenance seems to me to appear there most plainly and unmistakably" (Nishitani, *Religion and Nothingness*, 261).

5. Nishitani briefly defines nihilism as "that which renders meaningless the meaning of life" (*Religion and Nothingness*, 4).

6. Heisig, *Philosophers of Nothingness*, 215. Nishitani borrowed this idea from Nietzsche's *Thus Spoke Zarathustra*, which had a huge impact on his philosophical thought. He confessed that "he had carried around with him in his school years 'like a bible'" Nietzsche's book (ibid., 192).

7. Ibid., 215.

8. Winston King, "Foreword," in Nishitani, *Religion and Nothingness*, xiii.

9. Ibid.

10. Heisig, *Philosophers of Nothingness*, 216.

11. Nishitani, *Religion and Nothingness*, 33.

itself," and thus Nishitani denounced it as a "nothingness-at-the-bottom-of-the-self."[12] It is a nothingness set up by a self and made an "*object* of consciousness in representative form" with a self "still attached to it."[13] For Nishitani, true nothingness is that of Buddhism, in which "nihilizing emptiness" is itself emptied, and truly negates all attachments, "both the subject and the way in which 'things' appear as objects of attachment."[14] Although he found Nietzsche's position "far more comprehensive and penetrating than Sartre's,"[15] he categorizes it as yet another "standpoint of *relative absolute nothingness*."[16] In his view, the best resource to provide a solution to the problem of nihilism is Zen Buddhism. Its resources became the centre of Nishitani's philosophical commitment, which finds its best expression in his principal work *Religion and Nothingness*.[17] In this chapter I will examine Nishitani's solution for the overcoming of nihilism and the fruit it bears for Buddhist-Christian dialogue.

## 6.1 THE STANDPOINT OF EMPTINESS

Nishitani inherited and developed many views of his master Nishida.[18] As the founder of the Kyoto School could not separate philosophy from religion, neither could his disciple. What for Nishida was the "place of Absolute Nothingness (*zettai-mu no basho*)" becomes for Nishitani "the standpoint of emptiness" or "field of *shunyata*" (*ku no ba*) as the reference point, or "locus," for formulating his philosophical ideas.[19] Following his master, Nishitani is not merely a deconstructionist and does not use Zen just as

12. Ibid.

13. Ibid.

14. Ibid., 34.

15. Ibid., 55.

16. Nishitani, *Religion and Nothingness*, 66. Although Nishitani seldom mentions Heidegger in his writings, Waldenfels argues that Nishitani's refutation of Western nihilism is in fact an undeclared (because of their personal relationship) "fundamental confrontation with Heidegger" with the intention of taking "a great stride beyond him" (Waldenfels, *Absolute Nothingness*, 70, 74).

17. The Japanese edition was published in 1956, while the English translation appeared only in 1982.

18. James Heisig praises Nishitani's contribution to the Kyoto School by saying: "Without Nishitani's genuine feel for the heart of the philosophical problems that Nishida and Tanabe were dealing with . . . , I have no hesitation in saying that the term 'Kyoto School' would have little of the currency it now enjoys" (*Philosophers of Nothingness*,187).

19. Ibid., 186.

"an anti-ontological alchemy."[20] He is not satisfied with merely *seeing* things as they really are, empty of inherent existence, but is eager to define a way to *act* in the world once one acquires this knowledge. Therefore he affirms a difference between what he called the standpoint of nihility and that of emptiness. Since nihility is "an absolute negation aimed at all 'existence'"[21] and depends on the things whose "existence"[22] it negates, the standpoint of nihility is defined as "itself essentially a nihility."[23] In other words, the standpoint of nihility is merely deconstructing other views, and must itself be subjected to its own method. Once we understand this point, Nishitani takes us further to define the standpoint of emptiness, which is not just "simply negative negativity" but the standpoint at which negation becomes a "Great Affirmation"[24] and thus goes beyond seeing the self as empty to seeing emptiness as the self, and beyond seeing things as empty, to seeing emptiness as the things.[25] His approach follows Nietzsche's surpassing of a pessimistic nihilism generated by his famous saying "God is dead" and arrival at an "active nihilism," one that builds a new vision of the world.[26]

Like Descartes, Nishitani dared to challenge the grounds of Western philosophy, but unlike Descartes, who found a permanent self as the basis on which to build his philosophical system, Nishitani arrives at an even greater doubt, "the Great Doubt," which leaves no self at all as ground for a philosophical or religious inquiry. However, this does not prevent him from speaking of the "true self" as a non-substantial self whose ground is assumed emptiness and which is free of any kind of subject-object dualism.

20. Ibid., 249.

21. Nishitani, *Religion and Nothingness*, 137.

22. We must remember that in Zen "existence" is not an illusion, but rather a series of transformations which are not grounded on an inherently existing substance.

23. Nishitani, *Religion and Nothingness*, 138. Nishitani also says that "just as nihility is an abyss for anything that exists, emptiness may be said to be an abyss even for that abyss of nihility" (ibid., 98).

24. Ibid., 138.

25. Ibid.

26. A further direction for research, which I will not pursue, would be to assess to what extent Nishitani was influenced by Nietzsche's concepts of the "overman" and the "Will to Power." Nietzsche's nihilism is indebted to Heraclitus (whose philosophy he taught at Basel) and his principle of permanent change in the universe. Nishitani was pleased to find in Nietzsche's writings the concept of "Eternal return" (or "Eternal Recurrence") as the equivalent of *samsara*. He sees Nietzsche's version of the "Innocence of Becoming" as a modernized version of Heraclitus, and as coming "closest to the Buddhist standpoint of shunyata" (*Religion and Nothingness*, 215). However, in Nishitani's view, Nietzsche's "Will to Power" merely substitutes "the life-giving power of the Will for the God of Christianity" and thus is still not emancipated completely of a "being" (ibid., 216).

Since dualism fuels the illusion of a real ego, it deters one from knowing human nature as it is. Therefore the standpoint of emptiness offers the paradoxical perspective from which "the negation of the individual and his freedom would become the absolute affirmation of the individual and his freedom."[27] Heisig helps us understand Nishitani's thought by saying:

> Zen begins precisely at the point where Buber's I-you stops because it challenges a contradiction built into it, and indeed to all notions of interpersonal relationships based on a substantial ego.[28]

Nishitani constructs his view of human identity on the negation of such a substantial ego, but this does not mean that he is denying that humans are personal agents in the world. In his words, "Person is through and through real. It is the most real of realities."[29] What one has to realize is the emptiness of this "real person," which would lead to forsaking "the person-centred mode of grasping *person*."[30] As such, as Nishitani argues, the standpoint of emptiness is "indifferent to value judgments" and becomes "the standpoint of absolute love."[31] However, he does not show what this "absolute" love consists of, how it applies to contemporary social issues, or how absolute nothingness could "stimulate 'a moral energy' among citizens."[32] He simply

27. Nishitani, "The I-Thou Relation in Zen Buddhism," in Franck, ed., *Buddha Eye*, 51.

28. Heisig, *Philosophers of Nothingness*, 233.

29. Nishitani, *Religion and Nothingness*, 71.

30. Ibid., 71.

31. Heisig, *Philosophers of Nothingness*, 195.

32. Ibid., 210. An issue that I will not address here, as it does not directly concern my research, is the connection between the standpoint of *shunyata* and Nishitani's backing of Japanese imperialism. He justified Japanese expansionism in the war saying: "Not only is it (the war) a matter of the life or death of our own country, but of the life or death of the coprosperity sphere (East Asia), that is, of a new world order" (Heisig, *Philosophers of Nothingness*, 206). Japanese imperialism was seen by him as a must of that time: "The main thing is somehow to make them (the nations of the world) realize that Japan is now the leader in the construction of the Greater East Asia of today, and *must* be the leader as a matter of historical necessity" (ibid., 205). Nishitani inherited this superiority complex of the Japanese nation from Tanabe, who expressed similar thoughts (ibid., 134–46). Although I will not explore this issue here, one can hardly fail to notice the parallel with Nietzsche's *Beyond Good and Evil* and its use in backing the ideology of Nazi Germany in WWII. After the war, in 1958, Nishitani acknowledged his pro-war attitude and tried to justify it as "a kind of karma (he had) to cooperate" with (ibid., 212). But it seems he never gave up the superiority complex of the Japanese nation. In a 1967 essay he still affirms the "heavy responsibility" of the Japanese "to lay the foundations of thought for a world in the making, for a new world united beyond differences of east and west" (ibid., 214). It is not certain, however, that his nationalism

affirms that "to love others" following Jesus' command to "love your neighbour as yourself" is "the absolute negation of self-love."[33] In Nishitani's view,
un-selfishness translates as the need to negate a substantial self, while in
Orthodox Christianity it has nothing to do with such ontological assertions
on human nature. Jesus' command is not a mere negation of a substantial
self, but the demand to engage against egoism by one's opening towards
the practical needs of his or her neighbour, as illustrated in the story that
accompanies this command.[34]

In accordance with the Zen view of the inherent Buddha-nature, to
express the standpoint of *shunyata* is in fact a way of manifesting enlightenment.[35] According to Nishitani, one who is grounded in this standpoint
does not acquire new karma, and thus for him or her life is no longer "an
endless payment and reinstatement of a debt (karma)."[36] In other words,
once we are grounded in the standpoint of *shunyata* "each one of our deeds
is no longer something that produces being in a time without beginning or
end."[37] Such affirmations bear deep Buddhist overtones and as such evade
the realm of philosophical inquiry. They also lead us to assessing his understanding of several important Christian doctrines and his view of Buddhist-
Christian dialogue.

## 6.2 NISHITANI AND THE GOD OF CHRISTIANITY

As one can easily anticipate, for Nishitani the Christian God is of no help in
overcoming nihilism. In his view, a personal and transcendent God is not
only useless, but also the most embarrassing aspect of traditional Christianity.[38] It is a construct produced by the "'soul' or 'spirit' in man,"[39] as if
the five aggregates produce a sixth one, God. As a result, belief in God "as

---

was the result of the standpoint of *shunyata*. Further study is needed on this topic.

33. Nishitani, *Religion and Nothingness*, 278.

34. Jesus was asked by a teacher of the Law, "Who is my neighbour?" (Luke 10:29),
and in reply he told the Parable of the Good Samaritan (Luke 10:30–37). He emphasized the need to get practically involved in helping one's neighbour by concluding his
teaching of the parable with the words, "Go and do likewise" (Luke 10:37, NRSV).

35. We need to remember that according to Zen Buddhism we do not have to strive
for enlightenment, since we are *already* enlightened but do not realize it. This is why
practice is not a way of *attaining* enlightenment, but of *manifesting* it, as mentioned in
section 2.8.

36. Nishitani, *Religion and Nothingness*, 252.

37. Ibid.

38. Ibid., 37.

39. Nishitani, "Science and Zen," in Franck, ed., *Buddha Eye*, 114.

a *personal* Being possessed of a conscious 'will'"[40] is the core source of all problems with Christianity, especially of the self-centredness it fuels, and by extension, the fundamental cause of all problems in the Western world. This thought follows Toynbee's thesis of God being a projection of man's self-centredness, and "as the will of the self backed up by the will of God."[41] In Nishitani's view, Christianity is an "anthropocentric" religion,[42] and Western history, its outcome, is nothing but the pursuit of an illusion (*avidya*) "tied to the standpoint of karma and the fruits of karma."[43]

Following Western existentialism, Nishitani argues that the transcendent God of Christianity needs to be rejected in the context of the new worldview brought by the scientific method and its refusal to accept any "external authority."[44] Paradoxically, the very cause for which modern humanity advanced "in the direction of an estrangement from Christianity" would be the Christian way of seeing God.[45] Nishitani's solution for Western nihilism and for a reconciliation of science and religion would thus be for Christianity to "accept atheism as a mediation to a new development of Christianity itself."[46] In his opinion, "we must question the notion of the personal in God and inquire into the realm of the transpersonal."[47] If we continued to hold to the dualism stated by Christianity between God and creation, and between God and human beings, we would only further alienate ourselves from true existence and from knowing our true nature, that of emptiness.

40. Nishitani, *Religion and Nothingness*, 214.

41. Ibid., 203. In Nishitani's view, human self-centredness is "a permanent fixture in religions of the West" which is also found in "the guise of God's chosen people." He says: "Projected onto God is the conscious demand of the self to condemn other people" (*Religion and Nothingness*, 203). However, an elementary reading of the Old Testament would not back his thesis, for instead of the demand to condemn *other* people, God judges his *own* people for their unfaithfulness, which runs contrary to what we should expect from anthropomorphization.

42. Nishitani, "Science and Zen," 133.

43. Nishitani, *Religion and Nothingness*, 204. Buri also notes Nishitani's blame of Christianity for being "essentially responsible for this unwholesome course of history" (Buri, *The Buddha-Christ*, 190).

44. He says: "The emergence of the scientific worldview brought with it a freedom of thought from all external authority, which begins with a declaration of independence from God" (Heisig, *Philosophers of Nothingness*, 246).

45. Nishitani, *Religion and Nothingness*, 37.

46. Heisig, *Philosophers of Nothingness*, 246.

47. Nishitani, *Religion and Nothingness*, 61.

As we can see, Nishitani rejects the Christian solution against nihilism as God's intervention and revelation in human history.[48] Of a similar futility is the Pure Land Buddhist appeal to Other Power by invoking the name of the Amida Buddha (the reciting of the *nembutsu*).[49] What he demands, in the words of Heisig, is a "freeing of oneself from all dependence on liberation from another world or transcendent power."[50] In line with Zen Buddhism he calls for an awakening to the true nature of things, which means seeing things from the standpoint of *shunyata*. This awakening is called in Zen "the Great Death,"[51] because it is a death to ignorance and false beliefs, and implicitly to the stream of *samsara*. Through this Great Death one must "unburden himself of himself, give up his tiny, egotistic self and deliver it over to his 'unborn Self,'" which is one's true nature, emptiness.[52]

Nishitani is deeply troubled by a concept of a God who creates the world, sustains it in existence and then puts an end to history "in terms of divine punishment and divine judgment."[53] He says that such a view "must be flatly denied."[54] However, Heisig argues that we should not conclude that Nishitani advocates the simple replacement of the Christian God with the emptiness of Zen Buddhism. He found an equivalent of emptiness closer to the Western mind, in the form of "a more fundamental impersonality beyond the personality of God."[55] In Nishitani's words, a view of God that would be compatible with Zen is as a person "that appears out of what cannot itself be called personal and does not entail any confinement of self-being."[56] There is no doubt about the source which inspired in him this revolutionary view of the Christian God: Meister Eckhart.[57]

48. In Heisig's comment, "an act of faith in salvation from beyond is not to overcome the nihility but to dissociate oneself from it" (*Philosophers of Nothingness*, 220).

49. Heisig affirms that Nishitani is "openly critical of the adoption of the *nenbutsu* . . . as a *koan*" (ibid., 337). In his *Religion and Nothingness* Nishitani allows the invocation of the name of the Amida Buddha only if it "has nothing to do with the calculating discriminations of the observing individual himself" (ibid., 262). As such, the *nembutsu* must be "a mind at play" (ibid.), beyond subject-object dualism.

50. Heisig, *Philosophers of Nothingness*, 232.

51. Ibid., 231.

52. Nishitani, "Science and Zen," 124.

53. Nishitani, *Religion and Nothingness*, 214.

54. Ibid.

55. Heisig, *Philosophers of Nothingness*, 247.

56. Ibid.

57. D.T. Suzuki, the well known promoter of Zen in the West also acknowledged Eckhart as a bridge to Western philosophy and religion and called him "the leading Zen man in the West" (quoted in Winston L. King, "No-Self, No-Mind, and Emptiness Revisited," in Ingram and Streng, eds., *Buddhist-Christian Dialogue*, 161).

## 6.3 NISHITANI'S UNDERSTANDING AND USE OF ECKHART

Nishitani is thrilled to find in Eckhart the distinction between what traditional Christianity calls God and a more profound reality called the godhead (*Gottheit*), which "surpasses God as person."[58] This essence of God is taken by Nishitani to be the Western equivalent of *shunyata*, and the only locus where "man can truly be himself."[59] He argues that only in the nothingness of this suprapersonal godhead can the human being be brought "to a desert of absolute death,"[60] i.e., liberated from a dualist bondage to a transcendent God and renewed by the discovery of its own true nature, that of *shunyata*. This "absolute death" is the death of an illusion of a self, which then brings about a new vision of the world.

Nishitani is aware that in the *unio mystica* for which the Christian mystics strive there still lurks "a dualism of subject and object."[61] Therefore he is pleased to find in Eckhart a view of human perfection that goes beyond "being united with God (*Deo unitum esse*)" to "being one with God (*unum esse cum Deo*)."[62] In Nishitani's understanding of Eckhart, human perfection lies in seeing one's own nature as having the nature of the godhead, i.e., as constituted of what Zen Buddhism calls absolute nothingness.[63] In Nishitani's words, "It is the nothingness that Eckhart called the 'ground' of God in 'godhead' in which God is my ground and I am the ground of God."[64]

However, Nishitani's envisaged equivalence between Eckhart's view of the "godhead" and his Zen view of nothingness does not really make sense, since they bear different meanings. Surprisingly, the best correction for Nishitani's interpretation of Eckhart comes not from a Western theologian, but from another important figure of the Kyoto School—Shizuteru Ueda (b. 1926),[65] himself a disciple of Nishitani and his successor as professor at

---

58. Heisig, *Philosophers of Nothingness*, 195. Nishitani is aware that Eckhart was "markedly distant from orthodox Christian faith" and that he was seen as "heretical in his own times" (*Religion and Nothingness*, 66).

59. Ibid., 63.

60. Ibid.

61. Ibid.

62. Ibid., 62–63.

63. In Nishitani's words, "God must be encountered as a reality omnipresent in all the things of the world in such a way as to be absolutely immanent as absolutely transcendent" (ibid., 41).

64. Heisig, *Philosophers of Nothingness*, 194.

65. See Shizuteru Ueda's article "'Nothingness' in Meister Eckhart and Zen Buddhism," in Franck, ed., *Buddha Eye*, 157–68.

Kyoto University. Ueda pursued an intense study of Eckhart and found his view at odds with the Zen view of *shunyata*. Eckhart's nothingness of the godhead refers to a lack of attributes of a suprapersonal being, following the method of radical apophaticism. In stating his view of the godhead Eckhart was inspired by the One of Neo-Platonism, so it designates an unchanging and self-existing essence, and thus it cannot be taken as a Western equivalent of *shunyata*. Eckhart was still clinging to being, which is untenable for a Zen Buddhist. In Ueda's words,

> for Eckhart, to say that God is in his essence a nothingness is to treat nothingness merely as the epitome of all negative expressions for the purity of the essence of God, after the manner of negative theology.[66]

Eckhart's mysticism aims at union with this suprapersonal being, while in Zen no such union is conceivable, since there cannot be a real ultimate "godhead" or "One" with which one should be united. In other words, emptiness is not a substance with which one's essence could be reunited in a pantheistic way. Therefore Ueda criticizes Eckhart for not going far enough in his mysticism, for not overcoming mysticism itself.[67] Eckhart was seeking union with the suprapersonal godhead, while Nishitani's "impersonally personal (or personally impersonal)" God is not a being, but a concept which expresses absolute nothingness. It is to this concept that he is inviting Christians to convert.

## 6.4 NISHITANI'S INTERPRETATION OF THE KENOSIS AND OF OTHER RELATED CHRISTIAN DOCTRINES

An example which shows that Nishitani has some understanding of Christian doctrines is given by the way he sees the implications of creation *ex nihilo*. He is aware that in Christian theology God is absolutely distinct from creation, and that creation must be sustained by him in existence.[68] He acknowledges that the Christian view of creation has nothing to do with

66. Ueda, "'Nothingness' in Meister Eckhart," 159.

67. Fritz Buri, *The Buddha-Christ*, 255.

68. Nishitani, *Religion and Nothingness*, 39. An Orthodox Christian might agree with Nishitani that "the being of the created is grounded upon a *nothingness* and seen fundamentally to be a nothingness" (ibid.). But we must be careful what we mean by "nothingness." In Christianity the "nothing" out of which God creates is neither a preexistent substance, nor God's own nature (as in pantheism), nor Buddhist emptiness (as a fundamental truth). The only way in which a Christian could render the "nothing" out of which God created, would be the (physical) void, the non-existing.

pantheism, for God does not manifest creation out of his nature. Nishitani is right also on the fact that since all things owe their existence to God the human creaturely status should bear results in how human beings treat one another and the created world. They should not exploit and abuse each other and the environment, but be humbled by their condition, put themselves in the service of God and act responsibly towards his creation. These are applications every Christian should consider. However, his views deviate from Orthodoxy when he attempts to interpret the nature of God from the standpoint of emptiness.

As we have seen in the previous chapter on Nishida, one of the most appealing Christian doctrines for the Kyoto philosophers is that of the *kenosis*. Nishitani started developing his view on this topic by commenting on Jesus' words in Matthew 5:44–48 as representing God's requirement for attaining perfection.[69] He correctly observes that the term used in this text for God's indiscriminate love is *agape*, the same term used for the love displayed by Christ in his incarnation and service of humankind.[70] However, he then finds its equivalent in the Buddhist "non-differentiating love beyond enmity and friendship" which he calls "the indifference of love."[71] Such an interpretation is no longer consistent with Orthodox Christianity, for love is not passive equanimity, but must be expressed in action, by getting involved in practical ways in the welfare of other people, good and evil alike.[72]

Nishitani is again correct in seeing the link between the love of Christ and his "making himself empty" (according to Philippians 2:6–7), for he affirms that Christ was "taking the form of man and becoming a servant, in accordance with the will of God."[73] But from here he follows Nishida's understanding of the *kenosis*, saying that

> the very fact itself of God's being God essentially entails the characteristic of "having made himself empty." With Christ we speak of a deed that has been accomplished; with God, of an

---

69. Jesus said: "But I say to you, Love your enemies and pray for those who persecute you, so that you may be children of your Father in heaven; for he makes his sun rise on the evil and on the good, and sends rain on the righteous and on the unrighteous. . . . Be perfect, therefore, as your heavenly Father is perfect" (Matthew 5:44–48, NRSV).

70. As for instance in John 13:1 and 3:16.

71. Nishitani, *Religion and Nothingness*, 58. He said that such "indifferent love belongs rather to the realm of non-ego" which is "contained by nature in the perfection of God" (ibid., 59).

72. From the same text in Matthew 5:44–48 (God causing the sun to rise on the evil as well as the good) Nishitani defines God's attribute of "indifference of nature" (ibid., 58).

73. Ibid.

original nature. What is *ekkenosis* for the Son is *kenosis* for the Father. In the East, this would be called *anatman*, or non-ego.[74]

In other words, what we have seen explained by Stăniloae as a deliberate limitation of God the Son to express himself according to the (growing) capacity of a human nature, is taken by Nishitani (and the other representatives of the Kyoto School) as a necessity in the nature of God the Father himself. From a Zen point of view what one calls God or Ultimate Reality must be grounded in emptiness, and thus the *kenosis* of Christ must point to emptiness as the true nature of God the Father and the true source of his compassion.[75] In Nishitani's words, "compassion means a self-negation, a 'making oneself empty,' as a disclosure of the original emptiness."[76] As Heisig emphasizes, Nishitani distinguishes between the *kenosis* of God and the *ekkenosis* of Christ. The first is interpreted as "the nature of God to be self-negating, empty of self" while the second is taken as "a deliberate and free choice to act in accord with that nature." Because of this difference, one should say that "God *is love* and in Christ God *loves*."[77] However, this interpretation of the *kenosis* from the standpoint of emptiness cannot be reconciled with Orthodox Christianity. A mere coincidence of terms (*emptiness* in Buddhism and Christ making himself *empty*) is not enough to take these terms as equivalents.

As one can expect, Nishitani's unorthodox interpretation of the *kenosis* is followed by similar views of other key Christian doctrines. For instance, one of the topics of interest for him in Christian theology is the way human beings can relate to God. In essence, he argues that for a relationship between God and us to be possible both God and human beings must share the same nature and be grounded in emptiness.[78] He allegedly found a confirmation of this view in Brunner's way of defining the state of fallen humanity. In Nishitani's understanding, Brunner argues (similarly to Stăniloae

---

74. Ibid., 59.

75. This unorthodox understanding of the *kenosis* stems from viewing emptiness as "the original nature of the Eternal Buddha" (Nishitani, *Religion and Nothingness*, 288, footnote 4). Nishitani uses the doctrine of the three bodies of the Buddha in order to show that in *shunyata* lies the ground of the Buddha's compassion: "This Compassion is a compassion grounded in 'emptiness.' It is the so-called Great Compassion. Emptiness here takes on the quality and meaning of *anatman*, non-ego" (*Religion and Nothingness*, 288).

76. Ibid.

77. Heisig, *Philosophers of Nothingness*, 248.

78. Nishitani says: "it is only on the field of this same emptiness that God and man, and the relationships between them, are constituted in a personal Form, and that their respective representations are made possible" (*Religion and Nothingness*, 99).

in chapter 3) that the result of the fall was that likeness with God has been lost, while the image of God "survives the corruption to provide an *Anknüpfungspunkt* ('point of contact') with divine grace."[79] According to Nishitani's perspective, this point of contact between God and human beings must be found "*within* that complete corruption itself"[80] and is the lack of inherent existence of the self. This is the true locus "for receiving redeeming love."[81] However, since for the Swiss theologian the "point of contact" between human beings and God is located in human reason, Nishitani criticizes Brunner's view as incomplete, for his point of contact is "immanent in the self."[82] Hence he argues for a point of contact at which "the self is a nothingness, at which the self has ceased to be a self any longer."[83]

An *analogia entis* that requires that emptiness, however, stands at the foundation of *both* God and human beings is counterproductive for the Orthodox view of human perfection. As we have seen in chapter 3, Stăniloae argues that a personal relationship between a self-existing God and human beings created *ex nihilo* and held in existence by God is possible only by the grace of God. As a result, there is no need for *both* God and human beings to share the nature of emptiness, or for both to have a self (*atman*). From a Christian standpoint there is no need to interpret God's perfection as Nishitani does, as pointing "to something elemental, more basic than the 'personal.'"[84] Nishitani obviously draws inspiration from Zen and seeks the confirmation of his views in the mystical theology of Eckhart, and as a result reinterprets Christian doctrines in a way that even Eckhart in his radical apophaticism would not have backed.[85]

In Orthodox Christianity God has inherent existence as the tri-personal communion between Father, Son, and Holy Spirit. Personhood is first of all grounded in God's intra-trinitarian life, and only secondarily and

---

79. Ibid., 24. For Brunner the *Anknüpfungspunkt* is a point of contact for divine revelation within our nature, for the divine image is not completely lost and retains an idea of what sin and repentance means. Emil Brunner explains this view in his essay "Die Frage nach dem 'Anknüpfungspunkt' als Problem der Theologie," *Zwischen den Zeiten* 10 (1932) 505–32; later reprinted in Brunner, *Ein offenes Wort*, 239–67. In his debate with Brunner in the early 1930s, Barth contradicted this view, arguing that the point of contact itself is the result of divine revelation and is established by the Holy Spirit (Karl Barth, "Nein! Antwort an Emil Brunner," *Theologische Existenz heute* 14 (1934). Both essays are published in English as Barth et al., *Natural Theology*.

80. Nishitani, *Religion and Nothingness*, 25.

81. Ibid.

82. Ibid.

83. Ibid.

84. Ibid., 59.

85. For Eckhart, the ground of God, or what he calls *Gottheit*, has inherent existence.

contingently defined in human relationships. This means that one's relationship with God is an extension of the intra-trinitarian life of God. The arche-
type on which humans rest as relational beings is the Trinity, not a common
*shunyata* nature. In order that humans may be brought to perfection, i.e., to
reach the perfection of Jesus' human nature, they need the personal status
that God has granted them by creation. According to Orthodox theology
humans do not need to have inherent existence, but to be personal agents
in a (perfectible) relationship with the personal God. As for Nishida before
him, for Nishitani personhood is inherently associated with egoism, its sinful manifestation. Therefore he argues that both ego and ego-ism must go,[86]
while the Orthodox Christian perspective is to preserve personhood (an
ego) but without manifesting ego-ism. The two must be differentiated and
only egoism annihilated. Otherwise communion with God and other people cannot be possible, nor can attaining the Orthodox view of perfection.

   Another important Christian topic which is distorted when seen from
the standpoint of emptiness is that of faith.[87] Nishitani argues that one must
see the difference between the "ordinary sense of faith" and what it should
truly be when seen from the standpoint of emptiness. The first is "an *act*
performed by the self" and "arising from *within* the self as an intentionality
toward some object" and is always linked to the "field of consciousness and
self-consciousness."[88] This can be taken as the traditional view of Christian
faith. According to Nishitani this kind of faith has "debilitating effects" on
reason.[89] His understanding of faith invites us to reach the place where "the
framework of the 'ego' has been broken through." True faith would thus be
a "conversion from that sin (of not seeing the common ground of *shunyata*
that all beings share)" to a new way of seeing things. Rather than a "conscious act of the self," true faith consists in adopting a realistic way of seeing
things, as provided by the standpoint of *shunyata*.[90]

86. He argues that "the negation of person-centeredness must amount to an existential self-negation of man's person" (ibid., 70).

87. Nishitani allegedly found a confirmation of his view of faith in Eckhart's concept of returning "to the homeground of God" (ibid., 275), which obviously is not a
return to a personal relationship with God.

88. Ibid., 26.

89. Heisig, *Philosophers of Nothingness*, 195.

90. Nishitani, *Religion and Nothingness*, 26.

## 6.5 NISHITANI'S STANDPOINT OF SHUNYATA AND BUDDHIST-CHRISTIAN DIALOGUE

As we have seen, Nishitani's thesis is that the only reference point that would reconcile science and religion, and thus overcome nihilism, is the standpoint of *shunyata*. He is confident that the religion which displays a "universality analogous to that of science" and thus can lead the world to the overcoming of nihilism is Buddhism, especially Zen Buddhism.[91] However, his confidence is based on shaky foundations. On the one hand, one cannot claim that the Buddhist worldview is backed up by science. Karma, rebirth and enlightenment can hardly be reconciled with a scientific worldview.[92] On the other hand, nihilism in Western culture is not the natural product of Christianity or of the inadequacy of the Christian view of God, but rather the result of a shift in premises. What actually altered the place of Christianity in the Western world was not science itself, but rather scientism, a way of interpreting science and its resources, a philosophy that expects from science all answers to human problems.[93] Nishitani himself acknowledges that

> [t]he philosophical standpoint of "scientism," however, takes scientific certainty in itself to be the same as philosophical truth. . . . In philosophy, this is a dogmatism altogether divorced from science itself.[94]

Despite his openness to Christianity and his more thorough involvement in Buddhist-Christian dialogue than his master Nishida, Nishitani also performs a Zen hermeneutics of Christianity by attempting to accommodate Christian doctrines to his standpoint of *shunyata*. In Nishitani's vision, following the thought of his master Nishida, the future of Christianity lies not in its return to traditional beliefs and repentance for the misdeeds of the past, but in its complete reformulation, above all by forsaking its concept

---

91. Nishitani, "Science and Zen," 136.

92. As Keith Ward argues, the Buddhist view of the mind is "hard to reconcile with scientific views of the human mind and brain" (Ward, *Religion and Human Nature*, 111). Another author who questions the consistency of Buddhism with science is John Cobb. He complains that "If science disappeared, there would be little impulsion within Buddhism to renew it" (Cobb, *Christ in a Pluralist Age*, 208).

93. Nishitani was well aware of this philosophical issue, as he says: "In its essential structure scientific knowledge harbors the certainty that its method of experimental analysis can prevail, at least in principle, throughout the whole realm of natural phenomena, and this certainty is expressed in the scientist as a personal conviction" (Nishitani, "Science and Zen," 115).

94. Ibid.

of a personal God and replacing it with *shunyata*, emptiness.[95] As such, his contribution to Buddhist-Christian dialogue lies in demanding a reinterpretation of Christian doctrines that would lead to establishing a Zen version of Christianity, and not to a mutual understanding of the two religions. Therefore his views cannot be taken as a genuine basis for a dialogue of traditions that respect and help each other in pursuing their view of perfection.

95. Van Bragt summarizes Nishitani's view on the challenge Christianity faces in dialogue with Buddhism, saying that "it has to break free of its Western provincialism, to reassess its appreciation of its own values and reorient itself according to a deeper appreciation of the fundamental values of Buddhism" (Nishitani, *Religion and Nothingness,* xxxvii). As Heisig observed, he was disappointed to see that Christian theologians failed to follow his agenda of reforming Christianity in the light of *shunyata* (Heisig, *Philosophers of Nothingness,* 253).

# 7

## Masao Abe (1915–2006)

### The Work of a Zen Apostle to the Western World

THE NEXT REPRESENTATIVE OF the Kyoto School is quite different from Nishida and Nishitani. While they lived in Japan and were deeply immersed in European philosophy, Masao Abe spent much of his life in the West, as a teacher at many important universities. He was less active in raising awareness of Western philosophy for a Japanese audience than his forerunners at the Kyoto School, and as a result we find fewer references to European philosophy in his writings and a much deeper involvement in religious debates.[1] While Nishida and Nishitani were lay practitioners of Zen, Abe was a Zen teacher, and as such continued the work of D.T. Suzuki, the first "apostle" of Zen in the Western world. Although his major philosophical concern was the same as Nishitani's, to defend the role of religion in a world dominated by scientism and nihilism, he was more open to finding resources for it in dialogue with Christianity. While his predecessors at the Kyoto School limited themselves to an assessment of Christianity through Zen lenses, he argues that Buddhist-Christian dialogue should go beyond mutual understanding and enter the stage of mutual transformation so that they can both meet the challenge of modern nihilism.

The element that makes him one of the most important representatives of contemporary Buddhist-Christian dialogue, and thus especially important for this book, is that, unlike his predecessors, for whom Christianity

---

1. Nevertheless Abe still called himself a representative of the Kyoto School (Abe, *Buddhism and Interfaith Dialogue*, 112). Most references in European philosophy are made to Nietzsche, whom he found the best dialogue partner in Western philosophy.

was merely one of the many topics of philosophical interest in the Western world, Abe studied theology in the West and had much interaction with famous Roman Catholic and Protestant theologians. As a result, we find him going much further than his Kyoto School predecessors, entering into dialogue with Pannenberg and Küng, and seeking confirmation of his view of the *kenosis* in the theology of Moltmann and Rahner. No wonder then that Hans Küng called him (and John Cobb) "the primary initiators of a Christian-Buddhist dialogue upon a new, scholarly base."[2] Therefore this chapter will not have a section on the evolution of Abe's philosophical thought and use of Western philosophy. After a short section on Abe's biography I will proceed directly to assessing his vision of Buddhist-Christian dialogue. Since the topics he addressed are so vast and his interaction with Christian theologians so substantial, this chapter is considerably longer than the previous two.

## 7.1 THE RISE OF AN APOSTLE OF ZEN TO THE WESTERN WORLD

Masao Abe graduated from Osaka Municipal University in the late 1930s with a degree in economics and worked for four years at a trading company in Kobe. His work in the office made him feel he was living a futile and meaningless life. So he quit his job and in 1942 started to study Western philosophy at Kyoto University under Tanabe and Nishitani. The main influence on his philosophical thinking was Nishitani, so one can easily identify several themes that he inherited almost unchanged from his teacher.

In his youth Abe was a follower of Shin Buddhism, to which he was introduced by his mother, a devout worshipper of the Amida Buddha. However, during his student years in Kyoto his faith started to crumble in interaction with modern philosophy, especially in contact with Nietzsche's nihilism. The major blow to his faith in Amida came as a result of meeting the man who would have the most profound impact on his religious life: Shin'ichi Hisamatsu, a Rinzai Zen master associated with the Kyoto School who was extremely critical of Shin Buddhism and of any form of theism.[3] He challenged Abe's faith, but the young student had a religious experience of being overwhelmed by Amida's grace and felt that he could embrace any-

---

2. Hans Küng, "God's Self-Renunciation and Buddhist Emptiness," 208.

3. In Abe's words, Hisamatsu was for him "not only a lifelong teacher but also a life-changing and life-giving teacher" (Christopher Ives, "Introduction," in Cobb and Ives, eds., *Emptying God*, xv). According to Ives, Abe confessed of Hisamatsu's influence: "Without him I am not what I am" (ibid.).

one with his faith, so he decided that Shin Buddhism was the right religious path for him. However, the simple presence of Hisamatsu remained a challenge for Abe's faith, and he somehow felt attracted by the stern personality of this Zen master. Eventually Abe started practicing Zen and contributed to establishing a Zen Buddhist youth organization (the "Gakudo-Dojo"), from which later emerged the FAS Society.[4]

Jeff Shore tells the story of an incident in 1951 when during a Zen meditation session Abe "leaped up from his sitting cushions and raced toward Hisamatsu as if to attack him."[5] He nervously asked him: "Is that the True Self?," to which Hisamatsu replied affirmatively. Abe's challenge went further and during a tea break he slapped Hisamatsu, to which the teacher reacted by laughing.[6] Abe's final awakening came during another Zen retreat when he broke out of the line of a walking meditation and poured upon himself a bucket of ice cold water, crying "It's all a lie!"[7] This marked the end of his doubts and the moment he realized "the falseness of *everything*," including of his faith in Amida.[8] In the words of Christopher Ives, one of his editors, Abe came to realize that "even Amida and his unconditional mercy are sacred fictions."[9] So he became a zealous Zen Buddhist and followed an agenda of an "uncompromising rejection of theism,"[10] and of every view that states a form of a substantial Being as Ultimate Reality.[11]

Apart from the influence of Nishitani and Hisamatsu, and the indirect influence of Nishida,[12] I need to mention the influence of D. T. Suzuki, Nishida's life-long friend, with whom Abe had a close relationship during Suzuki's last ten years of life, and whose work of making Zen known to the West Abe successfully continued. Suzuki once confessed to Abe to being embarrassed by the zeal of Christian missionaries who willingly endured hardships to "propagate their faith" while in Buddhism "very few have risked

---

4. The FAS is a lay organization for the study and practice of Zen, with deep emphasis on relating Zen Buddhism to contemporary issues of Japanese society. Eventually Abe became its leader and influenced many generations of students by his views.

5. Jeff M. Shore, "The True Buddha is Formless: Masao Abe's Religious Quest," in Mitchell, ed., *Masao Abe*, 6.

6. Ibid.

7. Ibid.

8. Ibid.

9. Ives, "Introduction," in Cobb and Ives, eds., *Emptying God*, xv.

10. Cobb, "Preface," in Cobb and Ives, eds., *Emptying God*, xi.

11. Abe, "Kenotic God and Dynamic Sunyata," in Cobb and Ives, eds., *Emptying God*, 49.

12. Nishida's influence on Abe is indirect, as both Nishitani and Hisamatsu were Nishida's disciples.

their lives to transmit the Dharma."[13] Suzuki wished that such lack of commitment could change in the future, which for Abe was perceived "as if a thousand-pound weight had been brought to bear on my chest."[14] After the death of Suzuki, Abe became "the main representative of Zen Buddhism in Europe and North America,"[15] "the leading philosophical exponent of Zen to the West,"[16] "the exponent and disseminator of Japanese Buddhism for Western audiences"[17] and "the most active Buddhist participant in North American interfaith dialogue over the past four decades."[18]

Abe's Western mission started in 1955 when he went to Columbia University in New York to assist Suzuki and to study Christian theology with Tillich and Niebuhr at Union Theological Seminary and Columbia University. For the rest of his life he travelled back and forth from Japan to the West, teaching and lecturing at a large number of universities. In Japan he was associated mostly with the Kyoto, Otani and Nara Universities. In the United States, where he spent most of his life after 1980, he lectured at Claremont Graduate School, the University of Hawaii, Haverford College, the University of Chicago Divinity School, the Pacific School of Religion in Berkeley, Princeton University, and other academic institutions.

## 7.2 CONTINUING THE AGENDA OF NISHITANI AND SUZUKI

Abe stays in the line of discipleship opened by Nishida and continued by Nishitani, following the same approach on the major themes they addressed. As Nishitani saw the biggest threat to religion to be nihilism, Abe closely follows his thought by declaring that "the most crucial task of any religion in our time is to respond to these antireligious forces by elucidating the authentic meaning of religious thought."[19] The "antireligious forces" he refers to are the nihilism of Nietzsche and the philosophy of scientism, the view

---

13. Abe, "The Influence of D. T. Suzuki in the West," in Abe, ed., *A Zen Life*, 114.

14. Ibid.

15. Ives, "Introduction," in Cobb and Ives, eds., *Emptying God*, xiii.

16. John Hick, "Foreword," in Abe, *Zen and Western Thought*, ix. See also Steven Heine, "Foreword," in Abe, *Zen and Comparative Studies*, vii

17. Steven Heine, "Foreword," in Abe, *Buddhism and Interfaith Dialogue*, vii.

18. Christopher Ives, "Masao Abe and His Dialogical Mission," in Mitchell, ed., *Masao Abe*, 348.

19. Abe, "Kenotic God and Dynamic Sunyata," in Cobb and Ives, eds., *Emptying God*, 3.

that "the 'scientific' method constitutes the *one* and *only* criterion of truth."[20] Although he praises Nietzsche for having liberated the Western world from belief in a personal God, which is nothing but "an artificial construct, a self-deception,"[21] and "a 'sacred *lie*' produced by the instinct of theologians,"[22] he argues that simple irreligion cannot "fill the vacuum" created in the spiritual life of Western people.[23] Nietzsche's courageous *Übermensch* who faces nihility without God is a step forward in overcoming the superstition of theism, but not a satisfactory one, since it still bears traces of dualism and thus cannot be a successful substitute of religion. Nietzsche's will to power is still "something" which works by itself, i.e., it is "the seeking mind" which is "not free from objectification."[24] What modern men and women need is a religion beyond the active nihilism of Nietzsche, beyond "emptiness without God."[25] This religion is obviously Zen Buddhism and its standpoint of *shunyata*. Nishida had openly admitted the influence of Zen Buddhism on his philosophical thought only towards the end of his life, while Nishitani made this point clear in his masterpiece *Religion and Nothingness*. Abe felt no hindrances in affirming openly such a religious creed without hiding behind confusing philosophical constructions. He says: "*nirvana* is a realization of great freedom, both from theistic pietism with its dependence on God and from nihilism in a Nietzschean sense with its dependence on the will to power, making possible genuine self-determination by removing the illusion of a determinator."[26]

Abe was a man with a mission. He went beyond a mere criticism of Christianity from the standpoint of Zen philosophy and was the first to talk about a "mutual transformation of Buddhism and Christianity"[27] in order to provide "a spiritual foundation for future humanity in a global age."[28] In comparison with his forerunners, Abe had a much better understanding of Christian doctrines. This was the result of his long stay in the West and his direct interaction with leading Christian theologians such as Paul Tillich, John Cobb Jr., Hans Küng, Jürgen Moltmann and Wolfhart Pannenberg.

20. Ibid., 4.

21. Abe, *Zen and Western Thought*, 136.

22. Ibid., 146.

23. Abe, *Buddhism and Interfaith Dialogue*, 79.

24. Abe, *Zen and Western Thought*, 149–50.

25. Abe, *Buddhism and Interfaith Dialogue*, 79.

26. Ibid., 80; also in *Zen and Western Thought*, 211.

27. Abe, "Kenotic God and Dynamic Sunyata," in Cobb and Ives, eds., *Emptying God*, 3; "*Kenosis* and Emptiness," in Corless and Knitter, eds., *Buddhist Emptiness and Christian Trinity*, 5.

28. Abe, *Zen and Western Thought*, xxiii.

There are passages in his writings which prove he has a fair understanding of fundamental Christian theological issues. For instance, he defines the "kernel of Christian faith" to be "the belief that Jesus is the incarnation of the *Word* of God, that human sins are redeemed through his death on the cross, and that the severed relationship between God and man is also restored through his death and resurrection."[29] He is aware of the difference between Christianity and Buddhism concerning their reliance on a historical saviour, and that in Christianity there is no way of finding salvation by one's own power, but only by faith in God's initiative in Christ.[30] While in Buddhism historical acts of past teachers, including those of the Buddha, have no central role in one's enlightenment, since each of us can follow the same road, he notices that in Christianity salvation is possible "only through the historical event of Jesus' crucifixion and resurrection."[31] Abe knows the Christian claim that Christ is "the Redeemer of man's sin against God"[32] and describes well the image of Christian perfection as the restoration of the human being into God's likeness, which "has been demonstrated by the fact of the resurrection of Jesus Christ."[33] The resurrection of Christ, of which the Apostle Paul talks in 1 Corinthians 15:15–16, is in his words, "the receiving of a new life by conquering death," the resource in whom "all humankind fundamentally conquers death."[34] As a result, the perfected human being enjoys a personal form of existence "by the working of a new creation by God."[35] If no indication were given of the author of these sentences, one could well imagine that he was an Orthodox theologian, and not a teacher of Zen.

29. Abe, *Zen and Comparative Studies*, 120–21.

30. Several points where Abe departs from an orthodox Christian view can be corrected, amazingly, by his own explanations given in other parts of his writings. For instance, in one case he affirms that "Christians have *propounded* the necessity of faith in God" (Abe, *Zen and the Modern World*, 22, italics mine), which sounds as if faith in God were the invention of theologians, while in an earlier work he correctly emphasized that "the Christian participates in the eternal not by recollection (*anamnesis*) but by revelation (*Offenbarung*)" and that it is only through the revelation "of the word of God" that one can "recover the link with eternal life that has been lost as the result of sin" (Abe, *Zen and Comparative Studies*, 122–3). Therefore he corrects his affirmation that faith is "propounded" by Christians (as if it were their initiative) by saying it is a response to God's revelation. Unfortunately, the second affirmation predates the first, which means he departed from an original right view in favour of a postmodern interpretation of faith.

31. Abe, *Zen and the Modern World*, 27. This part was written in 1997.

32. Abe, "God, Emptiness, and the True Self," in Franck, ed., *Buddha Eye*, 67.

33. Abe, *Zen and Comparative Studies*, 123.

34. Ibid.

35. Ibid.

As we will see, however, Abe's view of Christianity is quite un-ortho-dox. In order to uncover his true understanding of Christian doctrines we must go beyond appearances and consider his doctrinal reference point, which is Zen Buddhism. Following his predecessors at the Kyoto School, who draw inspiration for their philosophical views from their practice of Zen, Abe's views emerge from "the immediate and mystical experience of Emptiness" which is the only locus where philosophical uncertainties can be "truly resolved (and, in a sense, dissolved)."[36] Since it is known that he strongly opposed theism, let me first assess his view of the Christian doctrine of God.

## 7.3 ABE'S VIEW OF GOD

As one could expect from a follower of Hisamatsu, Abe cannot accept the Christian concept of God as Ultimate Reality.[37] He follows Nishida's rejec-tion of God as subject, and insists on seeing God as "universal predicate," or as the "groundless ground," which is a synonym of the Buddhist *shu-nyata*.[38] He thus reiterates the predicate logic of Nishida, which does not leave room for a substantial Ultimate Reality, saying that "the true absolute is the absolute Nothingness, not the absolute Being."[39] All beings have their ground in *shunyata* and thus the personal God cannot be self-existing and *must* also have a ground. In Abe's words, "*Sunyata* or nothingness in Zen is not a 'nothing' out of which all things were created by God, but a 'nothing' from which God himself emerged."[40] This is the major premise on which he builds his entire perspective on Buddhist-Christian dialogue and from which he proposes his "humble suggestion towards an understanding of God today."[41]

36. Thomas P. Kasulis, "Masao Abe as D. T. Suzuki's Philosophical Successor," in Mitchell, ed., *Masao Abe*, 256.

37. He reminds us of his Zen assumptions when he says that "from the perspective of dependent co-origination, a notion such as the one God as the absolute good who must be independent is nothing but a reification and substantialization of something ultimate as the only entity that has its own being" (Abe, "Kenotic God and Dynamic Sunyata," in Cobb and Ives, eds., *Emptying God*, 49).

38. Abe, *Buddhism and Interfaith Dialogue*, 8.

39. Ibid., 118.

40. Abe, "God, Emptiness, and the True Self," 71. Although he finds Eckhart's *Got-theit* as "strikingly similar" to the Buddhist *shunyata* (Abe, *Zen and Western Thought*, 133), we must remember Ueda's warning that they cannot be viewed as similar. See Ueda's article "'Nothingness' in Meister Eckhart," in Franck, ed., *Buddha Eye*, 157–68.

41. Abe, *Buddhism and Interfaith Dialogue*, 10.

As did Nishida and Nishitani before him, Abe considers that as long as humans are bound to the idea of a personal God as Ultimate Reality they cannot overcome the root cause that generates divisions between religions and fuels humankind's anxiety. In his view, a personal God as in Judaism, Christianity and Islam necessarily "becomes authoritative, commanding, and intolerant," and as such generates "serious conflicts with other faiths."[42] Abe's solution is to find "a new understanding of monotheism"[43] by exhorting the adherents of monotheistic religions that they should emphasize "the self-negating, non-substantial aspect of their 'God.'"[44] This line of thought necessarily leads us to the views of Eckhart and Böhme, and to the doctrine of the *kenosis* as developed by Nishida and Nishitani, a topic that I will address in the next section.

Following his view on Ultimate Reality in Buddhism, Abe argues for a similarity between the Mahayana doctrine of the *Trikaya* (the three bodies of the Buddha) and that of the Christian Trinity. In his view, all historical religious teachers, including Siddhartha Gautama, Moses, Jesus, Muhammad and Buddhist masters such as Nagarjuna, Vasubanthu, Shinran, are forms of the *nirmanakaya*. The *sambhogakaya* corresponds to what these historical teachers have meant by "God." In other words, the *sambhogakaya* is what Jesus meant by God the Father, Muhammad by Allah, Shinran by Amida, etc. Beyond these personal gods stands the "impersonal, formless and nameless 'Nothing'" as the *dharmakaya*, the Ultimate Reality for all religions as "formless, colourless, nameless, unlimited, impersonal 'Openness' or 'Emptiness.'"[45] Since Abe is aware that in Judaism Moses cannot be a transformation body of Yahweh, nor can Muhammad be regarded in Islam as a transformation body of Allah,[46] he admits that his adaptation of the *Trikaya* doctrine is formulated especially for "the arena of Buddhist-Christian dialogue."[47] But, as we have seen in section 3.1, Abe's attempt to assimilate *sambhogakaya* with God the Father and *nirmanakaya* with God the Son

42. Abe, *Zen and Comparative Studies*, 217.

43. Ibid., 215.

44. Ibid., 217.

45. Abe, *Buddhism and Interfaith Dialogue*, 32–33. In Abe's words, "'Lord' roughly stands for *nirmana-kaya*, a historical religious figure that is the centre of faith; 'God' approximately represents *sambhoga-kaya*, a personal God who is suprahistorical but has a particular name and virtue(s); 'Boundless Openness' or 'Formless Emptiness' generally expresses *dharma-kaya*, Truth itself, which is also suprahistorical and is the ultimate ground for both a personal 'God' and a central historical religious figure as 'Lord'" (Abe, *Buddhism and Interfaith Dialogue*, 31).

46. Ibid., 32.

47. Masao Abe, "A Rejoinder," in Ives, ed., *Divine Emptiness*, 169.

is not tenable. Another problem in this parallel is that he cannot find the equivalent of the Holy Spirit in the Buddhist *Trikaya*.[48]

Abe's understanding of the Christian doctrine of God proves to be unorthodox again when he interprets the meaning of *homoousios*. First, he applies it to the two natures in Christ, saying that Jesus "has the nature of *homoousios*, consubstantiality, in which the immanence and transcendence are paradoxically one."[49] However, *homoousios* does not refer to the confusion or mixture of the two natures in Christ, but to the three *hypostases* of the Trinity as sharing the same divine nature. The second flaw in his interpretation of *homoousios* is seen in his difficulty of separating *ousia* and the three *hypostases* in the Trinity. In Abe's view, in order to avoid the need of seeing *ousia* as a kind of a *"fourth* being," he prescribes that "the oneness of this one God must possess the characteristic of zero."[50] In other words, only if *ousia* is seen as *shunyata* "can the doctrine of the Trinity be fully and dynamically realized" and be saved from "the haunting presence of the fourth being."[51] However, according to the Orthodox view the divine *ousia* is only in the *hypostases*, not beyond them, as the divine *hypostases* do not *possess* a common *ousia*, but rather *are* the common *ousia*.

## 7.4 THE KENOSIS OF CHRIST AND THE KENOTIC GOD

Abe finds in the hymn of Philippians 2:6–11 "one of the most impressive and touching passages in the Bible,"[52] which "deeply moved" him from

48. Abe formulates the equivalence between the Buddhist *trikaya* and Christian Trinity from an inclusivistic Mahayana Buddhist point of view. As he acknowledges in a footnote, Zen Buddhism does not need the *trikaya* doctrine for the realization of enlightenment (Abe, *Buddhism and Interfaith Dialogue*, 38, note 22).

49. Abe, *Zen and Western Thought*, 189. The confusion of the two natures in Christ contradicts Orthodox Christian doctrine as it goes against the Formula of Chalcedon (AD 451). Abe states again the confusion of the two natures in Christ, by arguing that in Jesus Christ "flesh and spirit . . . became identical" ("God, Emptiness, and the True Self," 67) and that "without the deeply dynamic nondual function of self-emptying, the consubstantiality of the divinity and the humanity in Jesus Christ cannot be properly understood" (Abe, "Kenotic God and Dynamic Sunyata," in Cobb and Ives, eds., *Emptying God*, 11). Since he says that the concept of *"homoousia"* does not simply indicate "'consubstantiality' of two substances, divine and human, as understood traditionally," but the "'non-dual function' of self-emptying or self-negation," his view on the nature of Christ is more complicated and will be dealt with in the next section, dedicated to the doctrine of the *kenosis* (ibid.).

50. Abe, "Kenotic God and Dynamic Sunyata," 24.

51. Ibid.

52. Ibid., 9. We find the major exposition of Abe's view on the *kenosis* in his article "Kenotic God and Dynamic Sunyata," (in Cobb and Ives, eds., *Emptying God*, 3–65),

his student days.[53] We already know how this passage is interpreted by his predecessors at the Kyoto School. In the words of Abe, Christ "abdicated his divine rank," undergoing a "complete and thoroughgoing" emptying of divinity for the sake of a disobedient humankind to God.[54] He rejects the Docetist view of Christ's incarnation as mere appearance, but goes to the other extreme, holding that in Jesus Christ God the Son abandoned his divine nature completely.[55] Although he seems to uphold the Protestant theological position of kenoticism, we will see that his view is thoroughly determined by the standpoint of *shunyata*. This must be the right reference point for understanding his thoughts on the *kenosis*.

Abe rejects the concept of the pre-existing Logos in John's Gospel as misleading, for emptiness does not leave room for a permanent Being through whom "all things came into being" (John 1:3). He also rejects a temporal sequence in Christ's becoming in order to achieve human salvation, the thought that "Christ was *originally* the Son of God and *then* emptied himself."[56] Instead, he argues that Christ's *kenosis* must be seen as representing the very nature of the Son of God as "*essentially* and *fundamentally* self-emptying."[57] In other words, one should not assume that he "*became* a person through the process of his self-emptying," but instead realize that what makes him a "true person and true God" is this "dynamic work and activity of self-emptying" itself.[58] In order for the concept of *kenosis* to make sense for Abe, he argues that Christ must be kenotic by his very nature, and thus "the historical incarnation is merely a disclosure of that nature."[59] Therefore one can understand why Abe is seeking a "new interpretation" of

---

which he calls a "milestone" in his participation in Buddhist-Christian dialogue (Abe, *Buddhism and Interfaith Dialogue*, 56).

53. Ibid., 55.

54. Abe, "Kenotic God and Dynamic Sunyata," 9–10.

55. He finds other passages in the New Testament that seem to confirm his view of the *kenosis*, but a careful reading of them indicates the limitation of the Son of God to a human nature (John 3:13): his incarnation and Ascension (John 16:28), and his obedience to the Father's will for our salvation (Romans 15:3; 2 Corinthians 8:9); so these passages do not confirm Abe's view of the total *kenosis* of the Son of God (in Abe, *Buddhism and Interfaith Dialogue*, 130).

56. Abe, "Kenotic God and Dynamic Sunyata," 10; also in Masao Abe, "Beyond Buddhism and Christianity: 'Dazzling Darkness,'" in Ives, ed., *Divine Emptiness*, 229; and in Abe, *Buddhism and Interfaith Dialogue*, 221–22.

57. Abe, "Kenotic God and Dynamic Sunyata," in Cobb and Ives, eds., *Emptying God*, 10.

58. Ibid.

59. Heisig, *Sunyata and Kenosis*, 9.

the theme of the "preexisting Logos" of John's prologue.[60] In his view, the Logos cannot pre-exist "as 'the Son of God' apart from us."[61] Instead, the Son of God "must be realized right here, right now, at the depth of our present existence."[62] In other words, "the Son of God" is the *process* of emptying that all humans must realize as operating at the core of their being as well.

For Abe the *kenosis* is not a matter of submission to the Father's will for the sake of *real* sinners, in the power of the Holy Spirit, according to the Orthodox view. As Heisig points out, "Abe refuses to allow himself to get entangled in the problem of how to determine *who* in the Trinity did *what* to *whom* and *when*."[63] In a way consistent with Zen thought, the event of the cross can be seen as having a saving effect on sinners only if "the sonship of Jesus is understood to be ultimately rooted in *Nichts* as Godhead."[64] Otherwise, if the cross is seen as part of the traditional view of human redemption from sin, it would fuel the illusion of eternal life as eternal communion with God. For Abe, as for Buddhism in general, real salvation can only be *out* of personhood, *out* of false theistic beliefs and towards the realization of nothingness. This is the reason why "the sonship of Jesus" must point to the *Nichts* of Eckhart. Otherwise Abe's position on the *kenosis* could not be reconciled with his rejection of theism, and with his reliance on Eckhart and Böhme for a more "realistic" view of God. Given these assumptions, Abe could only have rejected Stăniloae's emphasis on the realization in Jesus of the perfected *human* being in a perfect relationship with God. He keeps referring to the Son of God as emptying himself of his divine nature and completely ignores a discussion of the role of the two natures, the dynamics between them, and the ideal of elevating a true human nature to an unhindered relationship with God.

While Nishida and Nishitani built their view of the *kenosis* on Philippians 2:6–8 without paying much attention to the rest of the hymn (verses 9–11, on the exaltation of Christ), and were criticized for it by Christian theologians, Abe is aware that Christ's humiliation and exaltation cannot be separated.[65] However, he cannot agree with the traditional Christian inter-

60. Abe, "Kenotic God and Dynamic Sunyata," 10. Abe's justification for reinterpreting the traditional Christian meaning of the Logos is that he finds it "incompatible with the critical rationality and autonomous reason so important in the modern world" (Abe, "Kenotic God and Dynamic Sunyata," 13).

61. Ibid., 10.

62. Ibid.

63. Heisig, *Sunyata and Kenosis*, 9.

64. Abe, "Beyond Buddhism and Christianity," 230. Abe is obviously referring here to the *Nichts* defined by Eckhart.

65. Abe, "Kenotic God and Dynamic Sunyata," in Cobb and Ives, eds., *Emptying*

pretation that "the pouring out" of his self only serves the higher purpose of being "filled up" with the "fullness" of God,[66] for in Zen the self-emptying as Great Death cannot be followed by an even stronger bond with the personal God. Therefore we can understand the way in which Abe links Christ's humiliation with his exaltation only if we consider it from a Mahayana Buddhist perspective. He says that the inseparability of the two aspects finds its formulation in the following words: "The Son of God is not the Son of God; precisely because he is not the Son of God, he is truly the Son of God."[67] Although this enunciation may seem unintelligible, it points to the Son's alleged double orientation, as clinging neither to the *Gottheit* (in Abe's view, to Christ's divine nature), nor to his "form of a servant" in which he appeared as Jesus. Abe argues that Christ's humiliation and exaltation should not be seen as different states, but as "a single, dynamic one; that is, humiliation as it is is exaltation, and exaltation as it is is humiliation; kenosis as it is is pleroma, and pleroma as it is is kenosis."[68] This formula comes strikingly near to the *bodhisattva*'s simultaneous double orientation given by wisdom and compassion, which would translate here as "*pleroma*" and "*kenosis*." Thus in Abe's view Christ's humiliation *is* his exaltation, and his exaltation *is* his humiliation, which is another way of saying that the *bodhisattva* is enlightened in the midst of *samsara*, but is also moved by compassion for suffering beings despite his or her enlightenment.

As Nishida and Nishitani before him, Abe argues that the *kenosis* of Christ "inevitably leads us to face the problem of the *kenosis* of God."[69] We could have expected this position, for Zen Buddhism cannot accept a substantial Ultimate Reality. Only the *process* of emptying can be called Ultimate Reality, God, or Son of God, and therefore not only must the Son of

---

*God*, 13. In another version of this article, although he acknowledges the need to reconsider both aspects, he very briefly adds "I shall not, however, at this point, discuss his exaltation" ("*Kenosis* and Emptiness," in Corless and Knitter, eds., *Buddhist Emptiness and Christian Trinity*, 15).

66. Heisig, *Sunyata and Kenosis*, 10.

67. Abe, "Kenotic God and Dynamic Sunyata," 13. A similar formula is used below in the same essay: "God is not God (for God is love and completely self-emptying); precisely because God is not a self-affirmative God, God is truly a God of love (for through complete self-abnegation God is totally identified with everything including sinful humans) (Abe, "Kenotic God and Dynamic Sunyata," 16). What he means here is that Ultimate Reality is not the personal God, but the *process* of emptying, the *truth* of *shunyata*.

68. Abe, *Buddhism and Interfaith Dialogue*, 134.

69. Abe, "Kenotic God and Dynamic Sunyata," in Cobb and Ives, eds., *Emptying God*, 13. He also says: "Without the *kenosis* of God Himself, the *kenosis* of Christ is inconceivable" (*Buddhism and Interfaith Dialogue*, xviii).

God be kenotic by his very nature, but God the Father must be as well.[70] Following this assumption, Abe argues that the ultimate reason for the *kenosis* is "God's own fulfillment,"[71] which means expressing himself according to the law of dependent co-arising. In other words, God "fulfils" himself by following the process of self-emptying.[72]

Abe's interest appears to be clear. Since his fundamental assumption is that there cannot be a personal Ultimate Reality as the Christian Trinity, he interprets the doctrine of the *kenosis* in a way which suits his assumption. Therefore "the true God" for Abe, is not one that merely "had the Son of God take a human form and be sacrificed while God remained God," but one who is a "self-sacrificial God through total *kenosis*."[73] This "self-sacrificial God" that Abe has in mind is the ultimate *truth* of *shunyata*, which empties everything of inherent existence. It is only such a *view* that can release one from the bondage of false views and thus save "everything, including human beings and nature."[74]

In order to find confirmations of his view of the *kenosis* in Christian theology, Abe went further than his Kyoto School predecessors and entered into dialogue with important Christian theologians, such as Moltmann, Rahner, Pannenberg and Küng. Therefore I will continue this section with an assessment of his dialogue with them.

---

70. If we considered the *process* of emptying as the Ultimate Reality and called God the ultimate predicate, we would reach an agreement with Abe, but obviously not with the Orthodox Christian view, in which God is the ultimate subject.

71. Abe, "Kenotic God and Dynamic Sunyata," 16. In other words, Abe argues that the *kenosis* of God himself is "God's self-sacrifice for absolutely 'nothing' other than his own fulfilment" ("*Kenosis* and Emptiness," in Corless and Knitter, eds., *Buddhist Emptiness and Christian Trinity*, 19).

72. Following Nishitani, Abe also formulates the "divine indifference of God's love" towards all people, good or bad, from the text in Matthew 5:45 (*Buddhism and Interfaith Dialogue*, 14). In Abe's view, God's love for "the unjust and the sinner, natural and moral evil" ("Kenotic God and Dynamic Sunyata," 16) is not defined by his will, but by his emptying nature, and thus bears a different meaning from that in Orthodox Christianity.

73. Ibid.

74. Ibid. It is, however, puzzling how a *view* itself could be "self-sacrificial, abnegating love" (ibid.). These are prerogatives of persons, who can express love by their free will initiative. Pannenberg asks: "If there is no self-referential agent abiding in the process of negativity, how can one possibly speak of a 'compassionate aspect of Sunyata' and of 'wisdom realized in Sunyata'?" (Wolfhart Pannenberg, "God's Love and the *Kenosis* of the Son: A Response to Masao Abe," in Ives, ed., *Divine Emptiness*, 247).

## 7.4.1 Abe's Interpretation of Moltmann

One of the great names in Christian theology in whose writings Abe hoped to find a confirmation of his interpretation of the *kenosis* is Jürgen Moltmann. His challenging views of the event of the cross appeared to provide for Abe a bridge for Buddhist-Christian dialogue and a confirmation of his views of the kenotic God. However, one must be aware of the different orientations of the two authors. On the one hand, Moltmann's theology, formulated as "a theology after Auschwitz,"[75] seeks to present God deeply involved in human suffering through sharing in the suffering of Jesus on the cross. It explores the event of the cross as an event in the Trinity, rather than following the traditional understanding involving the two natures in Christ. On the other hand, Abe is seeking in Moltmann's writings a confirmation of his own views of the *kenosis* of Christ and of the kenotic God. In pursuing his goal, Abe starts from Moltmann's challenging declaration that "(God) also suffers the death of his Fatherhood in the death of the Son."[76] Then he is pleased to find Moltmann saying: "In the forsakenness of the Son the Father also forsakes himself. In the surrender of the Son the Father also surrenders himself, though not in the same way."[77] This seems to be close to Abe's view which links the *kenosis* of Christ with that of the Father himself.

However, Moltmann does not confirm Abe's thought of the kenotic God. As Abe is right to observe, "Moltmann emphasizes the deep community of will between Jesus and his God, which is expressed even in their separation."[78] The German theologian refers to the harmony of their wills, and does not explore an ontological change of God's substance. Therefore, although highly appreciative, Abe is not satisfied with Moltmann's trinitarian

75. Moltmann, "The Crucified God," 10; and *History and the Triune God*, 166.

76. Abe, "Kenotic God and Dynamic Sunyata," in Cobb and Ives, eds., *Emptying God*, 19, following Moltmann, *The Crucified God*, 243. Although this may look like the view rejected by the Church Fathers as Patripassianism, it cannot be applied to Moltmann, since Patripassianism is related to the early heresy of Modalism (or Sabellianism), which does not accept the Orthodox doctrine of the Trinity. This early heresy taught that Jesus was God himself incarnate, and as thus the Father himself suffered on the cross.

77. Abe, "Kenotic God and Dynamic Sunyata," 21, and *Buddhism and Interfaith Dialogue*, 20, following Moltmann, *The Crucified God*, 243. It is important to mention here that Moltmann and Stăniloae met several times at various ecumenical theological meetings and became good friends, and it was Moltmann who backed the translation of Stăniloae's *Dogmatics* into German. Moltmann acknowledged the influence of Stăniloae in his *History and the Triune God*, 173, 179) and dedicated this book to his Romanian friend.

78. Abe, "Kenotic God and Dynamic Sunyata," in Cobb and Ives, eds., *Emptying God*, 21.

theology and qualifies it as "merely one step into the interior and not a complete penetration into the depth of God's mystery."[79] He requires that Christians would make a further and decisive step towards acknowledging that the oneness of the triune God possesses "the characteristic of zero," or in other words, to acknowledge that "the one God in the Trinity must be the great zero."[80] One can easily recognize the Zen ground of his thought, seeing Father, Son, and Holy Spirit as having their origin in the *Nichts* of Eckhart.[81] This is the "still greater interior of the interior" towards which one should move, and the only way in which the event of the cross can be understood "in *both* trinitarian *and* personal terms," as Abe understands Moltmann's theological goal.[82] And since only in *shunyata* can a dynamical identity be stated between the "absolute interior" and the "absolute exterior" of God, Moltmann's theology is not sufficient to reach such a goal.[83] In his response to Abe, Moltmann rejects the insights of Eckhart and Böhme, and realizes that Abe's view is modeled on a "Buddhist understanding of ultimate reality."[84] As such it cannot find the right balance between person and nature. For the German theologian "in person, nature comes to itself" and "realizes him/herself."[85] In a way that reminds us of Stăniloae, he argues: "If one takes away the divine persons, then no divine substance remains."[86] In other words, there is no *ousia* beyond the *hypostases* (or nature beyond Persons).

In his dialogue with Abe Moltmann argued that the emptying of the Son of God is not based on an "arbitrary action,"[87] but in his personal initiative as response to the Father's will. Moltmann's view of the "loving surrendering" in the Trinity does not render obsolete the personhood of the *hypostases*, Father, Son, and Holy Spirit, but is one according to which they reciprocally fulfil each other, following the doctrine of the *perichoresis*.[88] He criticizes Abe for limiting his view of the Trinity to Tertullian's "*tres*

79. Ibid., 23.

80. Ibid., 24.

81. Ibid.

82. Ibid., 23–24.

83. Ibid., 25.

84. Moltmann, "God is Unselfish Love," in Cobb and Ives, eds., *Emptying God*, 120.

85. Ibid.

86. Ibid.

87. Ibid., 118.

88. Moltmann says: "The doctrine of perichoresis links together in a brilliant way the threeness and the unity, without reducing the threeness to unity, or dissolving the unity in the threeness. The unity of the triunity lies in the eternal perichoresis of the trinitarian persons" (Moltmann, *The Trinity and the Kingdom of God*, 175).

*personae—una substantia,*" while his view is based on the *"perichoretical community* of the three persons."[89] This model is similar to Stăniloae's view, for Moltmann argues:

> The Son does not exist in himself, but by virtue of his unselfish love entirely in the Father. The Father does not exist in himself, but by virtue of his unselfish love entirely in the Son. The Holy Spirit does not exist in himself, but entirely in the Father and the Son. So the three persons are by virtue of the essential surrendering different and yet entirely one.[90]

Another example in which Abe allegedly found a confirmation of his view of the *kenosis* in Moltmann's theology is in the following words:

> The divinity of the trinitarian God is *kenosis*. This divine *kenosis* is being as well as non-being. It is neither being nor non-being. It is the unfathomable secret of love, which one cannot comprehend, but rather only worship in amazement.[91]

What we have here is a case of misquoting and of ignoring the context of Moltmann's words. While one can understand why this text seems to confirm Abe's view of Ultimate Reality as beyond being and non-being, Moltmann has no such goal in mind. Abe did not quote the introductory "In this respect" of Moltmann's words.[92] "In this respect" is a reference to the preceding paragraph, in which Moltmann criticizes Eckhart's view of "the 'abyss' of the divinity behind the three divine persons," and points to the "hypostatic community" in which truly lies what Eckhart and Böhme were seeking, i.e., "unselfish love and surrender to the other as the highest form of *negation*."[93] Therefore it is in this "hypostatic community" that Moltmann sees the divinity of God as *kenosis*, unfathomable love beyond being and non-being, not in the predicative *shunyata*, which would render even the

---

89. Moltmann, "God Is Unselfish Love," in Cobb and Ives, eds., *Emptying God*, 119. Abe cannot accept as Ultimate Reality this perichoretical model of the Trinity, the "community in mutual interdependence and interpenetration" (Moltmann, "God Is Unselfish Love," 120). For him it would be just another way of reiterating Being as Ultimate Reality. For Abe *perichoresis* points to the nonsubstantiality of God: "Perichoresis becomes truly and fully perichoresis through the realization of the nonsubstantiality or emptiness of the one God" (Abe, "A Rejoinder," in Ives, ed., *Divine Emptiness*, 191).

90. Moltmann, "God is Unselfish Love," in Cobb and Ives, eds., *Emptying God*, 119.

91. Abe, "A Rejoinder," in Cobb and Ives, eds., *Emptying God*, 165, following Moltmann, "God is Unselfish Love," in Cobb and Ives, eds., *Emptying God*, 120.

92. The whole proposition reads: "In this respect the divinity of the trinitarian God is *kenosis*" (Moltmann, "God Is Unselfish Love," 120).

93. Ibid.

"hypostatic community" as empty of inherent existence.[94] Therefore, although Moltmann is a revolutionary theologian (and sometimes criticized for his daring views), one cannot find real confirmation of Abe's view of the *kenosis* in his theology.

## 7.4.2 Abe's Interpretation of Rahner

Karl Rahner is taken by Abe as advocating the concept of "the self-emptying God" in the following text: "The primary phenomenon given by faith is precisely the self-emptying of God, his becoming, the *kenosis* and genesis of God himself."[95] Could this mean that Rahner confirms Abe's view of the *kenosis* of God? Only if one ignores Rahner's theology as a whole. The German theologian holds firmly to the doctrine that God "is not subject to change in himself,"[96] that he is not bound to empty himself, but instead is *free* to change himself, having "the *possibility* of himself becoming the other, the finite."[97] Rahner says: "The mystery of the Incarnation must be in God himself, and precisely in the fact that, although he is immutable in and of himself, he *himself* can become something in another."[98] In other words, Rahner affirms that there is no external law (such as dependent co-arising) that could constrain God to change, but that God as the ultimate personal Being is free to assume a human, finite form. This has nothing to do with dependent co-arising as a law that generates God himself, but rather with God's freedom and his initiative of taking a different form for the sake of fallen humanity. In Rahner's words, God "possesses the possibility of *establishing* the other as his own reality by dispossessing *himself*, by giving *himself*

---

94. In another instance, Abe interprets Moltmann's view of creation as being "strikingly similar to the Buddhist notion of *pratitya-samutpada*" (Abe, "A Rejoinder," in Cobb and Ives, eds., *Emptying God*, 165). But when Abe paraphrased Moltmann as saying that "creation means that all existing things are contingent" (ibid.), he should have been aware that Moltmann referred to the view that creation is dependent on God's will for its preservation, a view similar to Stăniloae's (held in existence by grace). In this contingency on God's preservation lies the answer to Abe's question "What is the relationship between each thing and God?" (ibid.).

95. Rahner, *Foundations of Christian Faith*, 222, quoted by Abe in *Buddhism and Interfaith Dialogue*, 56.

96. Rahner, *Foundations of Christian Faith*, 220.

97. Ibid., 222, emphasis mine.

98. Ibid., 221 (Rahner's emphasis), quoted by Abe in *Zen and Comparative Studies*, 122.

away.["99] It is the will of a Person that prevails, not the inherent course of action of an impersonal law.

In his assessment of Rahner's theology Abe is displeased to find in it "traces of dualism" between God and human beings and argues that they are not really necessary for the Christian faith.[100] He wishes that Rahner had gone beyond his view of God becoming "*something else* by partial self-giving" and acknowledge that "God *is* each and every thing" through his "total self-emptying."[101] However, Rahner cannot be pushed into this Zen view. He does not abdicate from the doctrine of God as personal Ultimate Reality in favour of a deeper truth that would be "entirely beyond conception and objectification."[102]

## 7.4.3 Abe in Dialogue with Pannenberg

The next important theologian who engaged in dialogue with Abe, especially on the issue of the *kenosis*, is Wolfhart Pannenberg. Abe's debate with him follows the already known agenda: The *kenosis* of Christ must be seen as his emptying of divinity, and the "taking a human form" must signify "a renunciation of the Sonship of God."[103] As we have already seen, the "taking the form of a servant" in Philippians 2:7 cannot mean a mere change of "shape or appearance" but must necessarily imply "substance and reality."[104] In other words, one should acknowledge that "the Son of God abandoned his divine substance and took a human substance," and that this meant "a radical and total self-negation of the Son of God."[105] From the *kenosis*

---

99. Rahner, *Foundations of Christian Faith*, 222. This theme in Rahner's theology of God's "giving *himself* away" is also misinterpreted by Abe. It does not confirm his view of the kenotic God, but rather refers to the *perichoresis* of the three *hypostases*, an issue we have seen in chapter 2 explained by Stăniloae. In other words, Rahner is not referring to the impermanence of God here, but to the permanent intra-trinitarian relationships, the proper context where love is defined.

100. Abe, "Kenotic God and Dynamic Sunyata," in Cobb and Ives, eds., *Emptying God*, 15.

101. Ibid., 16.

102. Ibid.

103. Abe, "God's Total *Kenosis* and Truly Redemptive Love," in Ives, ed., *Divine Emptiness*, 254.

104. Ibid.; also in Abe, "Kenotic God and Dynamic Sunyata," in Cobb and Ives, eds., *Emptying God*, 10.

105. Masao Abe, "Kenotic God and Dynamic Sunyata," in Ives, ed., *Divine Emptiness*, 32; also in "God's Total *Kenosis* and Truly Redemptive Love," in Ives, ed., *Divine Emptiness*, 254–55.

of Christ Abe then proceeds to argue for the *kenosis* of the Father as did Nishida and Nishitani before him.

I have deliberately chosen to present first what seems to be Abe's introduction of his views to Pannenberg. However, the above arguments are presented in *response* to Pannenberg's comments to his initial article ("Kenotic God and Dynamic Sunyata"). My reason for doing so is to show that Abe is just reaffirming the initial arguments he presented in that article, while ignoring Pannenberg's response and despite being aware that Christian theology affirms that the *kenosis* of Christ does not involve a loss of his divine status and that there is no *kenosis* of the Father.[106] Despite all the criticism he received from Christian theologians, Abe usually just reaffirmed his interpretation of *kenosis*, proving that he did not pay much attention to what his Christian dialogue partners were saying. His reasons for rejecting the traditional Christian view of the *kenosis* are two: First, such a view can no longer cope with contemporary "antireligious ideologies," and second, it should be "deeply rooted" in the authentic spirit of Christianity, which affirms that "God is love."[107] In Abe's view, "God does not remain God while having the Son of God empty himself."[108] Instead he should become "completely identical with humanity, including sinful men."[109] Only if self-emptying were his fundamental nature, could God be called "love."

In his comment on Abe's "Kenotic God and Dynamic Sunyata" Pannenberg appears to agree with Abe's argument against the idea that "Christ was *originally* the Son of God and *then* emptied himself."[110] But this does not mean he follows Abe's view on the nature of the Son of God as "*essentially* and *fundamentally* self-emptying."[111] What Pannenberg agrees with is that the Apostle Paul is not referring in Philippians 2:6–7 just to the incarnation of the Son of God (i.e., just to the birth of Jesus), but to his whole earthly existence, which "as a whole . . . was characterized by emptying himself and by humbling himself in becoming obedient unto death."[112] Pannenberg was probably too quick to express his agreement with Abe here, as the Japanese philosopher was not referring to the birth of Jesus either. As mentioned

---

106. Abe, "God's Total *Kenosis* and Truly Redemptive Love," 256; also in Abe, "A Response," in Mitchell, *Masao Abe*, 389.

107. Abe, "God's Total *Kenosis* and Truly Redemptive Love," 256.

108. Ibid.

109. Ibid.

110. Wolfhart Pannenberg, "God's Love and the *Kenosis* of the Son: A Response to Masao Abe," in Ives, ed., *Divine Emptiness*, 247.

111. Abe, "Kenotic God and Dynamic Sunyata," in Cobb and Ives, ed., *Emptying God*, 10.

112. Pannenberg, "God's Love and the *Kenosis* of the Son," 247.

earlier in this chapter, Abe argued that one should not assume that Jesus "*became* a person through the process of his self-emptying," but instead to be aware that what makes him a "true person and true God" is this "dynamic work and activity of self-emptying" itself.[113] Therefore Abe was referring to the nature of the Son of God, not to his incarnation. Also, when Pannenberg affirms he agrees on this topic with Abe "even with regard to the trinitarian relations in the eternal life of God," he refers to the perichoretic relationships in the Trinity, and not to the kenotic God, as Abe does.[114]

According to Pannenberg's interpretation of the *kenosis* of Christ "in this process of self-denial Jesus Christ *continued* to be the Son of God."[115] Thus he rejects Abe's "complete and thoroughgoing" *kenosis*.[116] He explains that the Apostle Paul's intention in Philippians 2:6–7 was to explain the contrast between the way Adam had responded to God in Genesis 3 (the story of the Fall) and how Christ responded to God in all circumstances of his life. While Adam "hoped to become like God by grasping for the apple," in Jesus one should see the reverse course of action: "he was in fact like God . . . but he did not consider this something to be grasped."[117] Pannenberg follows a similar view to that of Stăniloae in explaining the *kenosis*, as he insists on Christ's accepting "an existence in obedience to the Father even when that obedience led to his own death."[118] This was the lesson the Christians in Philippi had to learn, not some new speculation about the true nature of God.

Thus there are three main corrections that Pannenberg brings to Abe's view of the *kenosis*: First, Jesus never ceased to be the Son of God. Second, Jesus' self-emptying does not mean denying the essential relationships he has in the Trinity.[119] And third, we cannot speak of a kenotic God, since "the emptying activity never denies the Father, but serves him."[120] As we can see, Pannenberg understands Abe's view of the kenotic God and disagrees with it. He explains that although "the self-emptying obedience of Christ has its 'origin in God' the Father," it does not necessarily lead to speaking

---

113. Abe, "Kenotic God and Dynamic Sunyata," 10.

114. Pannenberg, "God's Love and the *Kenosis* of the Son," 247.

115. Ibid., emphasis mine.

116. He affirms that in the process of *kenosis* itself "Jesus manifests himself to be the Son of God" (ibid.).

117. Ibid., 248.

118. Ibid., 247.

119. In Pannenberg's words, "it does not deny obedience to the Father, but, to the contrary, that obedience is kept uncompromisingly" (ibid., 248).

120. Ibid.

of "a self-emptying activity on the part of the Father himself."[121] He argues that there is no hint in the New Testament for such an interpretation, or that it would be a "logical implication" of the *kenosis* of Christ.[122] The *kenosis* points to the harmony of will between the Son and the Father, i.e., of the Father's will for the Son's emptying himself, and of the incarnate Son's will to remain in obedience to the Father.

Faced with the claim that Abe developed the idea of the kenotic God from "the Christian fundamental tenet that 'God is love,'"[123] Pannenberg argues that *kenosis* and *agape* cannot be related in this way. While the *kenosis* of Christ "is not connected with love for the world, but with obedience to the Father" and love in the New Testament "certainly involves an element of sacrifice," the idea of the kenotic God does not follow from here.[124] The *kenosis* "is only on the part of the Son" and "therefore, with regard to the inter-trinitarian life, one should not speak of a mutual *kenosis*"[125] as the equivalent of *perichoresis*, the mutual indwelling of the three *hypostases*. As he emphasizes, "only in the case of the Son does the self-differentiation from the Father become kenotic, and it is only in the incarnation that this kenotic dynamic becomes fully apparent."[126]

In his conclusion, Pannenberg affirms that the concept of *kenosis* "cannot function as a common denominator in Buddhism and Christianity."[127] While "the Christian idea of *kenosis* presupposes an agent, the Son, in relation to another agent, the Father, whose action is not kenotic,"[128] Abe's idea of the *kenosis* cannot accept such ultimate relationship, since he cannot admit the persons of the Trinity as having inherent existence. Therefore Abe declared that Pannenberg's view of the *kenosis* is limited to the "level of obedience and commission" and thus is "too narrow."[129]

## 7.4.4 Küng's Position on Abe's View of the Kenosis

Hans Küng admits that Abe is right when he affirms the crisis of religion in contemporary Western society and that we need to find resources to

121. Ibid.
122. Ibid.
123. Abe, "God's Total *Kenosis* and Truly Redemptive Love," 256.
124. Pannenberg, "God's Love and the *Kenosis* of the Son," 249.
125. Ibid.
126. Ibid.
127. Ibid., 250.
128. Ibid.
129. Abe, "God's Total *Kenosis* and Truly Redemptive Love," 257.

respond to the challenge of nihilism and scientism. However, he rejects Abe's solution of replacing the God of Christianity with Buddhist emptiness.[130] In his response to Abe's view of the *kenosis*, Küng emphasizes the following important points:

1. In the New Testament "God" always indicates God the Father "and never a divine nature consisting of several persons";

2. There is always a distinction in the New Testament between the Son of God and God the Father;

3. There is nowhere mentioned in the New Testament "an incarnation or a renunciation (*kenosis*) of God himself";

4. The *kenosis* of Christ is a "humiliation occurring in a unique, historical life and death on the cross";

5. The self-sacrifice of the Son is in complete harmony of will with the Father, for the redemption of humankind;

6. The resurrection of Jesus proves that one cannot speak of "the death of God" for there arises the question of "who brought this supposedly dead God back to life?"

7. "The renunciation of God himself in Buddhist shunyata" cannot be held in light of Jesus' resurrection and exaltation.[131]

What Küng fundamentally questions in Abe's interpretation of the *kenosis* is the effectiveness of his hermeneutics for contemporary Buddhist-Christian dialogue. He criticizes the Japanese Zen master for isolating key concepts from the text of the New Testament and for transplanting them in a Buddhist context, where they lose their original significance. Referring specifically to the issue of the *kenosis*, Küng criticized Abe for not seeing it as "ethical, exemplary humiliation," and instead transforming it into "ontological emptying, an emptying of God himself."[132] Küng's conclusion is that Abe's interpretation of Philippians 2:6–11 is an example of "Buddhist exegesis."[133] His method is selective and reductive,[134] and instead of doing an exegesis of

130. Hans Küng, "God's Self-Renunciation and Buddhist Emptiness," 213.

131. Ibid., 213-4.

132. Ibid., 214.

133. Küng, "God's Self-Renunciation and Buddhist Emptiness," in Corless and Knitter, eds., *Buddhist Emptiness and Christian Trinity*, 34. A similar conclusion is that of Ogden, who affirms that Abe's method "is controlled less by a historical critical exegesis of this passage than by his own Buddhist beliefs concerning the nature of ultimate reality" (Schubert M. Ogden, "Faith in God and Realization of Emptiness," in Cobb and Ives, eds., *Emptying God*, 128-29).

134. Küng, "God's Self-Renunciation and Buddhist Emptiness," in Ives, ed., *Divine*

the Christian text, he actually performs an *eisegesis* (i.e., introduces his own ideas into the text), which leads him to discover "his own world—even on foreign, Christian soil."[135] The origin of such hermeneutics is a Zen-induced predicate logic which must refuse by all means a permanent Ultimate Reality. In contrast, in his book *Does God Exist?* Küng emphasizes that one of the basic tenets of the Bible is that God is always "subject and not predicate," as he is "one who faces me, whom I can address."[136] As a result, one could have expected to reach irreconcilable positions between the Christian and the Buddhist views on the *kenosis*.[137]

## 7.5 KENOSIS AND HUMAN NATURE

Following Suzuki, Abe argues that the original nature of Adam and Eve was that of suchness (*tathata*), which expresses harmony with the ultimate truth of emptiness.[138] Accordingly, the Fall would not be the result of disobedience to God, but rather a loss of this vision of reality. In other words, the so-called sin of "eating the fruit of knowledge" is the emergence of self-consciousness, expressed by the making of "value judgments."[139] Self-consciousness fuels a dualist view of reality and leads one "to be involved in attachments"[140] such as love and hate. The dichotomy stated between one person and another transforms persons into "objects of emotion and volition . . . of like and dislike, love and hate," and as a result humans become "inextricably involved in the subject-object dichotomy and the persistent self-centeredness

---

*Emptiness*, 215.

135. Ibid., 214.

136. Küng, *Does God Exist?*, 634.

137. Another voice that reflects well what Stăniloae would have added to the chorus of criticism against Abe's view of the *kenosis* is that of Steve Odin, who reminds us of the ecclesial context in which this doctrine must be understood, i.e., the personal meeting of Christ by the believer in the Eucharist. Odin says: "The Kyoto School has generally neglected this essential connection between *kenosis*, the Eucharist, and the eschatological dimensions of Christianity; and to this extent, their understanding of *kenosis* is removed from authentic Christian experience" (Steve Odin, "A Critique of the Kenosis/Sunyata Motif," 77). Odin emphasizes that the doctrine of *kenosis* makes sense only in an ecclesiastical context, especially in relationship with "the Eucharist, which is itself the re-enactment of the mystery of Christ's sacrificial act of total self-emptying" (ibid., 84).

138. Abe, "Emptiness is Suchness," in Franck, ed., *Buddha Eye*, 204–5.

139. Ibid., 205. In another essay, Abe interprets the story of Adam and the forbidden fruit in a Gnostic manner, as a prohibition "from knowing the truth as God knows it" (Abe, *Zen and Western Thought*, 96).

140. Abe, "Emptiness is Suchness," 205.

engendered by it."[141] Such assertions stand in contrast with the position of Orthodox Christianity, whose representatives explain self-centredness in a different way from Abe and Suzuki. Human beings have not fallen from a non-dualistic perception of their emptiness, but from an unhindered relationship with God, while self-consciousness is the necessary condition for such a relationship to exist. Therefore self-centredness is not the necessary result of having self-consciousness, but of a wrong way of using it.[142]

As a result of such a difference in views on human nature, one finds different interpretations of what the restoration to the original nature of humankind represents. In Orthodox Christianity, as Stăniloae argued, the restoration is towards attaining likeness with God, which is an unhindered relationship with him.[143] Since for Abe self-consciousness "constitutes the fundamental ignorance inherent in human existence"[144] and the true nature of everything is emptiness, his view of human restoration is the return to the right perspective on reality, to what Nishitani called the standpoint of *shunyata*. This is the whole point of Abe's teaching of the *kenosis*. In his view, the *kenosis* of Christ and the kenotic God are not merely a bridge for Buddhist-Christian dialogue, but ideal teaching devices, so that one could himself or herself follow the process of self-emptying and attain enlightenment. Zen Buddhism teaches that "the true Self is empty and nonexistent,"[145] which means that one should strive for neither "absolute knowledge" nor for "salvation by God," but rather for "Self-Awakening."[146] His conclusion is that "each and every thing in the universe is also an incarnation of God together with Jesus Christ on the cross and his glorious resurrection."[147] Although this sounds unacceptable from the standpoint of Orthodox theology, it is logical for the Zen Buddhist since "each and every thing" has the nature of *shunyata*.

141. Abe, *Buddhism and Interfaith Dialogue*, 65.

142. In a way consistent with the Buddhist view on human nature, Abe advocates that "self-estrangement and anxiety are not something accidental to the ego-self, but are inherent to its structure. To be human is to be a problem to oneself" (Abe, *Zen and Western Thought*, 6). This is consistent with the Zen Buddhist view, but not with the Orthodox Christian one, which sees anxiety rooted not in being human, but in being a sinful human, alienated from God.

143. Although Abe speaks of "the self-sacrificial love of Christ for humankind disobedient and rebellious against the will of God" he does not connect it to a doctrine of human salvation by grace (Abe, "Kenotic God and Dynamic Sunyata," 9).

144. Abe, "Emptiness is Suchness," 206.

145. Abe, *Zen and Western Thought*, 9.

146. Ibid., 21.

147. Abe, "Kenotic God and Dynamic Sunyata," in Cobb and Ives, eds., *Emptying God*, 18.

As we can see, Abe's view of the *kenosis* cannot be reconciled with the traditional interpretation of the Apostle Paul's hymn in Philippians 2:6–11. His exhortation for the Christians in Philippi, in light of the *kenosis* of Christ, is that they need to refrain from ego-centredness and follow Christ's example of giving himself away for the benefit of others, so that they can inherit eternal life and thus follow him in his exaltation. Abe's vision of self-emptying is also soteriological, but points in a different direction. Instead of strengthening relationships, his view speaks of realizing one's *shunyata* nature, the way things really are. Instead of looking outside them and giving themselves away in relationships as Christ did, Christians should look inside them and understand that there is no true self. As a result, Abe's understanding of the regeneration of the believer in Christ (in Pauline terms the becoming of a "new person")[148] is the realization of one's own emptiness. Heisig captures well this thought when he says that for Abe, "conversion is not just a matter of loving one another because God has loved us in Christ, but of experiencing in ourselves the very *kenosis* that Christ experienced, of recovering in ourselves the kenotic nature that we share with Christ."[149]

Earlier in this chapter we have seen that Abe was able to formulate phrases that could easily be attributed to an Orthodox theologian. He continues to puzzle us by saying on the new life of the believer in Christ: "Without the total negation of our life, or the complete death of our ego-self, our new life as a manifestation of the life of Jesus is impossible."[150] Although these words could act as a good introduction to Stăniloae's view of human perfection as deification, they have encoded a different meaning. Abe argues that there cannot be any continuity between "the 'old person' and the 'new Person' in terms of a responsible subject in relation to God's calling,"[151] because ultimately there is no real God "calling," and no real "person" responding. In his view, both are mental constructs that one must get rid of through the Great Death of Zen, so that one may know his or her true nature of *shunyata*. Accordingly, the "true and authentic self" of which the Apostle Paul speaks in Galatians 2:20 is born out of the Great Death, and thus has

148. For Abe the renewal in Jesus Christ that the Apostle Paul speaks about in Romans 6:11 and 2 Corinthians 4:10 would consist in a new understanding of our being (Abe, "Kenotic God and Dynamic Sunyata," 11). But as we know from chapter 2, this new life in Christ is a relationship with God, not a metaphysical new knowledge of our nature.

149. Heisig, *Sunyata and Kenosis*, 10.

150. Abe, "Kenotic God and Dynamic Sunyata," 11. After reading Pseudo-Dionysius Abe wrongly assumes that *theosis* means "that man enters the godhead by getting rid of what is man," and that this "godhead" is the *shunyata* of Zen Buddhism (Masao Abe, "God, Emptiness, and the True Self," 68).

151. Abe, "Kenotic God and Dynamic Sunyata," 11.

the right perspective on how things really are.[152] When Abe says that "the Christian *participates* in the death and resurrection of Jesus Christ,"[153] he is not referring to the permanent renewal of the person and her eternal communion with God. By "death" he means the Great Death of Zen, which is a death to ignorance, to the belief of an enduring substantial self, which leads to a "resurrection" as a different stance to (present) life. In other words, one does not find in his view an affirmation of personhood, but an expression of the predicative self who realizes its own dependent co-arising. This self is by no means the deified human being in an eternal relationship with God.

Abe's statement that "the death of the human ego is essential to salvation"[154] is valid in both Buddhism and Christianity, but one must be aware that in Buddhism it means the death of personhood, while in Christianity the death of self-centredness. Therefore, an Orthodox Christian could not accept his statement that "no distinction can be made between Christian conversion and Buddhist awakening."[155] Christian conversion leads to the death of self-centredness and must be expressed in relationships, while Buddhist awakening is the death of an illusory substantial self, so it has to do with attaining the right sort of knowledge.[156] This is the right context from which one can assess Abe's claim to have found a confirmation of the concept of the Great Death in Paul's 2 Corinthians 4:10 and Galatians 2:20. Although he says that "Christ's death and resurrection is for Paul a spiritual fact which makes his own resurrection through death possible,"[157] which seems theologically correct from an Orthodox point of view, he insists that Christ's death is *exemplary*, not *life giving*. As Jesus set up an example by accepting his death, so Paul is inviting us to imitate his example as the "stand-

---

152. Ibid. In other words, the realization of the "new life through death" as seen in the resurrection of Christ is the Great Death of Zen (Abe, *Zen and Western Thought*, 189).

153. Ibid.

154. Masao Abe, "Man and Nature in Christianity and Buddhism," in Franck, ed., *Buddha Eye*, 154.

155. Ibid.

156. In the same paragraph, Abe proves to be aware of the personalist context in which salvation occurs in Christianity. He also presents an accurate contrast between sin and ignorance, and says that "in Buddhism man's death is not seen as the result of 'sin' in relation to something transcendent or supernatural, such as divine justice, but only as one instance of that transiency common to all things whatsoever in the universe" (ibid., 155). At the end of this essay, Abe acknowledges, in contradiction with his above view on no distinction between Christian conversion and Buddhist awakening, that "the 'direction' or 'location' of transcendence is not the same in Christianity and Buddhism" (ibid., 156).

157. Abe, *Zen and Western Thought*, 148.

point of the ontological self-realization of life."[158] As mentioned above, Abe's view of the Apostle Paul's "dying with Christ" is the Zen realization of the Great Death as giving up a false view of the world, while "rebirth" means awakening to seeing things as they really are, as having the nature of *shunyata*. This is why Abe can say that in Zen one "gains a new Life of rebirth through the realization of the Great Death" which "does not differ from the standpoint of Paul in essence."[159] The difference is in fact significant, as we face here two very different views of human perfection. One is through the Great Death of Zen, as freedom from a dualist way of seeing things, and the other is by participating in the death and resurrection of Christ, as freedom from sin and self-centredness towards a perfect relationship with God.[160]

## 7.6 TOWARDS A MUTUAL TRANSFORMATION OF BUDDHISM AND CHRISTIANITY

As mentioned earlier, Abe went much further in his dialogue with Christianity than his predecessors at the Kyoto School, who limited themselves to an assessment of Christianity through Zen lenses. In the beginning of his article "Kenotic God and Dynamic Sunyata" he argues that Buddhist-Christian dialogue is about to go beyond "mutual understanding" and enter the stage of "mutual transformation" so that they could both meet the challenge of modern nihilism.[161] We have already seen how Christianity should reinterpret itself in Abe's vision. Could there be room for a similar reinterpretation of Buddhism in its interaction with Christianity? Abe seems to suggest a positive answer and mentions two major issues in Buddhism which could be improved with Christian resources. The first would be for-

158. Ibid.

159. Ibid.

160. Abe doubts that "man's finitude in terms of sinfulness can be overcome by faith" (ibid., 190). His reason is that a true overcoming of finitude means realizing *shunyata*, the in-finite ground of everything. He says that human finitude is "so radical that it cannot even be overcome by faith, not even through the work of the divine other power" (ibid.). In his view human nature is determined by dependent co-arising, and thus its finitude can only be overcome by "the realization of absolute Nothingness" (ibid.). But as we have seen in chapter 2, in Orthodox Christianity there is no point in transcending finitude *per se*. The deified human being remains a finite being, knowing God in an unhindered relationship, but still as a finite being.

161. Abe, "Kenotic God and Dynamic Sunyata," in Cobb and Ives, eds., *Emptying God*, 3; also in "*Kenosis* and Emptiness," in Corless and Knitter, eds., *Buddhist Emptiness and Christian Trinity*, 5. In an article written in 1992 he calls for a "radical reinterpretation of each religion's own spirituality" in order to overcome present-day "fundamentalism and religion-negating ideologies" (Abe, *Buddhism and Interfaith Dialogue*, 5).

mulating a vision of time and history, and the second stating a ground for
ethics and social justice.[162]

## 7.6.1 Towards a New Buddhist Vision of Time and History

Since there is no Creator, creation or final judgment in Buddhism, its vision
of time and history is different from that of Orthodox Christianity. As Abe
says, "history in Buddhism is 'the history of the moment'" and of "discon-
tinuous succession."[163] From here follows the difficulty of being engaged in
history, social action and ethics, and as a result, Abe's awareness that "Buddhism is relatively weak in its view of history."[164] In his search for a solution
to this weakness, he found that it could come from applying the double
orientation of the *bodhisattva*, towards both the knowledge of emptiness
and the involvement in the world of *samsara*. He speaks of it as a "double
realization," for on the one hand wisdom proves that "life at this moment is
not a means to a future end, but is the end itself," while compassion teaches
that "life is an endless activity of saving others."[165] His view of time and history follows from the orientation given by compassion, from the urge to get
involved in saving all those who "despite *the fact of* universal salvation . . .
*believe themselves* to be 'unsaved.'"[166] This perspective creates a new vision
of history for the awakened one as the "endless process in which he or she
must try to actualize universal salvation in regard to those 'unsaved.'"[167] In
other words, what Westerners call history is for the awakened Buddhist the
process of saving those who are blinded by ignorance and cannot see things
as they really are. While a linear (Western) view of time is the product of
ignorance, a view consistent with Buddhism can be developed only by the
*bodhisattva*, the one who despite his or her realization of emptiness does not
cling to it, but gets involved in helping others to overcome spiritual ignorance. But since there are "innumerable (beings) at present and will appear

---

162. Ibid., 53. He also mentions the issue of formulating a view of the human being
which would take more seriously its freedom and "hence the possibility of doing evil"
(ibid.), but I failed to find any clarification of this thought in his writings.

163. Abe, *Zen and Comparative Studies*, 138.

164. Abe, "Kenotic God and Dynamic Sunyata," 59–60; also in *Zen and Comparative Studies*, 187.

165. Abe, *Zen and Western Thought*, 215.

166. Abe, *Buddhism and Interfaith Dialogue*, 85.

167. Ibid.

endlessly in future,"[168] the process is endless, and such a view of time and history is not of much practical help.

John Cobb, Abe's friend and best dialogue partner in the Christian world, criticizes Abe's solution to the Buddhist view of history for not allowing one to differentiate the future from the past and present, given the fact that compassion has the sole purpose of enlightening others, and thus is "the same at all times and places."[169] He argues that compassion should be focused on more pressing issues in our world today such as famines, and that we should be aware of the possible self-destruction of humanity, which lies "in the hands of unawakened people."[170] As for Abe's initial thought of finding help in Christianity for a new Buddhist vision of time and history, one can see that he did not use Christian resources at all, but instead relies totally on what the Zen tradition can offer.

## 7.6.2 Towards a New Buddhist Vision of Ethics and Social Justice

The next domain, not unrelated to history, in which Abe acknowledges that Buddhism could learn from Christianity, is that of ethics and social action. He admitted that "Buddhist history shows indifference to social evil,"[171] and that the Buddhist view of emptiness "often causes indifference to the problem of good and evil and especially to social ethics."[172] But although he admits that the Buddhist view needs improvement, he rejects the Christian view of justice as entailing judgement and punishment, because "judgment based on justice naturally calls forth a counter-judgment as a reaction from the side judged."[173] He obviously refers here to the dualistic view that feeds karma, by making judges to inherit bad karma and become victims of their own judgment in this or further lives. This is what he means by the "endless conflict and struggle between judge and judged."[174]

---

168. Abe, "Kenotic God and Dynamic Sunyata," in Cobb and Ives, eds., *Emptying God*, 60.

169. Cobb, "On the Deepening of Buddhism," in Cobb and Ives, eds., *Emptying God*, 96.

170. Ibid.

171. Abe, "A Rejoinder," in Cobb and Ives, eds., *Emptying God*, 179, and *Buddhism and Interfaith Dialogue*, 58. He also acknowledges that "traditional Buddhism lacks a concrete program of social transformation" because it is "more concerned with the ground or religious basis for social transformation rather than a practical program" (Abe, *Zen and Comparative Studies*, 186).

172. Abe, *Buddhism and Interfaith Dialogue*, 7–8.

173. Abe, "A Rejoinder," 180.

174. Ibid.

Abe's solution for ethics in Buddhism and "the basis for the transformation of society"[175] grows from the same source he used for building a view of history: the double perspective of the *bodhisattva*—involved in the sufferings of the world, but also aware of the emptiness of the beings who suffer. In his words, Buddhists "must learn from Christianity" how to improve their vision of ethics and social justice, but nevertheless to do it "in terms of the Buddhist standpoint of wisdom and compassion."[176] Ethics becomes meaningful in the *bodhisattva's* compassionate action, at the level of "conventional truth."[177] As Buddhist scriptures show, the *bodhisattva* often uses questionable ethical actions for bringing one closer to enlightenment.[178] Since good and evil have meaning only at the level of conventional truth, considering otherwise would lead us into "ignorance and falsehood,"[179] and therefore Abe argues for the emancipation from "the existential antinomy of good and evil and to awaken to Emptiness."[180] In the end, "in order to reach Emptiness ethics must be realized as 'ignorance' and be turned over completely."[181]

Further insights on Abe's view on social justice are revealed in his position on the Shoah. In his interaction with Christian and Jewish theologians on this issue, Abe stated that although he lived in Japan during the war, he shares a responsibility for what happened in the concentration camps,[182] because "the source of this historical evil is rooted very deeply

175. Abe, *Zen and Comparative Studies*, 186.

176. Abe, *Buddhism and Interfaith Dialogue*, 58 and "A Rejoinder," 180.

177. Abe, *Buddhism and Interfaith Dialogue*, 200.

178. See section 2.5 on the use of skilful means. Christopher Ives is not satisfied with Abe's solution for ethics as the *bodhisattva's* involvement in saving innumerable beings because his or her actions are meant to "lead oneself or others to awakening" and hence "are not necessarily ethically acceptable at the relative level" (Christopher Ives, "The Return to the Relative: Sunyata and the Realm of Ethics," in Ives, ed., *Divine Emptiness*, 168).

179. Abe, *Buddhism and Interfaith Dialogue*, 200.

180. Abe, *Zen and Western Thought*, 132. In Abe's view, the need of transcending ethical values is confirmed by the biblical text where God is said to love good and bad people alike (Matthew 5:45; Mark 2:17). Emancipation from the antinomy of good and evil is necessary for they "are completely antagonistic principles, resisting each other with equal force" (Abe, *Zen and Western Thought*, 132) and therefore Abe argues that in Buddhism it is "illusory to believe it is possible to overcome evil with good" (ibid.), while being aware that overcoming evil with good is precisely the exhortation of the Apostle Paul in Romans 12:21 (ibid.).

181. Abe, *Buddhism and Interfaith Dialogue*, 201.

182. Abe, "Kenotic God and Dynamic Sunyata," in Cobb and Ives, eds., *Emptying God*, 50.

*within ourselves.*"[183] The inner source he refers to is ignorance, expressed as the "endless thirst to live inherent in human existence."[184] All beings are inter-related in the collective karma of humanity, and thus one should not simply blame and punish the Nazis, but look beyond the historical facts and get a broader picture of all beings involved, and of all "events in the past and present of human history in which all of us, assailants and victims alike, are involved."[185] His solution for overcoming this huge issue that still torments humankind consists in realizing "its relationality and nonsubstantiality."[186] In other words, one should realize that all beings involved in the Shoah, victims and assailants alike, are related through their karma, and will forever exchange places in the everlasting manifestation of karma until they realize how things really are and attain enlightenment. Therefore, from a religious point of view the Shoah "should not be taken as an absolute but a relative evil."[187] As he did in formulating his view of time and history, Abe points (again) away from *action*, towards *understanding* the true nature of things. On the one hand he grounds his view on social responsibility in awakening, in realizing the nature of the true self, which is *shunyata*, but on the other hand, learning from his Western experience, he argues that one needs "objective knowledge of the social environment and historical change."[188] However, he does not show how this *objective* knowledge could be attained from the standpoint of Zen and how "the realization of true Emptiness" can become the basis for ethical life,[189] since awakening points to the non-dual (i.e., non-objective) perception of historical change. As a result, we can see that Abe did not use any insight from Christianity to solve the weaknesses

183. Abe, *Zen and Western Thought*, 255.

184. Abe, "Kenotic God and Dynamic Sunyata," 51.

185. Ibid., 52. Although Abe does not specifically formulate such a thought, an implication of karma might be that the victims of Auschwitz were receiving the right punishment for their deeds in previous lives, or that the shared responsibility we must feel for what happened there lies in the possibility of being ourselves the form in which the perpetrators of the Shoah have been reborn.

186. Ibid., 52.

187. Ibid., 53. Christopher Ives, Abe's former student, doubts that a realization of "collective karma" could "constitute a sufficient ethical response" to the issue of the Shoah or that it would lead to formulating "adequate, effective responses" (Ives, "The Return to the Relative: Sunyata and the Realm of Ethics," ibid., 166). He questions the "joint responsibility" that we should feel for such events as Abe's interpretation suggests (ibid.) and sees a serious ethical problem in undermining the distinction between victims and perpetrators (ibid., 167). Ives gives as example the ethical distinction that Abe fails to make between "a Jewish infant and a Nazi guard at Auschwitz" (ibid.).

188. Abe, *Zen and Western Thought*, 197.

189. Ibid., 132.

he acknowledged in the Buddhist view on ethics and justice. The only "help" from Christianity was to make him *aware* of the weaknesses of Buddhist ethics, and help him identify solutions inside his *own* tradition.

### 7.6.3 Is There Anything that Buddhists can Learn from Christianity?

Although Abe admitted there are issues in Buddhism that need improvement, he could not find help in Christianity for amending the Buddhist view of time and history, or for better dealing with ethics and social justice. To borrow any personalist approach from Christianity would be inconsistent with the Buddhist view of emptiness and would thus pose an obstacle to attaining enlightenment. Since Christian solutions would fuel a dualistic view of ethical issues and thus bring about karmic effects, Abe constantly insists on the realization of enlightenment as the true solution of all so-called problems. It is only enlightenment that can solve the problem of time and history, since in enlightenment "beginning and end, time and eternity, one and many, are not seen in duality but in dynamic oneness."[190] Since social evil has its source in "the human karma of each of us,"[191] the true and final solution for social action and overcoming evil is the "investigation of what the true Self is."[192] Once *nirvana* is reached in the very world of *samsara*, a human is no longer "confined by the endless process of endless transmigration," and becomes "master of the endless process of that transmigration."[193] As we can see, Abe's solution for ethics and social justice does not lead to action, but to withdrawal from social involvement, which leaves unsolved the initial issue that started the whole discussion.

190. Abe, *Buddhism and Interfaith Dialogue*, 84.

191. Abe, *Zen and Western Thought*, 255.

192. Ibid. Although he affirms that the solution to social evil is enlightenment, Abe proves to be very determined to condemn social and national evil in state relationships. He condemns unequivocally contemporary outbursts of imperialism, such as the Soviet invasion of Hungary in 1956 and Czechoslovakia in 1968, and the Vietnam War (ibid., 254). Although he declares that "sovereign states which oppose each other and claim that sovereignty resides with specific races or peoples must be negated" (ibid., 252), he ignores the position of Japanese imperialism in WWII. Not only has he not "apologized for his predecessors' support of Japanese aggression" (especially that of Tanabe and Nishitani), but it seems he completely ignored it (Steven Heine, "Introduction," in Abe, *Zen and the Modern World*, xv).

193. Abe, *Buddhism and Interfaith Dialogue*, 84. In Mahayana Buddhism *nirvana* is attained by cultivating non-attachment to both awakening, and to the world of unenlightened beings. Abe follows this doctrine, saying that "one can attain true enlightenment only through helping others become enlightened" (ibid., 236).

We could have expected that Buddhists cannot apply any Christian solution for the recognized weaknesses of their tradition, for Buddhism is grounded on a different ontology and axiology. As Abe is aware, the Christian view of God is not to be understood "merely ontologically, but also axiologically,"[194] and as a result, what matters most in Christianity "is not the issue of being and non-being, but the question of what I as a human being ought to do."[195] Axiology and ontology, ethics and theology, cannot work separately in either Buddhism or Christianity, so it is hard to ground a mutual transformation of them without fundamentally altering their theological/metaphysical ground.

## 7.7 CONCLUSION TO ABE'S VIEW OF BUDDHIST-CHRISTIAN DIALOGUE

Since Abe found nothing to change in Buddhism as a result of its interaction with Christianity, it obviously follows that the "mutual" transformation he envisages concerns only Christianity.[196] As Cobb observes, "Christians change but Buddhists remain where they are."[197] We have seen how several basic Christian doctrines should change in contact with Buddhism. In his essay "The End of World Religion," Abe argues that one can no longer "accept Christianity and Buddhism in their present historical forms as representing their *final* development."[198] While it is clear in which ways Christianity must change, it is not so clear whether he includes Zen among the forms of historical Buddhism that must further develop.

Being aware of the major controversies in contemporary interfaith dialogue, Abe requires a "*complete negation of both affirmative and the negative*

194. Abe, *Zen and Western Thought*, 193.

195. Ibid., 192.

196. Although in the beginning of his article "*Kenosis* and Emptiness," he proposed a "revolutionary reinterpretation of the concept of God in Christianity and the concept of Emptiness in Buddhism," in the end we see only the first objective fulfilled (in Corless and Knitter, eds., *Buddhist Emptiness and Christian Trinity*, 6).

197. John B. Cobb Jr., "Masao Abe, Process Theology, and the Buddhist-Christian-Jewish Dialogue," in Mitchell, ed., *Masao Abe*, 70. A similar thought is expressed by Thomas Dean: "Abe's approach to dialogue is so formulated as not to call into question the fundamentals of the Zen tradition. While Western thought is 'forced to a basic reexamination' of its fundamental ontological categories and presuppositions, Zen is asked only to 'internally embrace the standpoints of Western "Being" and "Ought" which have been foreign to itself.'" (Thomas Dean, "Masao Abe's Zen Philosophy of Dialogue: A Western Response," in Mitchell, ed., *Masao Abe*, 273, following Abe, *Zen and Western Thought*, 120).

198. Abe, *Zen and Western Thought*, 266.

*views,"* i.e., both of the views that hold on to the existence of a common denominator in world religions, and of those that reject it.[199] In his view the best variant of world religion is one that puts *shunyata* at its foundation, and as such is grounded on a "positionless position."[200] However, his option can hardly be truly "positionless" or "free from any statement."[201] It is just another position that invalidates all others, as any position could be rendered as either "positionless" or not, and as such still fuel dualism between itself and others.[202] Although he claims that his position is "non-substantial," it is conceptually very precise and exclusivistic. Therefore it cannot let "every other position stand and work just as it is," at least not in its traditional understanding.[203]

As one might have expected, for Abe the true religion which can challenge Nietzsche's nihilism and be *"beyond* active nihilism" is Buddhism, "which is based on *nirvana,"* or more specifically Zen Buddhism, since it must realize everything "as it is, in total dynamic reality."[204] Therefore his view of dialogue does not lead to deepening the "unique characters" of Buddhism and Christianity as he proposes,[205] but to an erosion of Christian distinctiveness, while preserving the Buddhist tradition untouched. Waldenfels expresses well the failure of Abe's method of dialogue when he argues that,

> he did not care much for the original Christian understanding, preferring conceptions that seemed adaptable to his own standpoint and confirmed by it. For although nondualism should imply an extreme richness of flexibilities, Abe's own standpoint appears nevertheless rather firm and inflexible. . . . Abe's thought seems to be unmovable and unmoved even amid the most challenging questions.[206]

In conclusion, one does not see fulfilled Abe's desire of realizing a mutual transformation of Buddhism and Christianity as a result of their

199. Abe, *Buddhism and Interfaith Dialogue*, 41.

200. Ibid., 42.

201. Ibid., 47.

202. Although Abe rejects "doctrines of absolute truth which exclude other views of truth as false" (ibid., 78), we can see that his view of *shunyata* as ultimate truth is also exclusivistic.

203. Ibid., 78.

204. Ibid., 79–80.

205. Abe, "Kenotic God and Dynamic Sunyata," in Cobb and Ives, eds., *Emptying God*, 61.

206. Hans Waldenfels, "Masao Abe's Intellectual Journey to the West: A Personal Reflection," in Mitchell, ed., *Masao Abe*, 61.

dialogue. His call for a "mutual" transformation proved to be addressed mainly to Christians, who should realize the nothingness of God, while there is little, if anything, to change in Buddhism. In light of my discussion of human perfection in Mahayana Buddhism, it is obvious that Abe is true to the *bodhisattva* ideal, and strives for the realization of a perfect balance between wisdom and compassion. His efforts in Buddhist-Christian dialogue prove to be the *bodhisattva*'s skilful means for introducing Zen to the Western world, but cannot be taken as a constructive way for a mutual transformation of Buddhism and Christianity. He successfully continued the efforts of his masters Hisamatsu and Suzuki as a Zen apostle to the Western world, but failed to deepen the uniqueness of Buddhism and Christianity in their common struggle against nihilism. However, what I find inspiring in Abe's view of a mutual transformation of Buddhism and Christianity is his methodology. When searching for a way in which Buddhism could change as a result of its dialogue with Christianity he did not use Christian resources, but instead searched for solutions in his own tradition and found them in the *bodhisattva*'s double orientation, towards both emptiness and the world of *samsara*. This way of dealing with criticism can be taken as a lead towards using comparative theology as a new approach in interfaith dialogue that would truly respect each religious tradition's uniqueness and make dialogue beneficial for all, despite fundamental differences. I will attempt to apply this approach in the last chapter of my book, after assessing the thought of another founding father of Buddhist-Christian dialogue.

# 8

# John B. Cobb Jr. (B. 1925)

## Process Theology as a Resource for Renewing
both Buddhism and Christianity

Unlike Nishida, Nishitani and Abe, who all belong to the tradition of Zen Buddhism, John Cobb does not represent either a Buddhist tradition or one of the major Christian traditions—Eastern Orthodoxy, Roman Catholicism or Protestantism. He is a representative of Process Theology, which appears to be much friendlier to Buddhism than traditional Christianity. Although, as Cobb is himself aware, participants in Buddhist-Christian dialogue cannot stand outside of both traditions, for otherwise it is questionable "whether they, in this way, achieve an understanding of either," we will see that he is a notable exception to this principle.[1]

Cobb was brought up in a Methodist family, studied theology at the University of Chicago and is an ordained minister of the United Methodist Church. He has a good understanding of Buddhism, as he had much interaction with Buddhist scholars over more than three decades of scholarly work in Buddhist-Christian dialogue. As we remember from the previous chapter, Hans Küng gave credit to him and Masao Abe as the founders of a scholarly Buddhist-Christian Dialogue.[2] Cobb issues several important challenges to traditional Christianity from his interaction with Buddhism and has formulated a similar goal to his friend Masao Abe—that of a mutual transformation of the two traditions. In his major work on Buddhist-

---

1. Cobb, *Transforming Christianity*, 161.
2. Küng, "God's Self-Renunciation and Buddhist Emptiness," 208.

Christian dialogue, *Beyond Dialogue*, he argues that the time has come for going beyond a mutual understanding of the two religions to their mutual transformation, which will eventually lead to "a new Christianity" and "a new Buddhism."[3] In this chapter I will analyze Cobb's method and assess whether he has come up with a more viable solution than his friend Abe. Since his proposal for Buddhist-Christian dialogue is formulated in the context provided by Process Theology, I must start with a short spiritual biography.

## 8.1 FROM METHODIST PIETISM TO PROCESS THEOLOGY. A SHORT SPIRITUAL BIOGRAPHY

Until the age of 15 Cobb's childhood was shaped in the context of a Protestant mission in Japan, where his parents were Southern Methodist missionaries. In 1940, when tensions rose between the US and Japan, the Cobb family returned to their home in Georgia. He grew up as a devout Christian in the tradition started by Wesley and planned to become himself a missionary. In 1944 Cobb Jr. enrolled in the army and served for three and a half years in the army's language school, owing to his knowledge of Japanese. But while he served in the army his spiritual horizons were broadened. At the University of Michigan, where his training took place, he met fellow soldiers from New York who had a quite different system of belief from his Methodist Pietism. As he says in his *Autobiography*, his worldview was for them just a "curious sociological phenomenon."[4] As the dawn of postmodernism posed a challenge to his faith and determination to become a missionary, the young Cobb lost his peace of mind and decided he must face this challenge and study the reasons for the rejection of traditional Christianity by the academic world. After the war, in 1947, he enrolled in the Humanities Division of the University of Chicago and immersed himself in the study of modern philosophy, determined to test his faith and expose it "to the worst the world could offer."[5] But after six months of struggle with alternative worldviews in which it seemed that his God had no place, his faith was "shattered" and the God of his youth "simply evaporated."[6]

This personal "death of God" experience led him to a fresh philosophical start with the University of Chicago Divinity School. There he met

3. Ibid., 48.

4. Cobb, *Autobiography*.

5. David Ray Griffin, "John B. Cobb, Jr.: A Theological Biography," in Griffin and Hough, eds., *Theology at the University*, 227.

6. Ibid.

Charles Hartshorne (1897–2000) with whose help he "was once again able to take the idea of God seriously."[7] Hartshorne was a follower of Whitehead's Process Philosophy, which seemed to offer a coherent worldview in which God and science would not exclude each other. The University of Chicago's Divinity School was the place where Whitehead's philosophy had a significant group of followers and as such provided for Cobb a new spiritual home.

Alfred North Whitehead (1861–1947) was a British mathematician and a philosopher of science who, after 1922, dedicated his life to formulating "a conceptuality through which every type of human experience could be understood."[8] His philosophy followed the tradition of William James and Henri Bergson, and although he had no primary interest in theology, he hoped that theologians would eventually "rethink his cosmological system in the categories of theological and metaphysical universals."[9] For Cobb he was "one of the greatest creative thinkers of all time"[10] and his perennial source of inspiration.[11] The endeavour to bring Whitehead's Process Philosophy into the realm of theology was one of Cobb's major intellectual achievements and made him the "chief builder, thinker, and leader of process theology,"[12] which he calls "the appropriate theology for the progressive church."[13] The pillars of his new worldview were not authority and tradition, as in traditional Christianity, but rather reason and logic, which were the instruments that helped him find a "more viable alternative"[14] of faith and a more "credible concept of God."[15]

After graduation Cobb spent three years teaching at a junior college in Georgia, five years at Emory University and thirty-two years at Claremont School of Theology and Claremont Graduate University, where he retired in 1990. He also served as guest professor at a number of other universities.

7. Ibid., 228.

8. Cobb, *Beyond Dialogue*, 147.

9. Gary Dorrien, "The Lure and Necessity of Process Theology," 319.

10. Cobb, *A Christian Natural Theology*, 16.

11. Ibid., 269.

12. Dorrien, "The Lure and Necessity of Process Theology," 316.

13. Cobb, *Autobiography*. Gary Dorrien calls Process Theology "the dominant school of thought in liberal theology today" ("The Lure and Necessity of Process Theology," 316).

14. Cobb, *Autobiography*.

15. Dorrien, "The Lure and Necessity of Process Theology," 323. An important contribution to this process was acknowledged to be the influence of Bultmann and his method of demythologizing the Bible (*July 2008 Question*), which helped Cobb to reach "reasonable judgments about what he (Jesus) did and said" (*April 2008 Question*). Cobb considers Bultmann "our century's greatest New Testament scholar" (Cobb, *God and the World*, 35).

In 1971 he launched at Claremont a journal dedicated to Process Thought, called *Process Studies,* with Lewis Ford, and in 1973 he founded the Center for Process Studies, with David Griffin. One of the declared tasks of the Center for Process Studies is to test the fruitfulness of Whitehead's philosophy to other religions. In 2001 this centre developed into the International Process Network, which has a significant following in China,[16] Korea and Latin America, and eventually generated its own church-like organization—Progressive Christians Uniting, in 2003.

Cobb found in Whitehead resources for more than Buddhist-Christian dialogue. In 1969 he was struck by the realization that our world is heading towards destruction and felt he must dedicate his life to finding alternatives "to the looming catastrophes of environmental collapse and social violence" which threaten our civilization.[17] He was very upset by the fact that academia did very little to tackle the plagues of modern society, so he decided to address these issues from the religious side by trying to "open the minds of religious people to the values of other traditions."[18] Cobb found Process Thought to be not only more credible from a philosophical point of view than traditional Christianity, but also "healing and transformative" for contemporary issues such as the environmental crisis, feminism and the global economy.[19]

As I need to limit the domain of this chapter to assessing Cobb's work in Buddhist-Christian dialogue, I will not refer to his work in other areas. We have already encountered some of Cobb's ideas expressed in his dialogue with Masao Abe in the previous chapter. In this chapter I will analyze Cobb's proposal for a mutual transformation of Buddhism and Christianity and Abe's reaction to it while keeping in mind the way human perfection is defined in Mahayana Buddhism and Orthodox Christianity. Let me start with an analysis of the similarities between Buddhism and Whitehead's philosophy.

## 8.2 PROCESS THOUGHT AND BUDDHISM ON HUMAN NATURE AND ULTIMATE REALITY

Whitehead's fundamental philosophical assumption is that the true nature of reality can be defined as a continuous process of becoming. As one

16. The Center for Process Studies has gathered a large following in China, where it boasts thirty-five million students (Cobb, *Autobiography*).

17. Paul F. Knitter, "Introduction," in Cobb, *Transforming Christianity,* 4.

18. Cobb, *Transforming Christianity,* 102.

19. Dorrien, "The Lure and Necessity of Process Theology," 327.

can expect, this assumption will generate many contact points with Buddhism.[20] The doctrines of impermanence, not-Self and suffering have close equivalents in Whitehead's philosophy. In a way that reminds us of Buddhist dependent co-arising, Whitehead refers to the stages of the causal flow as "actual entities" or "actual occasions." They have only momentary existence and constantly interact to build up new ones. The mechanism by which Whitehead defines the reciprocal interaction of actual entities is called "prehension," while the novelty that results from this interaction, or the new unity acquired by an entity, is a "concrescence."[21]

In Buddhism, we have seen that self-consciousness is the result of the flow of momentary experiences. Experiences do not belong to a subject but rather form the subject, as there is no substantial essence that would define personal identity. In a similar way, but following Whitehead's views, Cobb calls a particular moment of personal existence "an occasion of human experience,"[22] while the human being is defined as "a 'serially ordered society' of actual occasions of experience."[23] Each occasion of experience prehends the preceding one, and there is no constant subject that would witness the whole process. As Cobb emphasizes, Process Thought does not accept that the soul would be an enduring substantial entity which defines personal identity. By "soul" he refers to "a center of experience" but nevertheless one that is "nothing but the sequence of the experiences that constitute it."[24]

The ultimate objective of Whitehead's philosophy is to find peace, defined as "a positive feeling which crowns the 'life and motion' of the soul."[25] It is not a form of conscious survival after death but rather "a surpassing of personality."[26] Whitehead was aware that in Buddhism evil belongs to the "very nature of the world of physical and emotional experience" and that Buddhist wisdom invites one to find "release from the individual personality."[27] He affirmed that his philosophy is "entirely neutral on the

20. Although Whitehead's view of process is very close to the Buddhist doctrine of impermanence, it seems that his views were not inspired by Buddhism, but rather were developed independently. Nevertheless, he could have been influenced by Buddhism indirectly through the philosophy of William James.

21. Whitehead presents the categories of his philosophical scheme in his *Process and Reality*, 18–38.

22. Cobb, *The Structure of Christian Existence*, 33.

23. Cobb and Griffin, *Process Theology*, 15.

24. Cobb, *A Christian Natural Theology*, 48.

25. Whitehead, *Adventures of Ideas*, 285.

26. Ibid.

27. Whitehead, *Religion in the Making*, 49.

question of immortality," and that believing otherwise would require "more special evidence . . . provided that it is trustworthy."[28] Cobb follows Whitehead's position, saying that he is reluctant to consider "salvation in otherworldly terms," and instead prefers to focus on "what it means to be a Christian here and now."[29]

Further resemblances with Buddhism are found in Whitehead's view of suffering, as having its source in being "haunted by terror at the loss of the past,"[30] which in Buddhist terms translates as clinging to personal existence. However, there is a significant difference between the Buddhist and the Whiteheadian view of suffering. Whitehead did not intend his philosophy to become a religion, so his view of escaping suffering concerns only one's present life. Since he did not accept karma and rebirth, his meaning of peace does not refer to future lives.[31] His philosophy attempts to explain how "things really are" but without considering what may lie beyond this life. Since there is no point in speculating on a personal conscious survival of death, there is no need of compassionate *bodhisattvas* or Buddhas to help us, either.

Another significant difference between Whitehead and Buddhism is that for Whitehead the universe must have teleological direction, for the world as a sum of actual entities does not account for its order. In other words, there must be a reason why entities do not conflict or destroy each other, but rather seem to cooperate and mutually adjust for attaining their highest potential. This observation made Whitehead introduce the notion of creativity as a kind of supreme law that saves the world from chaos. Creativity is not God, but rather the ultimate ground of all entities, including God. According to Cobb, the Buddhist equivalent of creativity is the doctrine of dependent co-originating (*pratitya samutpada*). The two notions

28. Ibid., 107.

29. John B. Cobb Jr., "Whitehead's Philosophy and a Christian Doctrine of Man," *The Journal of Bible and Religion* 32/3 (1964) 216. In one of his monthly online answers, Cobb affirms that Griffin's studies in parapsychology led him to accept some form of "continued personal existence (after death) at least for a time" (*December 2004 Question*). Although he declares his openness to acknowledging the data from parapsychology, such data cannot be sufficient proof of immortality because, given his philosophical assumptions, "any form of creaturely existence enduring forever seems inherently implausible" (*June 1998 Question*).

30. Whitehead, *Process and Reality*, 400.

31. As a process theologian, Cobb affirms he can learn from Buddhism that religion must be salvific, not just a way of understanding the world (Cobb, *Beyond Dialogue*, 146). It is not clear however, whether he is willing to accommodate karma and rebirth in the Buddhist sense, or if he just expresses his concern for saving humanity from an imminent destruction. In light of his scepticism on immortality, the second option seems more plausible.

would be "alternative accounts of the same feature of the totality"[32] not because dependent co-originating has a teleological meaning in Buddhism (for it does not), but because of its all-encompassing nature. Unlike creativity, dependent co-originating just expresses how things really are, empty of inherent existence. As McFarlane emphasizes, creativity "implies more than just the interdependence of things—it also implies that the process of arising is an advance into novelty, and this aspect of the principle of Creativity is not present in the Buddhist doctrine of dependent arising."[33]

According to Process Theology the potentialities of creativity are actualized in an "actual entity" called God, or the principle of limitation.[34] Although this actual entity seems to be the equivalent of what humans worship in all religions, Whitehead's God is different. He is the only everlasting entity, capable of influencing all impermanent entities, for he is not located spatially or temporally. This explains why instead of the Orthodox doctrine of God holding the universe in existence by his will, we find in the philosophy of Whitehead the concept of God sustaining the world by "the power of himself as the ideal."[35] The way God intervenes in the world as principle of limitation is by calling all entities to fulfil their highest potential. In Cobb's words, God "lures the occasions of the world toward order and value."[36] Since it is not only humans that are lured to attain new possibilities, but the whole world, this would also explain the mechanism of biological evolution (God lures species to develop into new possibilities).

Between God and the world exists a reciprocal influence. God calls the world to order and fulfilment, but is also acted upon by the world. In other words, in Whitehead's vision God and the world shape each other.[37] God's

32. Cobb, "Amida and Christ."

33. McFarlane, "Process and Emptiness,"

34. God is the principle of *limitation* because out of the *many* possibilities that entities have for development God guides them towards the *best* fulfilment.

35. Whitehead, *Religion in the Making*, 149. In this book Whitehead attributes personal attributes to God such as wisdom (p. 154), consciousness and love (p. 152). However, he insists in the same book that God is not a person, since belief in a "personal being substitute to the universe" is the product of an intuition which lacks "evidential force" (pp. 62–63). In his *Christian Natural Theology* Cobb says: "Whitehead vehemently rejected the notion of a transcendent creator God who by an act of the will called all things into being out of nothing and continues to govern omnipotently from outside his creation" (p. 215).

36. Cobb, *A Christian Natural Theology*, 174. This concept has no parallel in Buddhism. As we will see in Abe's criticism, Buddhism cannot accept such a nontemporal aspect of God.

37. Whitehead says: "What is done in the world is transformed into a reality in heaven, and the reality in heaven passes back into the world. By reason of this reciprocal relation, the love in the world passes into the love in heaven, and floods back again

nature as an actual entity which is still capable of luring all others towards fulfilment is affirmed in Process Thought by the doctrine of the dipolar nature of God. It says that God has a primordial nature and a consequent nature. The first is eternal, unconscious and unaffected by change, although it can affect the world, while the second is everlasting and in constant change, in the sense that all that is happening in the world leaves its imprint upon God.[38] In Cobb's words, in God's consequent nature "everything about our experience makes an everlasting difference in the divine experience,"[39] which means that God's consequent nature "absorbs into itself what takes place in the world."[40]

Following Whitehead's concept of peace as ultimate goal, Cobb argues that "God offers to every occasion an ideal opportunity for its self-actualization or satisfaction."[41] God calls humans towards the fulfilment of their highest potential and permanently actualizes his call according to the choices they make (his consequent nature is in permanent renewal), and thus he is called "the great companion, the fellow-sufferer who understands."[42] Therefore there is no predestination for "actual occasions" as given by the Buddhist concept of karma, for there are two sources that shape human life. On the one hand there is the "physical pole," which represents the cumulative effects of an actual occasion's past and which cannot produce change, but on the other hand there is the "mental pole," which is the freedom to use the present for reaching a better future by following the call of God.[43] This "mental pole" is an effective solution against predestination. Cobb argues that, unlike in Buddhism, the new occasion that results from the old one "is not simply the vector resultant of the past occasions that come together

---

into the world. In this sense, God is the great companion—the fellow-sufferer who understands" (Process and Reality, 413).

38. Whitehead, Process and Reality, 409.

39. Cobb, July 2008 Question.

40. Ibid. We can find a clear formulation of the two natures in the words of Dorrien: "God's primordial nature is the universe of creative possibilities, the total potentiality of all existing entities at all moments of their actualization, while God's consequent nature is the accumulation of all actual choices. The primordial nature is conceptual and does not change, but the consequent nature is derivative and conscious, changing along with the world's creative advance" ("The Lure and Necessity of Process Theology," 318).

41. Cobb, A Christian Natural Theology, 226.

42. Whitehead, Process and Reality, 413.

43. Cobb expresses God's call and our freedom to respond in the following words: "God lures, urges, and persuades. We decide. If we decide to enter into the reality into which God calls us, we choose life. If we decide to refuse it, we choose death, a continual dying throughout life and a contribution to a planetary death" (Cobb and Griffin, Process Theology, 158).

to constitute it," for "there is an element of self-determination in each occasion" which makes us "responsible for some aspects of our beliefs, attitudes, and behavior."[44]

In Cobb's opinion Process Theology would be in continuity with the witness of Jesus and of the early Christians, although he admits that it is not "*the* Christian way of thinking about God."[45] To what extent Cobb's Process Theology can be reconciled with traditional Christianity is my next topic.

## 8.3 COBB'S CRITICISM OF TRADITIONAL CHRISTIAN THEOLOGY

Considering the basic tenets of Process Theology and Cobb's verdict on traditional Christian theology as being "incredible" and "harmful," obscuring the "biblical vision" and full of "ambiguity and mystification,"[46] there is no doubt that this would be his verdict on Stăniloae's theology as well. One of the reasons why an "open mind" should reject traditional Christianity is the contradiction between its concept of an omnipotent God and "the kind and quantity of the evil in the world."[47] In Cobb's opinion (following Whitehead), the concept of a good and omnipotent creator of the world cannot be reconciled with "so much cruelty, injustice, brutality, perversity, and deceit" in the world he has allegedly created.[48] Therefore, if God is called "the Lord of history," he must be seen as not only the one who allowed the Shoah to happen, but also as the one who actually caused it.[49] In order that God may become again part of one's "intellectual conviction" and secure the survival of Christianity, a reformulation of the doctrine of God would be a matter of urgent concern.[50] There is little doubt that this reformulation should take the form of the Whiteheadian God as "the One Who Calls us forward,"[51] which would be free of the weaknesses of traditional theism. Unlike the

44. Cobb, "Whitehead and Buddhism."

45. Cobb, *God and the World*, 64.

46. Cobb, *August 2002 Question*.

47. Cobb, *Can Christ Become Good News Again?*, 23. He argues that such a representation of God appeared when "the Church gave unto God the attributes which belong exclusively to Caesar" in the time of Justinian (*God and the World*, 39, following Whitehead's *Process and Reality*, 404). However, it goes without saying that omnipotence, as an attribute of God, is found in the Old Testament and in the early church as well, long before Christianity became the religion of the Roman Empire.

48. Cobb, *Can Christ Become Good News Again?*, 23.

49. Ibid., 24.

50. Cobb, *A Christian Natural Theology*, 14.

51. Cobb, *God and the World*, 61.

"Creator-Lord" and "Lawgiver-Judge" of traditional Christianity who is "a restrictive and repressive force over against man,"[52] in Cobb's alternative view God cannot be blamed for the evil in our world for he does not control the world, but rather calls it to new possibilities.

Since I have already described the Orthodox doctrine of God in chapter 3, I would only add here a few comments which could help us better understand how different it is from the view of Process Theology. From an Orthodox perspective, one could argue that Cobb's rejection of the traditional view originates in a wrong way of understanding God's omnipotence. Stăniloae did not formulate it as the obligation of a supreme dictator to "fix" all problems by his decree. Such a meaning of omnipotence would contradict his love. God's omnipotence is rather manifested in the creation and sustaining of the world,[53] and in the *kenosis* of the Son of God. When examined from the perspective of Orthodox Christianity, the fundamental element that is missing in Cobb's picture is God's love, as defined in the relationships in the Trinity and in Jesus Christ. Since God's fundamental nature is love, he truly is the one who calls, persuades and expects that humans would change. He displayed his character as supreme Caller and fellow-sufferer in Jesus' human life, from birth to passion and resurrection. As a result, human perfection itself is achieved in response to God's love, who calls us forward to eternal communion with him.

As one can expect, since there is no permanent "substance" in Process Theology, the doctrine of the Trinity as one "substance" in three "persons" is seen as inappropriate.[54] Cobb argues that the trinitarian way of seeing God "has done a great deal more harm than good" and that Jesus himself "had no thought of turning God into a triune deity."[55] Therefore the doctrine of the Trinity is for Cobb "an artificial game that has brought theology into justifiable disrepute."[56] The contrast between his view of God and that of

52. Ibid., 63.

53. Whitehead rejected the concept of creation *ex nihilo* and its consequent concept that the world would be kept in existence by God. In his view, "God is not to be treated as an exception to all metaphysical principles invoked to save their collapse" (*Process and Reality*, 405).

54. Cobb, *September 2009 Question*.

55. Ibid.

56. Cobb and Griffin, *Process Theology*, 109. What Cobb categorically rejects seems to be a form of Modalism, since he sees the three Persons "as aspects of that one substance" (*September 2009 Question*). He argues that the Western churches adopted this error from Augustine, while Eastern Christianity opted for "a tri-theism" (*September 2009 Question*). What I find intriguing is that he acknowledges a trend he calls "new Western Trinitarianism" which "grounds relationality and community in the nature of God" (*September 2009 Question*). Unfortunately it appears that he does not further

Orthodox Christianity is obvious. What Cobb defines as "an artificial game" is for Stăniloae "the supreme mystery of existence" which provides meaning to personhood and its perfection.[57] Since the ideal of human perfection in Orthodox Christianity is to be elevated to the trinitarian communion, the trinitarian way of seeing God and the Orthodox ideal of perfection stand or fall together.

We can find a similar difference between the theological foundation of Orthodox Christianity and that of Process Theology in their position on the nature of Christ. We have seen that in Orthodox Christianity the Son of God, one of the persons of the Trinity, was incarnated in Jesus and limited himself to the possibilities of a human nature in order to raise it to perfection. For Cobb, the concept of "Christ" has a different meaning. It is the *principle* which played a role in Jesus' existence, but which cannot be reduced to its function in Jesus. Cobb argues that the same "everlasting Wisdom" that is found in Jesus "is represented everywhere and at all times," and thus Jesus' words in John 14:6 cannot be taken to refer exclusively to a particular teacher.[58] They rather refer to the wisdom that Jesus incarnated. The same wisdom functioned in many other human teachers, including "Buddha or Amos or Paul or Eckhart," from whom Jesus is not "metaphysically different."[59]

In his response to an article written by Moltmann on the Trinity,[60] Cobb expresses his difficulty in correlating the history of salvation as depicted in the New Testament with the doctrine of the Trinity and the pre-existence of the Logos. He is shocked to find in Moltmann "the identification of Jesus as the second person of the Trinity," for this concept can only lead to Christian exclusivistic claims. The Orthodox theologian John Meyendorff replied to Cobb's article saying that "Christian trinitarianism can make sense only if one holds an *ultimately personalistic understanding of the persons or hypostases*" and that salvation means "entering into and participating in their interpersonal unity ('that they may be one in Us'—John 17:21)."[61] As we have seen in chapter 3, the trinitarian view of God and the incarnation of the Son of God in Jesus are essential for Orthodox theology. Its view of salvation cannot work unless one accepts the trinitarian view of

explore this concept in his writings.

57. Stăniloae, *Sfânta Treime,*7.

58. Cobb, *Transforming Christianity and the World*, 79–80.

59. Cobb, *January 2001 Question.*

60. Cobb, "Reply to Jürgen Moltmann's 'The Unity of the Triune God.'"

61. Meyendorff, "Reply to Jürgen Moltmann's 'The Unity of the Triune God,'" 187.

God and the double nature of Christ, which is the means through which the human being is elevated to personal communion with God.[62]

Not only Process Theology, but also Orthodox Christianity stresses the need of becoming responsive to the call of God. The major difference between them consists in the finality of this call. While for Cobb it leads to becoming *part* of God's consequent nature, for Stăniloae it leads to eternal *communion* with the triune God. Although an Orthodox Christian could agree with Cobb that Jesus did indeed introduce in the world "a final and unsurpassable structure of existence,"[63] it would bear for him or her a very different meaning. For the Orthodox Christian the new "structure of existence" is the Kingdom of God inaugurated by Jesus' resurrection, while for the Whiteheadian Christian[64] it is a new prehension of God which bears no effect on a conscious afterlife.

As a follower of Process Theology Cobb can only reject the Orthodox view of human perfection. In his view one attains the condition of "saintliness" by following the lead of God (as the principle of limitation) and by constantly deciding to open himself or herself to God's ideal aim.[65] This is an open path for anyone no matter what his or her religious or philosophical tradition may be. In Orthodoxy the image of perfection is the human Jesus who, according to Stăniloae, inaugurated a new humanity and conquered death as a man in full obedience to the call of God so that any human could also conquer death in union with him. Although Cobb says about Jesus that he was "fully responsive to the call of God,"[66] he was not perfect. To affirm Jesus' sinlessness would be a form of "pointless glorification" which can lead to religious sectarianism and hate for followers of other religions or even for "those who follow Jesus in a different way."[67] Cobb doubts that Jesus never sinned and gives a few examples that would prove the contrary, such as the cursing of the fig tree out of anger (Matthew 21:19) and the rejection of the Canaanite woman's plea to heal her daughter (Matthew 15:22–28).

62. James Carpenter concludes that Cobb's Christology generates more problems than it solves, for it does not solve the classic issue of giving an account "for God's unique presence in Jesus without displacing any aspect of Jesus' humanity" (Carpenter, "The Christology of John Cobb"). For Cobb the conflicts in the early church on the two natures of Christ and the attempts to find a solution in the Formula of Chalcedon are seen as consequences of "substantialist" categories of thinking (Cobb, *Christ in a Pluralist Age*, 167).

63. Cobb, "A Whiteheadian Christology," in Brown et al., eds., *Process Philosophy and Christian Thought*, 398.

64. Cobb uses this term in his online article "Whitehead and Buddhism."

65. Cobb, *A Christian Natural Theology*, 250.

66. Cobb, *April 2007 Question*.

67. Ibid.

These would be cases in which Jesus disobeyed God's call "to broaden his horizons."[68] Other "examples of many failures" in Jesus' life include his unwillingness to liberate John the Baptist from imprisonment, and then to resurrect him after his martyrdom as he did with other people.[69]

Further differences between the Christology of Cobb and that of Stăniloae can be seen in their position on the Cross and the resurrection. Cobb says almost nothing of the crucifixion,[70] while the resurrection is for him a mere "symbol of victory over loss and defeat" to encourage humans towards attaining their highest potential.[71] Although he argues that it is irrelevant what actually happened at Easter,[72] he admits to being "haunted by Paul's words in I Cor.15."[73] He is aware that for Paul "Jesus' rising from the dead was the foretaste of a glorious destiny," but still argues that belief in the resurrection does not depend on a *physical* resurrection of Jesus.[74] In Cobb's view, the resurrection should be seen as "a glorious transformation into a spiritual body," so it does not matter if the sightings of the resurrected body of Jesus were "convincing hallucinations" or "actual auditions and visions."[75] The most likely explanation for him would be that Jesus' resurrection was the sighting of a ghost, resembling "modern stories of ghost sighting."[76] He concludes his article on the resurrection by saying that what should matter for us is our "discipleship" and not "our opinions on such matters."[77] However, in Orthodox Christianity these opinions do matter a lot, since there is no sense in discipleship if there was no bodily resurrection of Jesus. For Stăniloae the resurrection is essential as it proves Jesus' sinlessness and his continuing relationship with his followers through the Eucharist for the renewal of human nature from the inside, so that they can share in everlasting communion with God.

68. Ibid.

69. Cobb, *April 2008 Question.*

70. He simply says "God used even Jesus' death for our salvation," but does not explain what he means by this (Cobb, "Who Was Jesus?").

71. Cobb, *May 2007 Question.*

72. Ibid. Pannenberg criticizes Cobb for not considering Jesus' resurrection as "the event that made this delay of the eschaton bearable for early Christianity" (Wolfhart Pannenberg, "A Liberal Logos Christology: The Christology of John Cobb," in Griffin and Altizer, eds., *John Cobb's Theology in Process,* 139).

73. "If for this life only we have hoped in Christ, we are of all people most to be pitied" (1 Corinthians 15:19, NRSV).

74. Cobb, *May 2007 Question.*

75. Ibid.

76. Ibid.

77. Ibid.

Not only is what happened to Jesus' physical body irrelevant for Cobb, but so is any discussion of the believer's resurrection. Since Cobb's view of immortality is that of becoming a part of God's consequent nature, the traditional doctrine of the resurrection of the body is deemed irrelevant and anachronistic.[78] This is another important contrast with the theology of Stăniloae. While for Cobb the resurrection is at most an open possibility, for Stăniloae it is a crucial element of belief, for the resurrected body is the very image of a perfected human nature. All these theological discrepancies between Process Theology and Orthodox Christianity will bear effects on how the two traditions can engage in dialogue with Buddhism.

## 8.4 COBB'S VISION OF BUDDHIST-CHRISTIAN DIALOGUE. TOWARDS A MUTUAL TRANSFORMATION OF BUDDHISM AND CHRISTIANITY

Among the most important reasons for Cobb's rejection of traditional Christianity stands its exclusivism. To proclaim Jesus Christ as the only means of salvation would not only compromise genuine dialogue, but also stand against Jesus' demand to love our neighbour.[79] However, his rejection of exclusivism does not mean that he is embracing a syncretistic unity of religions in which the best of each would form "a convincing synthesis" and function "as the soul of a truly global culture."[80] Cobb is aware that such an approach would in fact generate a new religion and would prejudice those who would resist it.[81] In the end it is an impossible road to take, since each tradition would see as "essential" elements that could not be reconciled with "essential" elements of other traditions and thus they could not form a synthesis. Another perspective in interfaith dialogue he rejects is Hick's attempt to define a common ground in world religions.[82] Such a proposal originates in a superficial understanding of religions and is categorized as paternalistic and a form of religious "imperialism," for it would inform adherents of other traditions "that the heart of their experience or the object of their attention is not what they have thought but rather something else."[83]

78. Cobb, *A Christian Natural Theology*, 67–68.

79. Cobb, *Transforming Christianity and the World*, 16.

80. Ibid., 58.

81. Ibid., 57.

82. Hick, *An Interpretation of Religion*. I will address Hick's view in the next chapter of this book.

83. Cobb, *Transforming Christianity*, 105. This affirmation goes against his own way of approaching traditional Christianity, as he seeks himself to reinterpret "the heart" of

A further difficulty lies in the fact that there is no consensus among those who hold this view concerning what may actually be the common essence of religions.[84]

Cobb is aware that Buddhist enlightenment and the renewed life in Christ are different goals that cannot easily be reconciled.[85] He disagrees that they could suit different people with different needs, for such a perspective would contradict "the universalistic character of both traditions."[86] He sees as equally wrong the option of reducing both goals to a secondary status, as this "would be a still more drastic break with their traditions."[87] Therefore it seems that the only option left would be that of religious pluralism. However, Cobb opposes a cheap pluralism that would simply assert the popular image of world religions being many paths to reach the same mountain peak, so that each of us could pick the path convenient to himself or herself.[88] He finds this form of pluralism as "not sufficiently pluralistic."[89]

Cobb's proposal for interfaith dialogue rejects all the above. Instead of exclusivism, syncretism and a simplistic pluralism, his demand is for recognizing the complementarity of religious traditions and the need for their mutual transformation. In his view one should allow different religious traditions to fulfil different needs for the *same* person. This is not syncretism, for he asks that both Buddhists and Christians remain faithful to their heritage while expanding "their understanding of reality and its normative implications."[90] Cobb argues that *as we are*, Buddhists *or* Christians, we can be renewed by the other tradition and benefit from dialogue by "enrichment and even positive transformation."[91] As an application, one can use both Buddhist meditation and Christian moral guidance and still be faithful to

---

traditional Christianity in favour of Process Theology.

84. Cobb, "Beyond 'Pluralism.'"

85. Cobb acknowledges that Buddhism is "the most different from Christianity of the great religious traditions" (Abe et al. "Buddhist-Christian Dialogue," 19) and that "much that Buddhists and Christians say is in marked conflict" (Cobb, "Christian Witness in a Pluralistic World," in Hick and Askari, eds., *Experience of Religious Diversity*, 159).

86. Cobb, *Christ in a Pluralist Age*, 207.

87. Ibid.

88. Cobb, *Transforming Christianity*, 55; also in Cobb, "Beyond 'Pluralism.'"

89. Cobb, "Beyond 'Pluralism.'" He says elsewhere: "A unity that omits the real belief and interest of most people is not the unity we sought" (Cobb, *Transforming Christianity*, 56).

90. Cobb, "Beyond 'Pluralism.'"

91. Cobb, *Transforming Christianity*, 66.

his or her tradition.[92] In his view Buddhism and Christianity respond to different questions and as such supplement each other. Buddhist emptiness is the answer to "what one is and what all things are," while God is the answer to questions such as: "Why is there an ordered world at all?" and "To what do I owe what is good in my life?" or "Where should I place my trust?"[93] Since the wisdom that Jesus incarnated was present in many other religious founders,[94] the transformation envisaged by Cobb would make Buddhism and Christianity resemble each other more than they do now. Hence he invites us to seek a deeper meaning of Buddhism and Christianity, which would allow one to follow both "Jesus as Lord and Savior" and "Gautama as guide to enlightenment,"[95] while still remaining faithful to one's own tradition, either Buddhist or Christian.

Cobb's major assumption in grounding this new path in interfaith dialogue is that the contradictions one sees between the traditions are given by the way they have been *formulated*, whereas the *truth* they express is not exclusivistic. He says:

> My goal is to transform contradictory statements into different but noncontradictory ones. My assumption is that what is positively intended by those who have lived, thought, and felt deeply is likely to be true, whereas their formulations are likely to exclude other truths that should not be excluded.[96]

By virtue of this principle, there is no fundamental or irreconcilable contradiction between Buddhist enlightenment and Christian salvation as "new life through faith in Christ."[97] One's quest should be to find that ultimate point of contact between the two traditions, the ultimate *truth* they express. By virtue of this principle, despite the great divide between Buddhists and Christians on the meaning and role of God, Cobb still finds that the two traditions can be mutually enriched on the very subject of God and non-attachment. He argues that

> the Buddhist could in principle acknowledge the reality of something worthy of trust and worship (the Christian God) without abandoning the central insight that attachment blocks the way

92. Ibid., 56.

93. Cobb, "Christian Witness in a Pluralistic World," 158–9.

94. Cobb's initiative of a mutual opening and transformation should not be limited to Buddhists and Christians. We could open ourselves to Islam and see Muhammad as "our prophet as well" (Cobb, *Transforming Christianity*, 60).

95. Cobb, *September 2001 Question*.

96. Cobb, "Beyond 'Pluralism.'"

97. Cobb, *Christ in a Pluralist Age*, 207.

to enlightenment. And the Christian could come to see that real trust (in God) is not attachment in the Buddhist sense.[98]

What he means is that, for Buddhists, the rejection of God is only skilful means for stressing non-attachment, while for Christians, the existence of God as a fundamental assumption is a means for emphasizing one's need for worship. In the end, at the level of *truth* "it is not impossible that both be correct."[99] The Buddhist may accept both "the reality of something worthy of trust and worship" and be committed to non-attachment, while the Christian could realize that his or her faith in God "is not attachment in the Buddhist sense." As such, both would "have learned what is most important to the other without abandoning their central concerns."[100]

Cobb's supposition in grounding a radical pluralism can be rephrased by saying that "there is more to truth" than what each tradition has expressed in its formulations.[101] In other words, there must be more to truth than what has been *so far* expressed. For the sake of progress Cobb's total pluralism demands total openness to other religious traditions so that more of the whole truth could be expressed. Faithfulness to Christ would then mean to recognize in other religious traditions anything of "worth and importance" that we cannot find in ours.[102] The result of such an approach is unpredictable:

> In faithfulness to Christ I must be prepared to give up even faithfulness to Christ. If that is where I am led, to remain a Christian would be to become an idolater in the name of Christ. That would be blasphemy.[103]

In conclusion, it appears that the true reference point for Cobb in Buddhist-Christian dialogue is none of the traditions but his own assumption

98. Cobb, *Transforming Christianity*, 74.

99. Cobb, "Beyond 'Pluralism.'"

100. Ibid.; also in Cobb, *Transforming Christianity*, 74. However, in his book *Beyond Dialogue* Cobb admits that in Buddhism "attachment to neighbor, Christ, God, is still attachment" and "just as binding as any other" (79–80).

101. Ibid., 61 and in Cobb, "Beyond 'Pluralism.'"

102. Cobb, *Transforming Christianity*, 45.

103. Ibid. As an example of how his perspective could really work, Cobb mentions the "positionless position" of Abe, which would relativize itself (Cobb, "Beyond 'Pluralism'"). But as we have seen in our assessment of Abe, this stand does not actually work. Although Abe proclaims his position as "positionless," he is very well fixed within the boundaries of Zen and is not open to adding anything from Christianity or to grounding a new position. Cobb himself, in an article written sixteen years earlier, expressed his doubt that such a "positionless position" could really work (see the discussion of his article "Ultimate Reality: A Christian View," *Buddhist-Christian Studies* 8 (1988) 75).

of a greater truth lying beyond the formulations of the existing traditions. This would be the basis for formulating what he calls a "new Buddhism" and a "new Christianity." Could they still be faithful to what the "old" traditions of Buddhism and Christianity have expressed as their ideal of human perfection?

## 8.5 WHAT COULD BUDDHISTS LEARN FROM CHRISTIANITY?

Not only is traditional Christianity targeted by Cobb's criticism, but traditional Buddhism as well. It too needs to develop into a "new Buddhism," and Christianity can offer important directions of adjustment. As we have seen in the previous chapter, Abe accepted some criticism from his Christian partners in dialogue (including Cobb), but did not actually use any of their specific suggestions for improving the acknowledged weaknesses of Buddhism. We will now see whether his friend Cobb is more successful in this attempt.

Two of Cobb's criticisms against Buddhism are similar to those made by Abe, and have already been mentioned in section 7.6—its view of history and the lack of interest in global social issues that affect us.[104] I will not return to these issues, but instead focus on a very original proposal for Buddhists, that of learning to see Amida as personal and ethical.[105] The link between Christ and Amida is seen as an important point of contact between Christianity and Buddhism for other important voices in Buddhist-Christian dialogue as well, such as the Dalai Lama and Robert Thurman. But while they argue for seeing Christ as one of the *bodhisattvas* and thus invite Christians to learn from Buddhism on the nature of Christ, Cobb invites us to consider the reverse direction as well. On the one hand, since Christ and the Buddha-nature are present in all things, he affirms that "Jesus might also have attained enlightenment" and Buddhists could see him "as another Buddha."[106] But on the other hand, unlike most Buddhist thinkers, Cobb emphasizes the reciprocal application as well, which demands that "Gau-

104. Cobb criticizes Buddhists in China, Korea and Japan for having "little responsibility for the social and political lives of their countries" (Cobb, *Transforming Christianity*, 155). An issue I will not address is Cobb's criticism of Buddhism for having no inner connection with science and for not stimulating scientific enquiry. He complains that "Buddhism has failed to nourish scientific enquiry and social ethics. . . . If science disappeared, there would be little impulsion within Buddhism to renew it" (Cobb, *Christ in a Pluralist Age*, 208).

105. Cobb, *Beyond Dialogue*, 129.

106. Cobb, *Christ in a Pluralist Age*, 205–6.

tama might also have incarnated the Logos in a redemptive manner." As a result, both Buddhists and Christians could reciprocally open themselves to "the normative figure in the other tradition."[107] In the rest of this section we will see how Buddhists could learn from the Christian view of Christ to see Amida in a different light.

Cobb is aware that if we stick to the traditional meaning of Amida and Christ we would reach the conclusion that they "do not refer to the same reality."[108] In Mahayana Buddhism Amida is one of the many Buddhas who attained *nirvana*, while in traditional Christianity Christ is "the preexistent one who took on human form in Jesus and then returned to the right hand of the Father, with or without his human body."[109] However, given his assumption that there is more to truth than traditions have so far expressed, Cobb affirms there still is a sense in which Amida and Christ "name the same reality."[110] Christ should be seen as the "creative and redemptive activity of God in the world"[111] which was "fully incarnate and redemptively effective in Jesus,"[112] but *not only* in Jesus. The same "Wisdom and Compassion" is present "everywhere," including (the legendary) Dharmakara who eventually became the Amida Buddha.[113] Therefore the universal presence of the Buddha-nature and of Christ would justify the equivalence between Amida and Christ.

In order to further explain his proposal, Cobb uses the Buddhist doctrine of the *Trikaya*, according to which Amida is an instance of the *Sambhogakaya*, which is a manifestation of the *Dharmakaya* or, in other words, of emptiness. The Ultimate Reality out of which both Amida and Christ emerged, whether one calls it creativity or *Dharmakaya*, is the same, but with an important qualification: While Whitehead's creativity provides a teleological drive towards "the realization of novel intensities of feeling" in us,[114] the Buddhist *Dharmakaya* has no such outcome. When comparing the dipolar nature of God with the nature of the Amida Buddha, Cobb finds an interesting equivalence. On the one hand, God's call (which originates in

107. Ibid., 206.

108. Cobb, *Beyond Dialogue*, 124.

109. Ibid. His statement here is at odds with traditional Christology, as the Son of God did not take just a human form, but a *complete* human nature, and ascended in a human body. As we have seen in chapter 2, his ascension in a human body is essential, not dispensable.

110. Cobb, *Beyond Dialogue*, 124.

111. Ibid.

112. Cobb, *Christ in a Pluralist Age*, 206.

113. Cobb, "Amida and Christ."

114. Cobb, *Beyond Dialogue*, 126.

his primordial nature) is equivalent to the vow of Amida to save all beings, as it was expressed by Shinran, and as such is analogous to what the Apostle John and the Patristic writers have called "the Word of God or Logos or Truth which is Christ."[115] On the other hand, since there is no similitude found between the consequent nature of God and the nature of Amida, Cobb argues that this consequent nature must be expressed by Amida's personal character, an aspect so far ignored by Buddhists. They can learn from Christianity to see Amida as both personal and ethical, for "as *a* Buddha he certainly retains personal characteristics."[116] In a similar way in which the consequent nature of God is modified by human acts, Buddhists should thus acknowledge that Amida is transformed by the prayers of his followers. This is an original contribution to Buddhist-Christian dialogue that I have not found in other authors.

As a result of this equivalence, not only can Buddhists learn of Amida's personal and ethical aspect, but also Christians can learn of Christ from the Buddhist way of understanding Amida. On the one hand, Cobb argues that nothing "of worth would be lost to Buddhists" if they would learn from the Christian view of Christ "that our lives are in this way of importance to Amida."[117] He invites Buddhists to learn this aspect and accept an influence upon Amida, which would eventually lead to formulating his consequent nature. Amida should be seen as *more* than skilful means for instructing us. Buddhists should see in him that it is really God "who calls us to compassionate action and to whom ultimate loyalty is due,"[118] and thus realize that the compassion they crave for is that of God. On the other hand, the application for Christians is that they should learn to be set free from a form of clinging which originates in seeing Christ as an absolute instead of "a feature of reality bound to particular times and places," for such faith in Christ is "idolatrous."[119] Christians should acknowledge that the same lesson about grace that Christians learned from the Bible and which culminated in Jesus "Buddhists have learned in a different way,"[120] i.e., through Pure Land Buddhism. This is the way in which Cobb argues how "Christians can gain

---

115. Ibid., 128.

116. Ibid., 129.

117. Ibid., 132.

118. Cobb, "Buddhism and Christianity." Cobb says: "Further, we believe that the God who comforts and calls also deserves our supreme loyalty, a loyalty that transcends that to any creaturely reality. This note of loyalty or commitment is lacking in Buddhism" (ibid.).

119. Ibid.

120. Cobb, "Amida and Christ."

further knowledge about Christ by studying what Buddhists have learned about Amida" and vice versa.[121]

What Buddhists should also consider as a result of being challenged by the (Whiteheadian) Christian understanding of Amida is his influence on the sphere of ethics. Amida should not only be worshipped in order to gain access into his Pure Land in the afterlife, but also taken as a stimulant for moral conduct and social involvement here and now. Cobb is unhappy with the present Buddhist lack of reaction against the threat of "unparalleled disaster and suffering if not actual extinction" that is looming over our world.[122] He defines the Buddhist problem in the area of ethics as a lack of a "trans-social norm by virtue of which society is judged" and formulates the requirement that Buddhists should be "in the forefront of movements of social protest."[123] They should learn and build into Amida's character the Whiteheadian view of the One who Calls.[124] As we have seen, this is possible by stating an equivalence between God's call (in Process Theology) and Amida's vow to save all beings (in Pure Land Buddhism). Therefore Amida's vow should be understood as not limited to the "immediate and private,"[125] i.e., to liberating humans from present suffering. If one could broaden his or her understanding of his vow, it would "introduce a space for human freedom" which is a real problem in Buddhism.[126] This freedom would be the necessary space for building "better concepts and theories" of social interaction and would help us become "more than we have been both for our sake and for the sake of others," which would be a serious gain for Buddhist ethics.[127]

However, Cobb's proposal can hardly be accepted by Buddhists, since Amida is not an actual entity in the Whiteheadian sense. Although Cobb's desire is to identify in Amida a primordial and a consequent nature, Pure Land Buddhism leaves no space for such a project to be realistic. On the one

---

121. Ibid.

122. Cobb, *Beyond Dialogue*, 133. He probably refers here to being more active against the threat of a nuclear war, as this book was published in 1982, when the threat of a nuclear war was still looming.

123. Ibid.

124. Ibid., 135.

125. Ibid., 136.

126. Ibid., 135. Cobb expresses his concern over the issue of freedom in Buddhism, saying that it is not clear "how an instance of dependent origination may involve an element of responsible freedom" (ibid., 106). In Process Theology the freedom of choice is given by the call of God and the actual possibility of an actual entity to prehend it or not.

127. Ibid., 135–6.

hand, if Amida were to have an (eternal) primordial nature as the White-headian God, it would mean he would escape impermanence, which is unthinkable in Buddhist terms. On the other hand, the events in the world of dependent co-origination cannot leave their mark upon Amida, for he does not stand in a relationship of reciprocal influence with the world. The grace by which Amida is able to help his followers is the result of merits accumulated in eons of previous lives, and nothing can be added to his wisdom by some present influence upon him by humans. In other words, even if one could speculate on a primordial nature of Amida (and defy im-permanence) as manifested in his call for all people to reach his Pure Land, there is no space for defining a consequent nature.[128] The God who Calls, in Whitehead's and Cobb's vision, is an everlasting entity whose role cannot be taken by Amida. Nothing in Buddhism can be seen as non-temporal, for otherwise it would become an object of attachment and ruin the Buddhist view of perfection. As a result, Amida and Christ cannot "name the same feature of the totality,"[129] even if one's analysis is limited to Process Theology and Pure Land Buddhism, which would be the most likely tradition to ac-cept Cobb's proposal.

## 8.6 WHAT COULD CHRISTIANS LEARN FROM BUDDHISM?

In light of his criticism of traditional Christianity, Cobb argues that dia-logue with Buddhism should help it move beyond its present provincialism and attain a "fuller universality."[130] In his book *Beyond Dialogue* he proposes four concrete directions for changing the way in which Christians see their faith. My assessment will follow his four questions which summarize these directions of change.[131]

---

128. From a more general Madhyamaka stand, we must remember that to see Ami-da as more than a product of the mind would betray a lack of wisdom and prove one is still trapped in illusion. It would be a major blow to the perfect wisdom a bodhisattva has to realize. For a Madhyamika Buddhist the image of a compassionate Amida is nothing more than skilful means for eliminating grasping and detaching from greed, aversion and delusion.

129. Cobb, "Amida and Christ."

130. Cobb, "Beyond 'Pluralism.'"

131. Cobb, *Beyond Dialogue*, 99. All the following quotations in this section, unless indicated otherwise, are from Cobb's book *Beyond Dialogue*, so page numbers will be given in the text.

1. "Can a Christian surrender all attachment, craving, and clinging even to Christ?"

Cobb is aware that in traditional Christianity faith means "cleaving to Christ" and that Buddhists interpret it as "a form of clinging" (p. 100). As with any form of belief in a deity, clinging prevents one from attaining enlightenment. Cobb suggests that Buddhism may provide the necessary help for Christians to realize a deeper understanding of faith that would not make it a form of clinging.[132] This help comes from Pure Land Buddhism, which insists on the need of resorting to Amida's grace for reaching enlightenment.

Cobb suggests there is an equivalence between Luther's view of salvation through faith as a free gift of God and not depending on one's "right mental and spiritual attitude" (p. 102), and that formulated by Shinran, who argued that Amida's grace is so efficient that one can be certain of his or her salvation by simply reciting his name. As such, the recitation of the *nembutsu* would be the Christian equivalent of participating in "the sacraments, prayer and Bible reading" (p. 101).[133] Yet, Cobb knows there are also significant differences between Luther and Shinran's teaching. While for the first faith has the meaning of trust manifested in "an interpersonal relation" (p. 103), for the second *shinjin* is more about realizing a proper attitude of mind and of recognizing "the true principle or depth of our own being" (p. 103). Since there is no true personal relationship between the Shin Buddhist and Amida, as that between the Christian and Christ, neither can there be a similar meaning of faith for Luther and Shinran.

However, the interpersonal imagery of faith is not essential for Cobb in order to build a renewed Christianity in dialogue with Buddhism (p. 103). Following Process Theology and its concept of the universal Christ, the separation between the Other (Christ) and the individual is blurred, and thus faith becomes "not only a relation to the source of grace" but also "the believing heart which that grace effects by its presence" (p. 103). This approach attempts to bring Christian faith closer to its Buddhist counterpart, but still does not make it its equivalent. Cobb argues that in order to accept a "common meaning of faith in the two traditions' one should recognize that both Buddhism and Christianity express by faith both "trust in a personal

---

132. A meaning of faith that is accepted in Zen Buddhism is that of having faith in one's master even when the disciple cannot make any sense of the teaching (p. 100). This kind of faith is useful only until the disciple realizes himself the truth of Buddhist doctrine, after which it is set aside (p.101).

133. However, Cobb omits that these acts are "means of salvation" (p. 102) only because they express a relationship with a self-existing God.

Other" and the element of "participation in a state of being" (p. 103). However, Buddhism cannot accommodate a true element of "trust in a personal
Other," nor that of "participating in a state of being" (i.e, contributing to
God's consequent nature) without being compromised. Despite Cobb's hope
that the two expressions of faith could be "most fruitfully related" (p. 102),
his project works only in Process Theology. It cannot work either in Buddhism, or in traditional Christian theology, in which faith is always about a
relationship with the Other (God) and never about becoming part of God.
The closer Cobb comes to the Buddhist view and affirms that "perfect faith"
is "complete letting go, not holding fast" (p. 104) the more he distances himself from the Orthodox view. And the more he emphasizes an external relationship (with the Other) the more he distances himself from the Buddhist
*shinjin*. Given this irreconcilable situation, his view of faith as "openness to
whatever happens" (p. 104) works well in Process Theology but cannot be
accepted by either Buddhists or Christians, and his question above must be
answered in the negative.

2. "Can a Christian accept as a goal the dissolution of personal
existence?"

Cobb reminds us that Buddhism does not accept a substantial self and
argues that there is no such idea to be found in the Bible either (p. 105).
But even if the self were not taken as substantial in traditional Christianity,
he observes that its image is still "real and strong" (p. 105). This sense of a
self constitutes a human's individuality against that of others and leads to
mutual isolation (p. 108). Therefore in order to truly love their neighbours,
following God's command, Christians should appropriate the doctrine of
not-Self from Buddhism. If Christians would realize that the person is a
product of the five aggregates, the barriers which separate humans would
break down and they would more naturally love each other. Cobb says: "The
Christian commandment to love the neighbour as the self is transformed in
the enlightened ones into a description of the actual relationship to others"
(p. 109).[134] In other words, it is the enlightened Buddhist who is able to fulfil
the command, so Christians should learn from him or her the meaning of
love for one's neighbour.

There are two aspects I need to discuss regarding this proposal. First,
Cobb's argument is similar to that of Shantideva for justifying compassion
in Buddhism. Since there is no self and no preservation of personal identity,

134. However, Cobb omits that the command to love others as "yourself" has an
ethical meaning (Matthew 22:39; Mark 12:31; Luke 10:27) and as such is irrelevant in a
discussion on the existence of a substantial self.

it is nonsensical that we love ourselves more than others. As we recall from section 2.5, this is what motivates the enlightened Buddhist to be compassionate. In a similar way, Cobb explains that as a result of blurring the differences between oneself and others we become "increasingly able" to inherit the influence of other persons following the way we are inheriting our own past (p. 110). In other words, the "empathy for one's own immediate past" will be transformed into empathy for others, and will manifest as openness towards the ideas of others, and as interest for their happiness (p. 110). This would be the meaning of true love for one's neighbour, and therefore Christians should move towards transcending "the personal structure of existence" (p. 110). However, as Williams has shown in section 2.5, Shantideva's argument is self-destructive. Since there is no self, we cannot talk of "my" or "his" suffering, and since there is no owner of pain, there is no pain either, and compassionate action loses any target of actual application. The same argument can be used against Cobb's resource for loving others. Since the "personal structure of existence" must be transcended and there are no real "others," the command to love one's neighbour loses its applicability.

A second way of assessing Cobb's proposal for transcending personal existence would be to refrain here from debating whether Christianity has a clear concept of a substantial self or not, and see whether his proposal would bring any results in Hinduism, where the self (*atman*) is taken as substantial beyond dispute. Could one argue that interpersonal relationships are significantly different in Hinduism because of the belief in a self? Or more plainly stated, can one witness more selfishness among Hindus than among Buddhists? It can hardly be said so. Against what one should expect from Cobb's argument, the relationships in a Hindu community (lay or monastic) work well despite the common belief in a self, while in a Buddhist community relationships are not much different. In other words, belief in a substantial self does not make Hindus more selfish than Buddhists. Therefore it is hardly self-evident that the Buddhist not-Self doctrine would be able to help Christians to improve social relationships. As regarding Cobb's second question in this section, the preservation of personhood is essential for perfecting a relationship with God, so it would be nonsensical to accept as a goal the "transcending personal existence" (p. 105).

3. "Can a Christian appropriate the vision of ultimate reality as Emptiness?"

Cobb's third direction of change for grounding a "new Christianity" concerns redefining its view of Ultimate Reality. He argues that a Christian is not in the situation of choosing between "identifying God with Emptiness" and "denying God altogether" (p. 110). A more appropriate solution for the Western world would be to admit a supra-personal essence as the source of God, or in his words, to realize the distinction "between Godhead and God" (p. 111). This approach resembles the view of Eckhart (*Gottheit* as the source of God), and of the Advaita Vedanta of Hinduism (Brahman as the source of Ishvara). He sees a similar subordination formulated in Buddhism, where a Buddha is a manifestation of the Buddha-nature (p. 111). This pattern should be accepted by traditional Christianity as well, by considering God a manifestation of a higher Ultimate Reality, not Ultimate Reality itself (p. 111). As such, it would liberate Christians from the pressure to worship a being or to be united with it.

The position from which Cobb makes his proposal is obviously that of Process Theology. From this perspective he rhetorically asks whether "anything essential to the Christian faith would be lost in rethinking God in Buddhist terms" (p. 113). His conviction is that "a Buddhized vision of God" would be more faithful to the way Jesus revealed God than would theological speculations on "God as being or Supreme Being" (p. 113). With the help of Process Theology and of the Buddhist insights on emptiness, he argues that "we Christians can rethink our belief in God" (p. 113) and affirm that "faith in God and realization of Emptiness can mutually fructify one another in living human experience" (p. 114).

Cobb acknowledges that his revolutionary view of God is "in tension" (p. 113) with traditional Christian theology, but this is an understatement. We have seen in chapter 3 how different the view of Orthodox Christianity is on Ultimate Reality and why, and therefore one could hardly accept that Cobb's insights would resonate better with the Bible than does the traditional view. Cobb's vision negates the communion of the Holy Trinity as Ultimate Reality and the image of human perfection as deification. Not surprisingly, his view of Ultimate Reality is in tension with Buddhism as well, for he argues for a reciprocal determination between God and the world. Only Process Theology allows one to affirm both that "there is no God apart from Emptiness" (p. 112) *and* that "it is equally true to say there is no Emptiness apart from God" (p. 113). His real interest must then be in the renewal of both Christianity and Buddhism in the likeness of Process Thought, which would be unfair to both traditions.

4. "Can a Christian enter fully into the sheer immanence of the moment?"

By the "immanence of the moment" Cobb refers to the Buddhist view of existence as a string of momentary stages of an endless process. He criticizes the Christian vision of the Kingdom of God, for it deters one from focusing on the present and instead invites to a passive "future orientation" (p. 117). In order to help Christians incorporate a sound vision of present and future, Cobb starts from the Buddhist prerequisite of focusing on "the here-now" and rejects any attempt to see the present from what he calls an "Archimedean point" (p. 116). He is probably referring to what in Christianity is called revelation, the input of a self-existing God who is both the creator and sustainer of the world, a concept which he considers misleading, as is the "naïve biblical view of beginning and end as objectively given" (p. 116). Instead he calls for building a "frame that provides hope without false confidence" and, probably referring to his own experience of realizing that we live in a dying world, for taking seriously "the appalling dangers of today's world" (p. 117).

In Cobb's vision, the traditional image of the Kingdom of God is nothing but a "postponement of gratification" given by a loss of belief in a "fulfilled immediacy" so that Christians need now "the encounter with Nirvana" as "a new way of conceiving the immediacy of blessedness" (p. 117). It is, however, surprising to hear from Cobb that Christians should learn from Buddhism how to build a more realistic vision of the future. He criticized Abe for *not* having the resources for a sound view of history.[135] Nevertheless he encourages Christians to go beyond the traditional view of the Kingdom of God and learn from the *bodhisattva*, the one who vows to save all beings before entering into *nirvana* (p. 118). This is the perfect example for Cobb of what it means to sit in the immanence of the present. It would lead Christians to formulate a "Christianized Nirvana" (p. 118) which should replace the traditional image of the Kingdom of God.

However, according to Orthodox Christianity the Kingdom of God is not a projection of human self-centredness or unfulfilled gratification, but the fulfilment of what Christ has started through his life, cross, resurrection and ascension. Therefore Cobb's view of a "Christianized Nirvana" cannot work, for these two terms cannot stand together. *Nirvana* is the dissolution of personal relationships, while the Kingdom of God is their perfection. In the Mahayana Buddhist tradition the ideal of the *bodhisattva* consists in realizing a perfect balance between wisdom and compassion in order that all clinging (to existence and non-existence) would be destroyed. The *bodhisattva* is not calling beings to the perfection of personal existence in relationship with God (or Amida), but to the realization of emptiness. Christ,

---

135. Cobb found a close connection between "the Buddhist analysis of reality, intimately connected to the quest for enlightenment" and "the absence of the social, ethical, and historical dimensions from its central self-understanding" (Cobb, *Transforming Christianity*, 156).

on the other hand, calls for the opposite, for the realization of a perfected relationship with God that would endure forever in the Kingdom of God. As such it is not compatible with either Buddhism or Process Theology. As with his other proposals, Cobb's exhortation for Christians to adopt a "Christianized Nirvana" is counterproductive for achieving perfection in the Orthodox tradition.

## 8.7 CONCLUSION TO COBB'S PROPOSAL FOR BUDDHIST-CHRISTIAN DIALOGUE

As we have seen, Cobb's proposal is that "a different Christianity" and "a different Buddhism" would emerge as a result of their mutual transformation.[136] This proposal originated in his assumption that there is a deeper level of truth than what the traditions have been able to express so far. If it is taken as an axiom, Buddhists and Christians *must* learn from each other and accept that it is a matter of "faithfulness to its past" that a tradition would be "enriched and transformed in its interaction with the other traditions."[137] We have now arrived at a point of final assessment of this proposal. Let us first see what his friend Abe thinks about it from a Buddhist point of view.

In the previous chapter, we have seen that Abe rejects any compromise to Zen teaching and any improvement that might be supplied from the Christian side. Process Theology is much closer to Zen than traditional Christianity, but Abe still considers it insufficient. One can easily guess his point of discontentment: it is Cobb's view of God. Although God is not substantial in Process Theology, for Abe it is still "a relative kind of nothingness"[138] not absolute Nothingness, which alone is consistent with the principle of dependent co-origination (*pratitya samutpada*). Although Cobb argues that "nothing in Whiteheadian theism" would be "fundamentally in conflict with the deepest and most widely accepted Buddhist insights"[139] it appears he is wrong. For Abe it is unacceptable to see God as "*somewhat* beyond the interdependence of everything in the temporal world."[140] He is obviously referring to what Whitehead defined as the primordial nature of God, and the view that God is "the only actual entity which is *not* an actual occasion."[141]

---

136. Cobb, *Beyond Dialogue*, 52.

137. Cobb, "Beyond 'Pluralism.'"

138. Abe, *Zen and Western Thought*, 159.

139. John Cobb, "Whitehead and Buddhism."

140. Abe, *Zen and Western Thought*, 158.

141. Ibid., 164.

Abe cannot accept such an exception, for it means that "a trace of dualism still remains."[142]

Abe's conclusion is that the differences between Process Theology and Buddhism are "essential, fundamental, and intrinsic."[143] Therefore he asks for a complete overcoming of dualism in Process Theology, by seeing God as both an actual entity and an actual occasion. In Zen terms this should be stated as follows: "God, then, is no longer the principle of limitation, and instead, the 'no principle of limitation' is 'God.'"[144] But if God were no longer the principle of limitation, the world would no longer have its teleological drive and call towards fulfilment. Such a condition for a "different Christianity" is unacceptable even for Process Theology. Therefore Cobb's expectation that Buddhism would not deny "the existence of God as Whitehead conceives deity"[145] is not met.

There is not much left to add on assessing the "different Christianity" Cobb envisages. He ends his book *Beyond Dialogue* with the claim that the "new Christianity" that would emerge from its interaction with Buddhism is not "less Christian" from what is now Christianity in the West.[146] However, in light of what we have seen throughout this chapter, one can hardly reach the same conclusion. The "multiple transformations" that one should follow "in faithfulness to Christ" would make Orthodox Christianity a very different religion from what Stăniloae has described in chapter 3.

The traditions of Buddhism and Christianity are obviously too far apart for Cobb's project of a "different Christianity" and a "different Buddhism" to be realistic. Therefore to follow both "Jesus as Lord and Saviour" and "Gautama as guide to enlightenment" is a contradiction in terms. The same conclusion applies to his proposal for Buddhists "to have faith in Christ" and for Christians to "engage in the practice of Zen meditation as a means of realizing their Buddha-nature."[147] Against Cobb's expectation, such projects cannot remain a "promising direction for the future."[148] The Kyoto philosophers were at least devoted to their Zen tradition and did not compromise it in dialogue with Christianity, while Cobb's proposal for Buddhist-Christian

142. Ibid.

143. Abe, "Mahayana Buddhism and Whitehead," 415.

144. Ibid., 427.

145. Cobb and Griffin, *Process Theology*, 140.

146. Cobb, *Beyond Dialogue*, 149.

147. Cobb, *Transforming Christianity*, 158. Cobb argues that his proposal has found a following among Whiteheadian Christians who adopted traditional Buddhist meditation. He affirms there are "hundreds if not thousands" who are living out this double orientation "especially among Catholics in Japan" (Cobb, "Whitehead and Buddhism").

148. Cobb, "Whitehead and Buddhism."

dialogue must be rejected by both Buddhists and Christians. My analysis has shown that neither Buddhists nor Christians have reasons to assimilate elements of the other tradition in following their path to perfection.

Since Cobb's proposal for Buddhist-Christian dialogue is not faithful to either of the two traditions, one can suspect that he follows a different agenda from that of improving one with the resources of the other. Although Cobb argued for total pluralism in Buddhist-Christian dialogue, since his views are not consistent with either traditional Christianity or a traditional form of Buddhism, the best option which could represent him would probably be inclusivism. However, it would be an inclusivism that is neither Christian nor Buddhist. It would rather be a kind of Process Thought inclusivism, i.e., one that sees the many traditions as being fulfilled by Process Thought. In other words, what appears to be his real interest in dialogue is a transformation of traditional Christian theology into the likeness of Process Theology. The "different" or "new" Christianity that would be the fruit of dialogue with Buddhism is the one he found through the philosophy of Whitehead.[149] As such Cobb is advocating for a third position, different from both traditional Buddhism and Christianity, one that would in fact be a *new* religious tradition.[150] It has already taken shape as the church-like organization called Progressive Christians Uniting.

Given the methodology of my research, of assessing Buddhist-Christian dialogue through the lens of human perfection as defined in Mahayana Buddhism and in Orthodox Christianity, I can expect that Cobb would certainly reject such an approach, for he would see it as leading inevitably to exclusivism. In his view, the traditional beliefs of both religions would make dialogue impossible. Cobb says: "If Christianity is understood to be forever what it has been in the past, fixed in its own language and system of meanings, and if Buddhism thought of in the same static way, no terms of one system can be translated adequately into the terms of the other."[151] As a result,

149. In the "Postscript" to his book *Beyond Dialogue*, Cobb proves to be aware that this is a legitimate suspicion, for he rhetorically asks: "Am I not inviting other Christians to adopt the Whiteheadian philosophy in the guise of asking them to learn from Buddhism?" (*Beyond Dialogue*, 145).

150. The feeling that Cobb is starting a new tradition is acknowledged by Abe as well when he says: "Whenever Cobb emphasizes the complementarity relation between the ultimacy of 'Emptiness' and the ultimacy of 'Yahweh,' where is he taking his own stand? Is he taking the ultimacy of 'Emptiness,' the ultimacy of 'Yahweh,' or some third position as his own stand? Since it is impossible to *properly* talk about *complementarity* between two items by merely taking *one of them* as one's own position, we must assume that Cobb is consciously or unconsciously taking some *third* position as his own" (Abe, *Buddhism and Interfaith Dialogue*, 25–26).

151. Cobb, *Transforming Christianity*, 161.

Christians and Buddhists engaged in dialogue would no longer be able "to learn from one another about the fuller meaning of their own faith."[152] In the next chapter of this book I will argue that such a fatalistic stand is wrong and that despite the significant doctrinal differences that persist between the traditions of Buddhism and Christianity in their original forms, Buddhists and Christians should not give up dialogue. Cobb's failure to justify a middle ground between Christian and Buddhist traditions in the form of Process Theology indirectly points to comparative theology as a way to surpass the shortcomings of his approach and make Buddhist-Christian dialogue still possible and beneficial to both sides, with both Christians and Buddhists still remaining true to their own ideals.

152. Cobb, "Amida and Christ."

# 9

# Comparative Theology and
# Buddhist-Christian Dialogue

In the previous chapters we have seen that the Kyoto philosophers were eager to enter into dialogue with Christianity, but in the end they remained convinced there is really nothing for Buddhists to learn from Christianity. At best, dialogue can only evoke a tradition's own resources in dealing with recognized weaknesses.[1] Their position is that Buddhists have the right vision on reality while Christians should convert to the standpoint of *shunyata*, or to the "positionless position" expressed by Abe. They pleaded for the opening of Christianity to the Buddhist concept of emptiness, while Cobb used Buddhism as skilful means for the opening of traditional Christianity to Process Theology.

This situation leads us back to the perennial issue of who should actually change in Buddhist-Christian dialogue. The Kyoto philosophers have shown it is always the Christians. When it comes to "mutual" transformation, it seems only Christians have to open their minds to new perspectives. In fact, excepting the Kyoto philosophers and a few other Buddhist scholars, there is very little interest among Asian Buddhists in getting involved in interfaith dialogue at all. Paul Ingram observes that there are very few Buddhist centres that are interested in studying Christianity and concludes that Buddhist-Christian dialogue tends to be a "Christian monologue."[2] In his view, "the interesting fact is that even though Christians are usually re-

---

1. Let us remember Abe's recognition of the Buddhist weakness in its view of history and social action and his reliance on the *bodhisattva* vow as solution in section 7.6.2.

2. One notable exception is the Eastern Buddhist Society founded by D. T. Suzuki.

garded as more doctrinally intolerant than Buddhists, it is Christians who have more openly and systematically responded to the challenge of Buddhist religious experience through interfaith dialogue."[3] Abe acknowledged already in the first issue of *Buddhist-Christian Studies* that the interest for dialogue is always much greater from the Christian side, while "Buddhists are passive" and "take little initiative in seeking dialogical opportunities." Cobb consented by saying that "the initiative has been almost entirely from the Christian side."[4]

Cobb recognized as early as 1987 an increasing trend towards exclusivism and a resurgence of fundamentalism in most world religions. He expressed his disappointment at not seeing fulfilled his expectation for a "mutual appreciation and a softening of boundaries" between religions.[5] Given this situation, it seems that the only practical reason for dialogue would be that of seeking a common stand for global concerns such as the environmental crisis, world peace, poverty, crime, abuse, justice, etc.[6] For a Christian these are valid goals, justified by the fact that the Christian faith must bear fruit for *this* life as well. But although there can be no compromise in fulfilling one's duty to the world, my aim is to look for a way of grounding a real theological exchange between Buddhism and Christianity.

## 9.1 A CONTEXTUALIZED USE OF COMPARATIVE THEOLOGY

An approach which demands that the other tradition must be more open to change and reinterpretation than one's own cannot lead to a genuine interfaith dialogue, for it compromises the identity of at least one of the dialogue

---

3. Paul O. Ingram, "Interfaith Dialogue as a Source of Buddhist-Christian Creative Transformation," in Ingram and Streng, eds., *Buddhist-Christian Dialogue*, 91.

4. Abe and Cobb, "Buddhist-Christian Dialogue," 14. A similar attitude was witnessed by Winston King in his encounter with Burmese Theravada Buddhists. In his words, they manifested a "polite but total *dis*interest in Christianity." Their reason must have been "their absolute confidence that Buddhism embodied the ultimate and perfect religious truth so there was no need to be interested in or concerned about anything else in the way of religion" (King, "Buddhist-Christian Dialogue Reconsidered," 5).

5. Cobb, *Transforming Christianity*, 51.

6. Pope John Paul II argued that interfaith dialogue would help people belonging to different religious traditions "to build a more just and fraternal society" (*Redemptoris missio*, 57). A practical application developed by a Catholic theologian is Hans Küng's "Global Ethic Project," which seeks to formulate a common ground in the ethics of all religions as a way towards world peace. Some of his publications on this issue are: *Global Responsibility, Yes to a Global Ethic*, and *A Global Ethic for Global Politics and Economics*.

partners. However, this does not mean that interfaith dialogue is a blind alley or a long detour that would eventually lead to exclusivism. The time has come to argue for a different approach in interfaith dialogue, one that, paradoxically, will confirm that there is some truth worth exploring in Knitter's thought of looking to other religions in order to "find something that is vitally, maybe essentially, important for the job of understanding and living the Christian faith."[7] I find that this thought complies well with the method of comparative theology. Therefore, in this chapter, I will argue from the side of Orthodoxy that a comparativist approach to Buddhist-Christian dialogue is one that truly respects each religious tradition's uniqueness and makes dialogue beneficial for all participants, despite the doctrinal differences between them.

In the Preface to his book *Beyond Dialogue*, Cobb affirms that there are two major options in interfaith dialogue regarding the place assigned to Jesus Christ. One is to hold the position of "Christian superiority" and turn Christ "into an instrument of our arrogance," while the other is "to see Jesus as one saviour among others" and thus abandon the view of his uniqueness.[8] So far we have encountered both positions in this research. In chapter 3 I followed Stăniloae advocating for "Christian uniqueness," although his concern was not that of formulating a theology of religions, while in chapters 5 to 8 we have seen the three Kyoto philosophers and John Cobb justifying the second option, that of seeing Christ as one of the many saviours. The two positions remind us of Kiblinger's warning that a certain theology of religions is always at work in a theologian's mind. If one would attempt to formulate a theology of religions in light of the way human perfection is defined in Orthodox Christianity and in Mahayana Buddhism, it seems that "closed" inclusivism would be the most realistic option.[9] This view is not far from that of the founders of comparative theology, Clooney and Fredericks, who are "open" inclusivists. Once stated, the theology of religions which results from my inquiry of human perfection in Orthodoxy and Mahayana Buddhism, and in light of my assessment of the work of the founding fathers of Buddhist-Christian dialogue, I can now proceed to formulate an Ortho-

---

7. Knitter, *Without Buddha*, xi.

8. Cobb, *Beyond Dialogue*, viii.

9. We need to remember here Kiblinger's classification of inclusivism as "closed" and "open" inclusivism. The two categories differ by the role of other religious traditions in one's salvation (Kiblinger, "Relating Theology of Religions and Comparative Theology," in Clooney, ed., *New Comparative Theology*, 28). While for both groups Jesus Christ is the normative revelation of God, for the first group other religionists are saved despite their religion, while those of the second group admit the attainment of salvation through the following of a non-Christian religion itself.

dox Christian contribution to comparative theology. But first let me remind here of the principles of this approach and some of the ways in which I can apply it.

Comparative theology was developed by Clooney and Fredericks as primarily oriented towards a parallel examination of texts in two religious traditions.[10] As Fredericks reminds us, "comparative theology proceeds dialectically" from "critical study of another religion," which means reading its texts and engaging in personal dialogue with its adherents, to "conversation within the home tradition in which its classic texts, art, rituals, ascetic practices, etc., are reinterpreted in light of the study of the other tradition."[11] I have attempted a parallel reading and reflection on several texts of early Buddhism and of the gospels in an earlier book. A first parallel reading in this book is from the *Parable of the Pearl of Great Price* as we find it in Matthew 13:45–46 and from a famous Mahayana sutra, the *Perfection of Wisdom in 8000 lines*.[12] Both parables invite believers to abandon anything that makes them ignore the "pearl" (the Kingdom of God and the truth of emptiness, respectively). Then I have compared two parallel episodes in the life of Jesus and of the Buddha in which they expressed care for suffering fellow human beings. In one pair of texts we find the founders of the two religions meeting a woman who lost her only son (Luke 7:11–16 and *Therigatha* 10—a text in the *Khuddaka Nikaya*).[13] In a second pair of texts I compared the content of Mark 5:22–42 with the *Ekaputta Sutta* (*Udana* 2), both on a father who lost his child and went to the supreme teacher for help.[14] A more thorough comparison follows what both traditions call the 'Parable of the Prodigal Son,' as it appears in Luke 15, and in the *Lotus Sutra*, chapter 4. Both parables have a similar message on the human need for spiritual transformation, and I have compared the context, the characters, the actual story of the "prodigal son," and the teaching of the parable in the two traditions.[15]

However, as Clooney suggests, comparative theology must not be restricted to comparing texts. My intention for the next sections is to follow his invitation to extend the domain of comparative theology to "a comparison of doctrines" which "may also include evaluations, from one tradition's

10. For instance, in his *Theology after Vedanta*, Clooney performs a parallel reading of texts from the Hindu *Uttara Mimamsa Sutras* and from the *Summa Theologiae* of Thomas Aquinas.

11. Fredericks, "Introduction," in Clooney, *New Comparative Theology*, xiii–xiv

12. Valea, *The Buddha and the Christ*, 131.

13. Ibid., 167–8.

14. Ibid., 168–9.

15. Ibid., 171–9.

perspective, of two traditions' doctrines placed next to one another."[16] Although I have found many doctrinal differences between Orthodox Christianity and Mahayana Buddhism in my study of human perfection (chapters 2 and 3), this should not discourage dialogue, since, as Clooney argues, "[t]o utilize discovered similarities while overlooking obvious differences accomplishes nothing."[17] Fredericks sustains this insight and reassures us that the comparative exercise will sometimes "be a recognition of similarity, sometimes of difference."[18]

Since comparative theology is a young discipline, Clooney invites theologians to get involved and expand its use, for his work does not offer "the definitive theory" of it.[19] Given the lack of involvement of Orthodox theologians in interfaith dialogue, Fredericks' words could be taken as stimulating for them for he says that "comparative theology may lead Christians to see the challenge posed by their non-Christian neighbors not as a threat, but as a blessing in the deepest sense of the word."[20] In the following sections I will attempt to show how this "blessing" may work from an Orthodox perspective. To use Fredericks' words, I will look for ways in which "[t]he truths of non-Christian religions can stimulate Christians to look into their own religious tradition with new questions and emerge, perhaps, with new insights."[21]

We have already found some hints pointing to such an approach in the writings of Abe. For instance, in his *Zen and Western Thought* he argued that the effort to disclose differences among religious traditions can stimulate not only "mutual understanding," but also "inner development of themselves."[22] I will not follow his proposal for the renewal of Christian doctrines, for we have seen that it would lead one to unacceptable changes of the meaning of Christian doctrines (for instance his view of the *kenosis* requires the emptying of God the Father himself).[23] Instead I will follow Abe's way of dealing with criticism addressed to Buddhism. Although he acknowledged to "have been stimulated and inspired" in his understanding of Buddhism as a result of his interaction with several leading Christian

16. Clooney, *Comparative Theology*, 52.

17. Clooney, *Theology after Vedanta*, 165.

18. Fredericks, "Introduction," in Clooney, ed., *New Comparative Theology*, xi.

19. Clooney, *Comparative Theology*, 162.

20. Fredericks, *Faith among Faiths*, 9.

21. Ibid.

22. Abe, *Zen and Western Thought*, 186.

23. As Clooney emphasizes, "Comparative theological reading does not require the abandonment of any particular doctrines, nor a revisionist interpretation of the meaning of any particular doctrine" (Clooney, *Theology After Vedanta*, 189).

theologians,[24] when he faced criticism on the Buddhist position on history, ethics and social justice, he did not use Christian resources to find solutions, but instead searched for them in his own tradition and found them in the *bodhisattva*'s double orientation towards both wisdom and compassion.

Heisig, one important author who provided great help in my assessment of the Kyoto philosophers, appears to express a similar vision with that of comparative theology when he argues that the interaction of religious traditions could reveal the "blindspots" which are not apparent to one's own tradition, but obvious to "those who view it from the outside."[25] In other words, he suggests that "the Christian looks through the lens of the Buddhist faith to have a second look at Christian faith" and vice versa.[26] Such a "second look" or "looking back" at our own tradition in light of what we know from the other is what I propose as an Orthodox contribution to comparative theology. In the next sections I will address several key areas of Christian belief and practice where it could bear thoughtful results, and then look for ways in which Buddhists could use it. As we will see, there are questions we pose ourselves only after we become familiar with other traditions, with their assumptions, doctrines, stories and parables and understand how they work in their given context. Comparative theology demands that we know the other religious traditions on their own terms, but is not limited to just informing adherents of different religious traditions of how different others' beliefs are. It is rather about examining our own beliefs and practices in light of the other's, and about learning something in the process of comparing texts and doctrines. I will discuss several concrete applications of such learning, and see whether understanding the tenets of Buddhism sheds some light on one's Christian faith by disclosing things that are assumed to belong to his or her tradition, but in fact do not.

Comparative theology would thus make a Buddhist a better Buddhist and a Christian a better Christian. It is not a path towards becoming a Buddhist Christian or a Christian Buddhist. One cannot engage seriously in interfaith dialogue and give up a firm footing in a tradition, for he or she will no longer be a genuine dialogue partner of a real religious tradition. Dialogue needs firm partners who know their own tradition, follow it and are not prone to make easy compromises that would disqualify them as representatives of that tradition. In the end, a reciprocal influence between religious traditions can only be of two kinds: It can lead either to syncretism, the corruption of at least one of them, or to the sharpening of one's own,

---

24. Abe, *Buddhism and Interfaith Dialogue*, 53.
25. Heisig, *Dialogues*, 116.
26. Ibid., 116–7.

once differences and commonalities are better understood. For an Orthodox Christian comparative theology can only work by taking the second
stand. This stand would require to start from one's own tradition and devote
himself or herself to it in practice, then to examine other traditions and
understand them on their own terms, and finally to come back to one's own
tradition to share a fresh perspective as a result of the comparative study.

As Clooney suggests, a comparativist approach to interfaith dialogue
must not be reduced to acknowledging similarities between different religious traditions. It can also help us learn from differences. Although he is a
comparativist who privileges similarities, he encourages other theologians
"to highlight differences, even with respect to the same texts."[27] Following
his openness to see theologians doing "comparative theological work stub-
bornly focused on differences,"[28] and his suggestion to expand this method
to analyzing concepts and doctrines, in the next sections I will attempt to
highlight practical outcomes of Buddhist-Christian dialogue for Christians
in three fundamental aspects of practice: compassion, prayer and faith.
Clooney argues that we should not expect that comparative theology will
"produce new truths," or revolutionary changes to traditional beliefs, but
instead we should let it help us to get "fresh insights into familiar and re-
vered truths, and new ways of receiving those truths."[29] In my attempt to
find concrete ways of applying this thought, I will start with examining a
parallel of the Buddhist and the Christian view of compassion.

## 9.2 BUDDHIST AND CHRISTIAN COMPASSION. WHAT CAN CHRISTIANS LEARN FROM THE BUDDHIST VIEW OF COMPASSION?

In the second chapter of this book we have seen that the Mahayana Buddhist view of perfection is the becoming of a Buddha, one that has realized
perfection in both wisdom and compassion. The two domains are meant to
balance each other in order to avoid clinging either to *nirvana*, or to involvement in the world of suffering. As Williams reminds us, the *bodhisattva*
knows that, on the one hand, ultimately there is no enduring "being who is
helped," and on the other hand, that the impermanent "beings" experience
suffering as something very real.[30] Compassionate action for their sake not

---

27. Clooney, *Comparative Theology*, 77.
28. Ibid., 76.
29. Ibid., 112.
30. Williams, *Mahayana Buddhism*, 56.

only is possible due to the *bodhisattva*'s wisdom, but also is the way in which the *bodhisattva* avoids a selfish attachment to *nirvana*. In this section I will return to the Buddhist concept of compassion and see what outcome it can have for Buddhist-Christian dialogue from a comparativist point of view. We will see what Christians can learn about their own view of compassion once they see how compassion works in a Buddhist framework.

Buddhist compassion (*karuna*) displayed by Buddhas and *bodhisattvas* and Christian love (*agape*) displayed by Christ do not have the same meaning. Since there are no inherently existing beings *karuna* is a skilful way of getting involved in the sphere of suffering, and seeing things differently would be attachment. Etymologically compassion translates as "suffering with" someone, which is incompatible with the Buddhist view on how "beings" can be helped. A Buddha or a *bodhisattva* acts compassionately as an actor in a film. He acts *as if* beings and their suffering were real, but ultimately knowing there are no beings that have inherent existence. A film drama can depict a lot of suffering, but both actors and spectators know that ultimately nobody is hurt, nobody really dies and all actors are well. Like actors in a film, *bodhisattvas* use skilful means for getting involved in the world's "drama," but ultimately know that suffering beings and their suffering are mere momentary stages in the flux of continuous becoming. The goal to which their compassionate action must lead is to help these beings see "how things really are." The ultimate end is to find enlightenment (either here, or in a Pure Land) by following the *right teaching*, not the *right relationship*.

One of the most important exponents of Buddhist compassion in our world today is the Dalai Lama. He defines it as "*a state of mind* that is non-violent, nonharming, and nonaggresive," or in other words, as "*a mental attitude* based on the wish for others to be free of their suffering."[31] While this is a wonderful thought that could be followed by anyone, whether religious or not, I must emphasize the "mental" aspect of this definition. Since there is no constant subject of suffering and the "person" is just a constant transformation of physical and mental states, it is difficult for the Dalai Lama to define a strong link between compassion and practical engagement in the service of others. We recall here the criticism faced by Abe on the deficiency of social action in Buddhism (section 7.6.2) and Knitter's surprise of not finding in Buddhism a "theory of justice."[32] One example given by the Dalai Lama on how he personally practices compassion is that in his morning meditation he focuses on the ignorance of Chinese invaders of Tibet, and

31. Dalai Lama and Cutler, *The Art of Happiness*, 114, (emphasis mine).
32. Knitter, *Without Buddha*, 181.

mentally absorbs their vicious deeds into himself.[33] Although he acknowledges that the cultivation of Buddhist compassion should mean more than
quietly sitting and meditating and that it "should be expressed in deeds,"[34]
there is very little effective involvement of Buddhists in curing the social
diseases of our world. As a result, one can hardly find concrete forms of acting compassionately for the needy, such as hospitals, schools, orphanages,
asylums, etc., established by Buddhists.[35] One can see many meditation
centres and temples around the world, but not many Buddhist charities.[36]
This suggests that there is no real interest for social action in Buddhism,
for what really matters is liberation from illusion. Therefore the real goal
of Buddhist compassion is the perfection of one's own mind, establishing
a renewed way of seeing things, of thinking about others, not necessarily
a concrete involvement in their lives. Although the Dalai Lama defines the
Tibetan term for compassion (*nying-je*) as connoting "love, affection, kindness, gentleness, generosity of spirit, and warm-heartedness,"[37] these virtues

33. Dalai Lama, *How to Practice*, 39.

34. Dalai Lama, "The true expression of non-violence is compassion." In the same
article he says: "As a Buddhist monk, the cultivation of compassion is an important part
of my daily practice. One aspect involves merely sitting quietly in my room, meditating. That can be very good and very comfortable, but the true aim of cultivation of
compassion is to develop the courage to think of others and to do something for them.
For example, as the Dalai Lama, I have a responsibility to my people, some of whom are
living as refugees and some of whom have remained in Tibet under Chinese occupa-
tion. This responsibility means that I have to confront and deal with many problems."

35. Although the Dalai Lama says that "One important aspect of charity is the giving of material things such as food, clothing and shelter to others," we do not find much
practical initiative in this direction in the Buddhist world (Dalai Lama, *The Heart of
Compassion*, 76). Neither do we find concrete ways of following his thought of giving
"our time and energy . . . to those with mental or physical disabilities, to the homeless,
to those who are lonely, to those in prison and those who have been in prison" (Dalai
Lama, *Ancient Wisdom*, 121).

36. One important example of a Buddhist charity that would make a difference is
the Order of Interbeing (Tiep Hien) founded by Thich Nhat Hanh in 1964 during the
Vietnam War. Its aim was to help the victims of war, while after the war it contributed to
the rescuing of Vietnamese refugees (the "boat-people"). Nhat Hanh was denied return
to Vietnam and lives in southern France, where he founded a community (the Plum
Village) to promote Zen meditation. In 1982 he began to travel worldwide with two
main goals—the revival of Zen Buddhism in the contemporary world and the promo-
tion of peace. In Harvey's view, contemporary forms of "engaged Buddhism" find their
roots "in the meeting of Buddhism with Western values in the colonial era." Buddhists
(especially in Sri Lanka) "responded to Protestant Christian domination, and criticism
of Buddhist social passivity, by a Buddhist resurgence. This borrowed some of the characteristics of the Christianity it was fighting against" (Harvey, *Introduction to Buddhist
Ethics*, 112.)

37. Dalai Lama, *Ancient Wisdom*, 78.

are hardly expressed in practical terms.[38] The reason for this is that "most importantly *nying-je* denotes a *feeling* of connection with others."[39]

In his research on love and sympathy in Theravada Buddhism, Harvey Aronson reached similar conclusions. Charitable action is left to Buddhist lay people, and mostly for the sake of the *sangha* (the Buddhist community of monks), while monks practice compassion as an attitude of mind. Aronson says:

> Love is epitomized, however, by the wish, "May all beings be happy," which stops short of *necessary* commitment to action. The reason for this is perhaps that in the discourses the teachings on love and compassion involve the cultivation of these attitudes in meditation.[40]

I must emphasize here that this is not a criticism addressed to the Buddhist vision of compassion, but rather an attempt to get the proper picture of this key concept. The Buddhist view of compassion is not similar to the Christian view, and *cannot* be its equivalent. Since the framework in which compassion works in the two religious traditions is different, their views of compassion *must* be different. The comparativist approach argues for consistency between one's beliefs and practices, and is not an attempt to show which view is superior or better. In Clooney's words, the specific insight on a certain point "will not be decisive regarding which religion is truest or best."[41] One's attitude towards social issues is right or wrong only if it is consistent or not with one's own philosophical premises, not if it simply sounds better than the other from an (illusory) neutral point of view.

Now let me turn to the Christian meaning of compassion and then draw my comparativist application. As mentioned above, given its Latin origin, the word compassion means "to suffer with," or to share in the suffering of others. While in Buddhism it has primarily a mental meaning, in Christianity compassion must have a practical outcome. The difference

---

38. In discussing the method of putting oneself in the place of others in order to attain the awakening mind (*bodhicitta*), the Dalai Lama says that others' miseries are "mentally taken on ourselves" and "we generate a strong wish that all those who lack joy and happiness immediately be endowed with it." The purpose of this exercise is "to develop the power of our own mind, to strengthen the force of compassion" (Dalai Lama, *Activating Bodhicitta*, 29. On the same theme see Dalai Lama, *Kindness, Clarity, and Insight*, 33–38.

39. Dalai Lama, *Ancient Wisdom*, 78–79 (emphasis mine). Lama Thubten Yeshe reiterates this view arguing that "true love does not depend on physical expression" for it is "a feeling deep within you" (Yeshe, *Silent Mind*, 24).

40. Aronson, *Love and Sympathy*, 64.

41. Clooney, *Comparative Theology*, 112.

is perfectly represented by the founders of the two religions. While the Buddha expressed his compassion through the teachings he gave to his followers in order to help them escape suffering and rebirth, Jesus embodied the Christian ideal of compassion by the way he practically cared for his neighbors. Jesus truly shared in human suffering, for he was born in a world of suffering, poverty and injustice, and presented to us an embodied life of compassion, up to the point of giving up his own life on the cross for the sake of humankind. This different version of compassion in Christianity originates in the affirmation of human beings as real subjects in relationship with a permanent God. Compassion and love (*agape*) for one's neighbour are interchangeable notions and require practical engagement, by following the example of Christ.

Stăniloae sees an indissoluble connection between the relationship with God and that with other human beings. Neither could work properly without the other. In his words, "the disappearance of the one entails the disappearance of the other."[42] Unlike Buddhist *karuna*, Christian *agape* leads to a deep attachment to neighbours, as there is no other way of sanctification and growth into perfection. Stăniloae says that "God wants us to respond not only to others' need of salvation" (which would be the Buddhist position), but "also to their earthly needs."[43] He argues that Christ commanded his followers to live a compassionate life when he said that eternal life in communion with him "will depend upon the help we have given to the sick, hungry, naked, and persecuted (Matthew 25: 32–46), for by helping them, we helped him."[44] Salvation itself, in his view, depends on living a compassionate life, for "God humbles himself and honours us, making our salvation dependent on our efforts to find him in those who suffer."[45] As a result, Christian compassion leads to social action and the pursuit of social justice. It is a different attitude from what Knitter means by not taking sides against anyone,[46] and from Nhat Hanh's demand that one should not take sides, "not even with the poor."[47]

Following Buddhist teaching, Knitter argues that when facing injustice and poverty, Buddhist compassion asks us to accept reality "as fully as we can," to "surrender to what is going on," for "we don't try to control it; indeed,

42. Stăniloae, "The Faces of Our Fellow Human Beings," 33.

43. Stăniloae, *Studii de Teologie Dogmatică Ortodoxă*, 210.

44. Ibid., 211.

45. Ibid.

46. Knitter argues that considering some people evil means to "take sides against them" and this would "cut off connectedness—and the possibility of understanding and feeling compassion for them" (*Without Buddha*, 188).

47. Nhat Hanh, *Living Buddha*, 79.

we embrace it."[48] Such an attitude is very different from the Christian ideal of compassion and social action. As we have seen in chapter 3, deification is achieved in relationship with God and is certified by a renewed relationship with one's neighbours. As Stăniloae boldly says, "without responding to the call of others, one cannot be truly human."[49] Jesus Christ, the image of Christian perfection, did take sides and made very harsh judgements on the religious hypocrites of his day, the Pharisees. He did not "embrace" their reality, but condemned it in very un-"compassionate" terms. Following his example, Christians need to take sides against hypocrisy and social injustice in practical compassionate ways. They need to change the world from its present misery, not embrace it as it is.

When we look back at how compassion works in Buddhism and Christianity we can start making comparativist applications by answering the following questions: How can it be that Christians so often practice a Buddhist view of compassion, as a mental benevolence towards those in suffering, which lacks practical involvement? Why have Christians forgotten to take sides against the suffering of their neighbour? Why are they content with wishing well to those who suffer, but reluctant to do something practical for them, something that may require time, money and the loss of comfort? These are important insights for all Christian denominations, for all Christians face the threat of growing cool towards the needs of our world. They follow as application to Buddhist-Christian dialogue, for one cannot follow a Buddhist pattern while pretending Christian belonging. What in Buddhism works well in the name of non-attachment, in Orthodox Christianity is wrong in light of its ideal of perfection.

## 9.3 A COMPARATIVIST VIEW ON PRAYER IN BUDDHISM AND CHRISTIANITY. THE *JESUS PRAYER* IN ORTHODOX CHRISTIANITY AND THE *NEMBUTSU* IN SHIN BUDDHISM

Prayer in Buddhism is a difficult topic to deal with, for there is no ultimate God to pray to. Unlike theists who pray to God, Buddhists train their mind through meditation in order to realize how things really are. For this section I have chosen to comment on a theme of special relevance for Orthodox Christians, that of the *Jesus Prayer*,[50] as I found it interpreted in an impor-

48. Knitter, *Without Buddha*, 161.

49. Stăniloae, *Chipul Nemuritor al lui Dumnezeu*, vol. 1, 100.

50. The *Jesus Prayer* is a short prayer developed by the Orthodox tradition of *hesychasm* which says: "Lord Jesus Christ, Son of God, have mercy on me, a sinner."

tant book on Buddhist-Christian dialogue on prayer and meditation. The book itself has a very telling name: *Christians Talk about Buddhist Meditation, Buddhists Talk About Christian Prayer*.[51] In his article "Jesus Prayer and the Nembutsu,"[52] Taitetsu Unno (a Shin Buddhist) finds an important point of contact between Shin Buddhists and Orthodox Christians in the use of the *nembutsu* and the *Jesus Prayer*. In order to assess this claim we need to locate the two practices in their original doctrinal context.

In the second chapter of this book we have seen that Pure Land Buddhism started as an easier way towards Buddhahood, open to everyone, monastic and lay person alike. Shinran taught that we live in an age of depravity (*mappo*) in which the force of delusion is so great that one cannot earn enlightenment by his or her own resources (*jiriki*). One can be enlightened only by resorting to the Other Power (*tariki*) of Amida's grace, which is made available by calling his name (the practice of the *nembutsu*). Since the *Jesus Prayer* is also about repeating a formula (the invocation of Jesus), Unno concludes that the two practices are similar ways by which Other Power is working in us. As a confirmation of his view, he quotes bishop Kallistos Ware saying that the goal of the *Jesus Prayer* is to "Become what you are,"[53] which for Unno translates as "discovering grace that works within each person."[54] But while for Unno to "become what you are" means the discovery of one's innate Buddha-nature, or *shunyata*,[55] Ware does not back such an import into Christian theology. In the article quoted by Unno, Ware speaks of becoming "what you already are *potentially* and secretly, by virtue of your creation according to the divine image and your re-creation in Baptism."[56] For the English Orthodox bishop the *Jesus Prayer* points to a relationship, not to discovering an essence, for the "divine image" is given by God for the purpose of having a relationship with him, and baptism in Orthodoxy is the first step towards restoring this relationship. He dispels any doubt about this relational aspect of the *Jesus Prayer* by saying that its final objective "may aptly be described by the Patristic term *theosis*, 'deification,'"[57]

---

51. Gross and Muck, *Christians Talk about Buddhist Meditation*.

52. Taitetsu Unno, "Jesus Prayer and the Nembutsu," in Gross and Muck, ed., *Christians Talk about Buddhist Meditation*, 109–17.

53. Ibid., 112. See also Ware, "The Power of the Name," 186.

54. Unno, "Jesus Prayer and the Nembutsu," 112.

55. While Unno does not make this correlation in the immediate context, he speaks of the transformation brought by the Buddhist point of view "that sees impermanence, flux, and change as elemental and all phenomenal reality as devoid or empty of enduring essence (*sunyata*)" (ibid., 115).

56. Kallistos Ware, "The Power of the Name," 186, emphasis mine.

57. Ibid., 199.

which brings us back to the theology of Stăniloae. In agreement with Ware, the Romanian theologian affirms that the *Jesus Prayer* points to "realizing the presence of Jesus, of our own sinfulness and our need for Jesus' mercy."[58] Since Unno fails to realize the Orthodox perspective on its own terms, it is no surprise that he cannot understand why an Orthodox anthology on the *Jesus Prayer* fosters dualism between good and evil, and the need to fight against evil.[59] He admits that such a view "presents a sharp contrast to Shinran."[60] However, it is in no contrast to the spirit of Orthodoxy. Therefore the equivalence found by Unno between the *Jesus Prayer* and the *nembutsu* is highly questionable.

Another Romanian Orthodox theologian who examines the parallel between the *Jesus Prayer* and the *nembutsu* is Nicolae Achimescu in his book *Budism și Creștinism* [*Buddhism and Christianity*]. He expresses his disagreement with Enomiya-Lassalle's attempt to use *Zazen* in Christian meditation, and as preparation for those who are engaged in the practice of the *Jesus Prayer*.[61] He calls this attempt an "exaggeration"[62] and warns that while in Zen one needs to transcend the duality between the practitioner and the object of his or her concentration, in the practice of the *Jesus Prayer* Christ the Lord remains the constant reference point.[63] The aim of practicing the *Jesus Prayer* is a deeper personal relationship with Christ and therefore the Orthodox "does not follow a process of internalization in order to give up self-consciousness, but seeks to discover Christ inside him, whom he has already received by the grace of Baptism."[64] In other words, while in Zen one seeks union with *shunyata*, the Orthodox seeks to be united with the personal Christ, by his grace. In order to achieve the desired union, the Zen practitioner contemplates emptiness, while the Orthodox contemplates the living God, or more precisely, what God allows one to be known of him.[65]

Achimescu reminds us that inner purification in Orthodox practice is achieved in harmony between own effort and the divine grace bestowed upon the believer by Christ.[66] In saying the *Jesus Prayer* the Orthodox

---

58. Stăniloae, *Ascetică și Mistică Creștină*, 237.

59. Unno, "Jesus Prayer and the Nembutsu," 115. The anthology he refers to is Chariton of Valamo, *The Art of Prayer*.

60. Unno, "Jesus Prayer and the Nembutsu," 115.

61. Achimescu, *Budism și Creștinism*, 292–303.

62. Ibid., 293.

63. Ibid., 296.

64. Ibid., 275–6.

65. Ibid., 300.

66. Ibid., 299.

believer addresses Christ in order to ask for his mercy and forgiveness of sins.[67] It demands full cooperation of the believer with Christ, who does not annul one's own contribution and free will, while for Shinran the recitation of the *nembutsu* is a complete work of the Amida Buddha. Otherwise it could not be seen as the complete Other Power of Amida acting in the believer.[68] Therefore Achimescu questions the very character of the *nembutsu* as prayer in the proper sense of the word, as a true conversation between the human and the divine.

Given the uneasy task of building bridges between Buddhism and Christianity in the area of prayer and meditation, it seems that Mahinda Deegalle (a Theravada Buddhist) is right when he says that "'Prayer' is not a traditional Buddhist term."[69] He argues that the usual Buddhist prayers, such as meal prayers, should be taken as "contemplative practices" rather than as addressing a god, a *bodhisattva* or a Buddha.[70] Although even Zen Buddhists use a "thank you for the lovely meal" thanksgiving formula similar to the Christian custom, it does not mean that there is a permanent "you" to whom it is addressed.[71] In Deegalle's view, the thanksgiving rather has the role of reminding "of one's good intentions and asserts the wish that everyone may reach Buddhahood."[72] In order to be consistent with the Buddhist view of Ultimate Reality, one must thus see Buddhist prayers as skilful means which foster the detachment from illusion of the one who is "praying." As Rita Gross justly argues, although Buddhists pray for the same things as Christians do, as for instance for the "renewal of negative fortunes, health, wealth, and well-being in general," since there are no inherently existing beings, the meaning of such prayers is that of "making aspirations and wishes, in which no one is addressed."[73] Although this is hard to grasp by Christians, it is the way in which skilful means do work. Gross affirms that the role of very important prayers in Mahayana Buddhism, such as the formula of The Four Immeasurables,[74] or the dedication of merits at the end

67. Ibid., 288–9.

68. Ibid., 287

69. Mahinda Deegalle, "Buddhist Prayer? A Reflection," in Gross and Muck, ed., *Christians Talk about Buddhist Meditation*, 118.

70. Ibid., 126.

71. Ibid., 127.

72. Ibid.

73. Rita Gross, "Meditation and Prayer: A Comparative Inquiry," in Gross and Muck, ed., *Christians Talk about Buddhist Meditation*, 91–92.

74. The Four Immeasurables formula is an aspirational prayer uttered by the *bodhisattva* which says: "May all sentient beings have happiness and its causes, May all sentient beings be free of suffering and its causes,

of a ceremony, is to have an effect "on the one who *says or thinks them*," for ultimately "there is no being who could hear or react."[75] We meet here the same logic seen in the meaning of compassion, for saying the Four Immeasurables has the effect of transforming the one who prays into "a person who can actually manifest them."[76] This means transforming his or her mind towards seeing things as they really are. Buddhist prayer and compassion have the same role, to train one's mind, not to develop a relationship.

Terry Muck, one of the editors of *Christians Talk about Buddhist Meditation, Buddhists Talk About Christian Prayer*, affirms that the assignment given to the contributors to this book was to explore in what ways Buddhists and Christians could learn from the spiritual practices of the other tradition.[77] Rita Gross, the other editor of this book, observed that Christians were much more open to learning from Buddhist meditation, while most Buddhists proved to be more conservative and "simply couldn't find anything to say" about Christian prayer.[78] The Buddhists who did contribute barely made reference to Christian prayer.[79] Given their different doctrinal foundations, Christian prayer for a Buddhist, or Buddhist meditation for a Christian could hardly work. On the one hand, as Gross argues, prayer in Buddhism is a "'skilful method,' something designed to propel the practitioner into recognition of reality as quickly as possible."[80] This reality is obviously *shunyata*, not the personal God. On the other hand, in Christianity the practice of prayer is part of one's relationship with God, so a Christian needs to pray for experiencing this relationship, and for acknowledging his or her dependence on God. Since one must reject syncretistic attempts to reconcile Christian prayer and Buddhist meditation, let us now see how we can apply the approach of comparative theology and learn from differences.

A definition of prayer given by the Dalai Lama would probably be very challenging at this point. Although he could have defined prayer as a way of relating to the many *bodhisattvas* and Buddhas of Tibetan Buddhism, he calls prayer "a simple daily reminder of your deeply held principles and

---

May all sentient beings never be separated from bliss without suffering, May all sentient beings be in equanimity, free of bias, attachment and anger" (Buddha, The Four Immeasurables).

75. Gross, "Meditation and Prayer," 95.

76. Ibid.

77. Terry C. Muck, "Introduction," in Gross and Muck, eds., *Christians Talk about Buddhist Meditation*, 9.

78. Rita M. Gross, "Conclusion," in Gross and Muck, eds., *Christians Talk about Buddhist Meditation*, 150.

79. Ibid.

80. Gross, "Meditation and Prayer: A Comparative Inquiry," 98.

convictions."[81] This definition can easily trigger a series of comparativist applications, for it can work well in a Buddhist context, but not for a Christian. Christians can (and should) repeat their convictions, as for instance in the form of the Apostles' Creed, but they must be aware that such formulas should not replace personal prayer. Nor should prayer be replaced by getting *information about* God, for prayer is about staying in personal communion with him. Therefore several comparativist applications can be found by answering questions such as: Have Christians reduced prayer to a "reminder" of "principles and convictions"? In other words, is it a monologue or a dialogue? Has prayer become a ritual of repetitive formulas that helps Christians ease their conscience, or does it really address God, leading to the confession of sins and to changing their life following the example of Jesus? Are Orthodox Christians facing the possibility of transforming the *Jesus Prayer* into a monologue in their individual practice? Have Evangelical Christians transformed the formula "In Jesus' name we pray" into a magic key which can open any lock in heaven, similar to the use of the *nembutsu* for getting the grace of Amida, while ignoring what would be obvious to do with the resources they already have at hand?[82] Such questions should challenge Christians to re-evaluate their view and use of prayer, as well as to correct syncretistic views they have already accepted.

## 9.4 COMPARATIVE THEOLOGY AND FAITH IN BUDDHISM AND CHRISTIANITY

As we have seen in chapter 2, in early Buddhism faith expresses trust in the *dharma*, in the fact that by following the Noble Eightfold Path one would eventually reach *nirvana*. As indicated in the oldest Buddhist scriptures, to have faith in the effectiveness of the Buddhist path is the first condition for practice.[83] The act of taking refuge in the Buddha has the same meaning. According to Williams, "in taking refuge in the Buddha one takes refuge in just this *dharmakaya*, those qualities which the Buddha's doctrine sets forth and teaches."[84] From the perspective of Zen Buddhism, Nhat Hanh explains

81. Dalai Lama, *The Art of Happiness*, 298.

82. This is not an invitation to replace prayer with works, but to avoid becoming superficial and hypocritical when the things we pray for are already at hand, as for instance in the case of praying for the needs of our neighbour. If we already have the necessary resources it is unconceivable to just pray "in Jesus' name" that this neighbour may get help from elsewhere.

83. *Sutta Nipata* 182–3, in Müller, trans., *The Sacred Books of the East*, 30.

84. Williams, *Mahayana Buddhism*, 175.

it as taking refuge "in the Buddha within myself,"[85] which is one's innate Buddha-nature. In his words,

> When we take refuge in the Buddha, we express trust in our capacity to walk in the direction of beauty, truth and deep understanding, based on our experience of the efficacy of the practice. When we take refuge in the Dharma, we enter the path of transformation, the path to end suffering. When we take refuge in the Sangha, we focus in our energies of building up a community that dwells in mindfulness, harmony and peace.[86]

As I concluded in chapter 3, perfection as deification is a very different view from the perfection of wisdom and compassion stated in Mahayana Buddhism. In contrast to the Buddhist view, in Orthodox Christianity human perfection is represented by the human Jesus and his relationship with God, and therefore Christian faith (Greek *pistis*) can be defined only in the context of relationships. Stăniloae argues that God's love awaits the response of our love, the opening of our person towards communion with him as "an agreement between two freedoms."[87] Christian faith is the act of opening believers towards God and his redemptive initiative in Christ. It is the personal response of human beings to follow Christ and be regenerated by him. In other words, Christian faith is a matter of trust in God, as reliance on a Person. Given the different orientation of faith in Buddhism and Christianity, for a Buddhist to express faith in a *bodhisattva* or a Buddha in the Christian sense would represent clinging to false concepts, which is a form of delusion.[88] As Abe justly emphasizes from a Zen Buddhist perspective, in the theistic religions "*will* is included on the side of both man and God as the essential factor of their relationship" and thus faith is expressed as the human will responding to the will of God, while "the Self-Awakening of *Dharma* in Buddhism is completely free from will and intellectualization, whether human or divine."[89] In other words, in Christianity faith is a way of knowing God and a commitment to follow him, while in Buddhism it is an interior power meant to enable one to attain a correct way of seeing reality.

85. Nhat Hanh, *Going Home*, 111.

86. Nhat Hanh, *The Heart of the Buddha's Teaching*, 162.

87. Stăniloae, *Teologia Dogmatică Ortodoxă*, vol. 2, 209.

88. Cobb criticizes the traditional view of Christian faith for containing the "element of clinging" to the personal and *permanent* God, and asserts that "Christians have much to gain" from the Buddhist view of faith in the sense of adopting a "nondual thinking about God" (Cobb, "Faith," 40–41). However, in light of my assessment of Cobb's thought in chapter 7 we cannot follow this proposal, for his "nondual thinking about God" can work only in the framework of Process Theology.

89. Abe, *Buddhism and Interfaith Dialogue*, 189.

The only exception to this view of faith in Buddhism seems to be that of Pure Land Buddhism, for it requires faith (*shinjin*) in the Amida Buddha, who saves all who call his name. But since Amida is not a self-existent deity, does not create the universe and does not uphold it in existence, one's relationship with him cannot be the equivalent of Christian faith. Malcolm Eckel noticed the reluctance of Shin Buddhists to translate *shinjin* as "faith." While translating Pure Land scriptures into English at Harvard University, they argued that "*shinjin* should be left untranslated to avoid confusion with the Christian concept of faith" for *shinjin* should be seen as "the human reflection of the mind of Amida Buddha."[90] A better Japanese equivalent for Christian faith would be the Shinto term *shinko* which, according to Kenneth Lee, "indicates the mind to have faith in a certain God or gods."[91] The Buddhist term *shinjin* cannot imply a dichotomous relationship as in theism, for this would be "contrary to the central Buddhist teaching of emptiness and nonduality."[92] As Lee explains, *shinjin* involves "the awakening of the inherent Buddha-mind in beings by Buddha's activity" which dissolves the duality between Amida's mind and the practitioner's mind.[93] In the conclusion of his article "Faith in the Buddhist Tradition," Robert Traer says that "faith is central to the Buddhist tradition, as *an attitude of the mind*."[94] This conclusion is consistent with my findings in the previous sections. Not only are Buddhist compassion and prayer to be seen as skilful means towards enlightenment, but faith as well.[95] Therefore a Christian could hardly follow Paul Ingram's suggestion that Pure Land teachings "provide Christians with an experiential entry point for 'passing over' into Buddhist experience."[96]

90. Eckel, "Perspectives on the Buddhist-Christian Dialogue," 48.

91. Lee, "Comparative Analysis of Shinran's *Shinjin* and Calvin's Faith," 174. Relevant here is that in the Japanese translation of the Bible we find the word 'faith' translated as *shinko*.

92. Ibid.,

93. Ibid., 175. In traditional Christianity to awaken to our true nature would mean to realize we are all sinners. Unlike in Buddhism, human beings do not have a common nature with that of God, or eons of time to achieve salvation.

94. Traer, "Faith in the Buddhist Tradition," 109, emphasis mine. This aspect is emphasized by Buddhadasa, who argues that faith "does in fact imply a concentrated mind" (Buddhadasa Indapanno, *Christianity and Buddhism*, 40).

95. Abe became well aware of the difference between Christian and Buddhist faith. He realized that "The faith in Jesus Christ is inseparably connected to the realization of man's sinfulness." Therefore he concluded that for a Christian "the Zen expression, "Encountering a Buddha, kill the Buddha. Only thus does one attain liberation,' may sound blasphemous" (Masao Abe, "Self-Awakening and Faith—Zen and Christianity," in Griffiths, ed., *Christianity through Non-Christian Eyes*, 175. Abe is right. Christians cannot dissolve God into emptiness, or else Christian faith loses its meaning.

96. Ingram, "Faith as Knowledge in the Teaching of Shinran Shonin and Martin

Being aware of the meaning of faith in Buddhism and Christianity, I can draw several applications for Christians on the topic of faith in the form of the following rhetorical questions: Has our faith become a way of awakening to and knowing an innate hidden nature? Have we become "islands unto ourselves," relying on our inner potential, as the Buddha asked his disciples,[97] instead of relying on Christ as our image and source of perfection? Do we see Christ just as a symbol to stimulate faith in ourselves and establish a peaceful state of mind? Given the way faith works in Buddhism and Christianity, Christians should reconsider the focus of their trust, and practice a faith that opens them towards God and other people, instead of one that isolates and limits them to the cultivation of inner strength.

## 9.5 COMPARATIVE THEOLOGY FOR BUDDHISTS

In the preceding sections we have seen three comparativist applications that Christians should consider as arising from Buddhist-Christian dialogue. A similar approach can be used by Buddhists. They too can look back at their own tradition after knowing the way things really are in Christianity and see their traditional beliefs in new ways. In section 7.6.2 we have seen Abe facing criticism for the deficiency of social action in Buddhism and finding a *Buddhist* solution in the *bodhisattva's* perfection in both wisdom and compassion. His approach can be taken as a comparativist application done by a Buddhist. Several other such applications will be proposed in this section, with the reservation that they should be taken as provisional thoughts, as only Buddhists themselves are entitled to perform a comparativist critique of their own tradition.

The insights we have seen in the last three sections can be considered by Buddhists as well, but obviously from the opposite direction. For instance, the comparativist application to prayer for a Theravada Buddhist would consist in remembering that prayer is not about relating to some divine being, but skilful means for dealing with greed. With the exception of Pure Land Buddhism, faith should not seek the help of *bodhisattvas* and Buddhas, but be kept as skilful means for detaching oneself from clinging to self-power. As for compassion, even if one is involved in practical social works, he or she should be aware that the "beings" that are out there to be helped are mere instances of a flux of empty *dharmas*, and therefore compassionate deeds should not develop personal attachments. Otherwise one would run into the Christian view of prayer, faith and compassion, and in

---

Luther," 33.

97. *Mahaparinibbana sutta*, in Walshe, *The Long Discourses*, 245.

the whole personalism and entanglement in relationships that the Christian faith requires.

Other important comparativist applications for both Buddhists and Christians would probably arise from an examination of prayer and meditation in the monastic traditions of Buddhism and Christianity.[98] However, the use of comparative theology by monks in dialogue is a topic beyond the reach of this book and should be left to monastics themselves.[99] I would only note here the affirmation of the Orthodox theologian John Garvey that the most promising contact point between the two religious traditions could be found by Buddhist and Christian monks, who in prayer and meditation "encounter the false moves the mind makes in the effort to protect the ego."[100] In his view, it is fascinating to find "resemblance between the Buddhist sense of mindfulness and the various ways of the Orthodox *Philokalia* addresses the idea of guarding the heart" as they both "caution against allowing either aversion or attraction to mislead us."[101] However, in order to be consistent with the method of comparative theology, this kind of dialogue should be limited to matters of monastic practices, such as obedience to rule, celibacy, ascetical life, and would not encourage the reciprocal appropriation of ends (as for instance touching a common Ultimate Reality). In other words, it would concern the use of similar means to reach different goals, not a uniformization of doctrine.

An important comparativist application to be considered by Buddhists would concern the meaning of language. Since there is no enduring "I" or

98. A monastic Buddhist-Christian dialogue in Europe started in 1979 at the Benedictine monastery in St. Ottilien, Germany (see Thomas Josef Götz, OSB, "Catholic Monk, Buddhist Monk: The Monastic Interreligious Dialogue with Japanese Zen," in May, ed., *Converging Ways?*, 15–16.

99. An important representative of Buddhist-Christian dialogue between monks is the Trappist monk Thomas Merton (1915–1968), a good friend of D.T. Suzuki, Nhat Hanh and the Dalai Lama. His views of interfaith dialogue could make the object of an entire new research. In a letter to D.T. Suzuki he wrote: "It seems to me that Zen is the very atmosphere of the Gospels, and the Gospels are bursting with it. It is the proper climate for any monk, no matter what kind of monk he may be" (Shannon, *The Hidden Ground of Love*, 561). For a comparison of monastic traditions in Buddhism and Christianity see Henry and Swearer, *For the Sake of the World*. Another good resource for such inquiry would be the dialogue initiated at the Abbey of Gethsemani, Kentucky. See Mitchell and Wiseman, *The Gethsemani Encounter*. I would also mention that a challenging comparativist project would be to examine Küng's affirmation that "*monasticism is the foundation of Buddhism, not of Christianity*" and thus is "more central and essential to Buddhism than to Christianity" (Küng, *Christianity and World Religions*, 347).

100. Garvey, *Seeds of the Word*, 121.

101. Ibid., 121–2.

"you" as a continuous subject to be identified as a "person" in the Christian sense, one must be careful with the use of personalist language in order to avoid attachments to false views. Since humans are not subjects held in existence by a permanent God, language of personal identity must be seen as a misleading convenience. In the words of Williams, language of beings is a "merely practical convenience that can easily mislead and engender attachment and consequential suffering."[102] A precise use of language by Theravada Buddhists would require that instead of persons they should name numerous physical and psychological *dharmas* with no permanent status and in constant interaction and transformation, or at least to keep in mind that this would be the proper way of speaking of persons. Given the difficulty of always having to keep in mind that ultimately there are no "persons," a personalistic language as the following, used by Abe, could lead one away from realizing "how things really are." He says:

> [w]e are bound by our own *karma* which shares in and is in-separably linked to *karma* operating in the universe but, on the other hand, we, as beings with self-consciousness and free will, have the opportunity to be liberated from *karma* through our own free act performed by our personal choice.[103]

We should notice how often Abe uses here the personal pronouns "we" and "our," which must not be understood as referring to a permanent subject and, as such, significantly complicate one's proper understanding of Abe's exhortations.

These are just several suggestions of what Buddhists could gain from a comparativist approach to Buddhist-Christian dialogue. As said above, they should be assessed and rephrased by Buddhists themselves. What is of utmost importance is to seek faithfulness to one's own tradition, and not "adaptations" that could corrupt it.

## 9.6 COMPARATIVE THEOLOGY AND HINDU-CHRISTIAN DIALOGUE

Although the task of this book is to draw attention to comparative theology as a proper approach to Buddhist-Christian dialogue, it must be remembered

---

102. Williams, *Buddhist Thought,* 120. In the words of Ward, "The story of personal rebirth is a myth for those who cannot achieve the sophisticated understanding of the no-self theory" (*Religion and Human Nature,* 89).

103. Abe, *Zen and Western Thought,* 214.

that it works in other pairings of interfaith dialogue as well.[104] In this section I will briefly propose ways of extending its use to a comparison of themes in Hindu-Christian dialogue, being obviously aware that the pioneer and leading theologian to formulate a comparativist approach to this area of interfaith dialogue is Clooney.[105] Since I focused on a comparison of doctrines, rather than of texts, I would draw attention to the resources comparative theology can provide for examining a parallel of the theme of the incarnation of the divine in Christianity and theistic Hinduism. While in Christianity we speak of the unique incarnation of God the Son in Jesus Christ, the Hindu god Vishnu is said to have ten incarnations (*avatars*), of which nine have occurred already and one is still to come. Since only Christianity and Vaishnava Hinduism hold this concept of the divine incarnation, exploring a parallel of their views would lead to interesting comparativist applications.

The most important aspect of the *avatars'* mission, as it appears in the classic texts,[106] is that they came to restore the cosmic order which was perturbed usually by a demon who gained power over the gods, by means of performing austerities. As a result, the way by which the *avatar* fulfils his role is by performing a clever trick which takes the demon by surprise and defeats him. For instance, one of these *avatars* (the ninth) is the Buddha. According to the Hindu version his mission was to deceive the demons by preaching false views against the Brahmanic sacrificial system. As soon as the demons abandoned the Vedas (by becoming Buddhists) they were weak enough to be killed by the gods. Surprisingly, one can find parallels to such a view of saving humankind in Christianity as well. Some early Church Fathers ascribed to Jesus the role of a trickster-like figure who deceived the devil in order to liberate humankind from its captivity.[107] However, in light of the way in which salvation through Christ has been defined by Stăniloae in chapter 3, such views should be reconsidered.

104. A good overview of sources for a study of other areas of interfaith dialogue is Clooney, "Comparative Theology."

105. Let me recall here Clooney's work of comparing Hindu and Christian texts in his books *Theology after Vedanta* and *Hindu God, Christian God*. Other good resources for a comparativist study of Hindu-Christian dialogue would be Vempeny, *Krishna and Christ*; and Jaswant Raj, *Grace in the Saiva Siddhantham and in St. Paul*.

106. The main Hindu texts in which we find this theme are the *Puranas* and the great Hindu epics—the *Ramayana* and the *Mahabharata*.

107. One of them is Gregory of Nyssa. He says that the "Deity was hidden under the veil of our nature, that so, as with ravenous fish, the hook of the Deity might be gulped down (by the Devil) along with the bait of flesh, and thus, life being introduced into the house of death, and light shining in darkness, that which is diametrically opposed to light and life might vanish" (Gregory of Nyssa, *The Great Catechism*, 24).

A whole new book could probably be written exploring a parallel between the divine incarnation in Christianity and in Hinduism from a comparativist perspective. Several questions that may yield comparativist applications would be the following: Could one consider that Jesus fulfilled the role of a Hindu *avatar*? Did the *avatars* of Vishnu have a similar goal to that of Jesus? What would the Christian doctrine of the *kenosis* tell us in light of the Hindu concept of the *avatar*? To what extent can we speak in the case of the Hindu *avatars* of the union of the two natures in a Chalcedonian way? Should we rather see the Hindu *avatars* as skilful means to teach one a lesson for his or her own spiritual growth? What connection is there between the *avatar* and the Docetic view of Christ? How, whom and why does the divine incarnation save?[108] Of what importance is the historicity of the divine incarnation? How much does it matter whether the *avatars* and Jesus have a historical basis or not? The result of pursuing a comparativist approach to these issues would probably lead to a challenging outcome for both Christians and Hindus.

## 9.7 CONCLUSION. COMPARATIVE THEOLOGY AS A CONSTRUCTIVE APPROACH IN INTERFAITH DIALOGUE

Following Clooney, we have seen that the approach of comparative theology can be used for investigating both similarities and dissimilarities between religions. For instance, in another important pairing in interfaith dialogue, that of Islam and Christianity, the major dissimilarities are related to the nature of God, as mono-personal vs. tri-personal, and to the role of Jesus, as prophet vs. Son of God and saviour. Dialogue cannot reach a middle point on these issues, for a compromise would ruin both traditions. Rather, as a comparativist approach proposes, we could better understand our own tradition in light of the reasons the other tradition has for rejecting ours. In the case of Muslim-Christian dialogue a Christian should learn the reasons why the view of God as tri-personal is vehemently rejected by Muslims by undertaking an in-depth study of the Muslim view of the oneness of God (the doctrine of *tawhid*), and only then come back to the doctrine of the Trinity and reaffirm it in light of what it is not. The reciprocal application for Muslims would be to require an in-depth investigation of the Christian view

---

108. The most striking difference from Hindu *avatars* regards Jesus' death. As Fredericks observes, "[t]he difference between an *avatar*, as Hindus say, and the incarnation, as Christians say, is nowhere more apparent than when Hindus learn about the death of Jesus on the cross" (Fredericks, *Faith among Faiths*, 146).

of the Trinity, rather than its simple rejection as polytheism, and then to reaffirm the Muslim view of *tawhid*. The discussion of the role of Jesus in the two religions would then naturally follow from that on the nature of God.[109]

As I have shown, comparative theology is not a method of reaching superficial agreements or of softening differences, but of examining religious traditions on their own terms and of learning from differences. An Orthodox contribution to comparative theology would thus emphasize its use as a way of better treasuring one's own tradition after having learned those of others or, in other words, as a way of better understanding one's own tradition by learning what it is not. As Abe correctly suggests, "an attempt to disclose the differences, if properly and relevantly done, promotes and stimulates mutual understanding and inspires both religions to seek further inner development of themselves."[110] An Orthodox comparativist approach to interfaith dialogue would have exactly this role of providing a better understanding of one's own tradition when considered in the light of the other. When we look back on ourselves through someone else's eyes, we may better understand and even correct our own tradition, while using internal resources for doing the necessary corrections.

In this chapter I have suggested several issues on which Christians should reflect in light of contemporary debates in Buddhist-Christian dialogue. As a result of knowing Buddhism on its own terms, comparative theology draws attention to the need of clarifying the practices of compassion, prayer, and faith. It reminds Christians that they cannot carry out a Buddhist view of compassion, prayer and faith, for the doctrinal context in which these practices are defined makes the interchange hardly possible. Christian compassion requires concrete involvement in the needs of our suffering world, not just teaching the right doctrines and wishing well to those who suffer. The Orthodox *Jesus Prayer* is not exclusive "Other Power" at work in the believer towards realizing his or her true nature, but a means for deepening a personal relationship with Christ through his grace. Christian prayer cannot be the equivalent of reciting the *nembutsu*, for Christians need to relate to a permanent self-existing God in a personal way. Neither can faith become a way of evoking Own Power in disguise, a way of establishing a peaceful state of mind, or of trusting inner resources, instead of trusting God. Although I suggested some Buddhist applications concerning compassion, prayer and faith and the proper use of language, it is expected that Buddhists themselves would clarify these aspects. Despite the opposing

109. Some good resources for applying a comparativist approach to dialogue between the three great monotheistic religions would be Burrell, *Knowing the Unknowable God.*

110. Abe, "Self-Awakening and Faith—Zen and Christianity," 172.

views of the two religious traditions in matters of human perfection, and despite standing back to back on most fundamental doctrines—an opposition mirrored even in their places of worship, with the Orthodox church entered from the West and a Buddhist temple from the East—their dialogue is still fruitful and rewarding for both. In the last section I attempted a brief excursus into Hindu-Christian dialogue, and suggested that a comparativist approach would strengthen critical aspects of Christian doctrine such as the nature of the incarnation of Christ, as a result of seeing it in light of the incarnation of the Hindu *avatars*.

An Orthodox contribution to comparative theology would emphasize the uniqueness of all religious traditions in dialogue and oppose syncretism. Other traditions have the role of inviting one to reflect on the weaknesses of his or her own tradition, not to offer solutions to correct them. Correction or clarification must come from one's own tradition, by means of going back to its *own* resources. Comparative theology would thus make a Buddhist a better Buddhist and a Christian a better Christian. As such, it fosters a real interfaith dialogue, by debating specific issues with adherents of other traditions and making sure we have the right picture of these issues, by restating our views in a clearer manner, and finally by applying what we have learned, but without compromising our own tradition. Dialogue can be sincere and fruitful only if partners remain convinced partners, not converts to another view, or half-converts that no longer belong to any tradition. As such, an Orthodox contribution to comparative theology encourages its use as a door opener for interfaith dialogue in our pluralistic religious world without fostering religious pluralism.

# Conclusion

IN THIS BOOK I have focused on assessing contemporary Buddhist-Christian dialogue from the perspective of a real theological exchange between the two traditions and suggested that comparative theology would provide the best balanced approach. An Orthodox contribution to comparative theology would emphasize the need of knowing the traditions on their own terms, of rejecting syncretism and learning from differences. Let me recapitulate the flow of my argument.

In the first part of the work I set the stage for assessing Buddhist-Christian dialogue by pointing to the impasse to which the current theologies of religions lead. Exclusivism cannot be called a form of interfaith dialogue, for it does not even consider worth undertaking a serious study of other religious traditions. To my surprise, I noticed that exclusivism not only characterizes a significant portion of Christian theologians who look at other religions, but it is a common trend among Buddhist scholars as well. Inclusivism performs an *a priori* judgement of other traditions and tends to ignore what is particular to them. Pluralism proposes that the true goal of religion is beyond what has been formulated so far by the individual traditions, and that they would still converge at some point. The major difficulty of the pluralist approach is that its adherents criticize all particular traditions, but fail to grasp their own limitations and be critical of their own assumptions. Not only pluralists, but also exclusivists and inclusivists approach other religious traditions with a soteriological interest and often apply evaluating criteria that are irrelevant for the existing religious traditions. As a result, the current theologies of religions hardly offer a solid basis for building an interfaith dialogue of theological exchange that would benefit all participants.

In order to be true to the religious traditions of Mahayana Buddhism and Orthodox Christianity and avoid a syncretist approach in dialogue that would compromise both, I proposed as a criterion for assessing the current positions expressed in Buddhist-Christian dialogue the extent to which they respect the view of human perfection as it is formulated by the original traditions. I followed Stăniloae to present the Orthodox view of human perfection as deification, and several scholars of Buddhism to present the Mahayana view of perfection as Buddhahood. Since both Christians and Buddhists strive for human perfection, the positions they express in dialogue should be consistent with the ideal of perfection of the original traditions. The two views of perfection appeared to be very different. On the one hand, Buddhahood is becoming a Buddha and teaching other beings to escape suffering and ignorance by giving up thirst for personal existence. On the other hand, deification is reaching the perfection of the human nature in Christ, by attaining the most intimate communion with God. There is no surprise in finding such a difference. The two traditions started from very different premises on the nature of Ultimate Reality and built worldviews that are consistent with these premises.

However, this does not mean that exclusivism would be the only option left for Buddhist-Christian encounter. A far better approach is that of comparative theology, given its strong emphasis on knowing other religious traditions on their own terms and on learning from them in a non-syncretistic way. As I have seen it defined by Clooney and Fredericks, comparative theology would truly respect the two views of human perfection and make dialogue beneficial for both parts involved.

In the second part of this book, in light of the impasse reached by the current theologies of religions, I felt the necessity to return *ad fontes* in Buddhist-Christian dialogue, and perform an assessment of its founding fathers. As practitioners of Zen Buddhism, the three representatives of the Kyoto School attempted to find equivalence between the Christian view of God and the Buddhist *shunyata*, by way of interpreting the doctrine of the *kenosis* of Christ as requiring the *kenosis* of God the Father. Nishida argued that the true Absolute must be seen as a predicative truth which negates any substantial Ultimate Reality, including the concept of God as self-subsisting. Nishitani, the next important figure of the Kyoto School, concluded that the Christian view of God cannot be a resource for counteracting phenomenon of nihilism as occurring both in the West and East and that the solution would come from adopting the standpoint of emptiness. Following his master Nishida, he argued that the future of Christianity lies not in its return to traditional beliefs and repentance for the misdeeds of the past, but in forsaking its concept of a personal God and replacing it with *shunyata*, emptiness.

A different approach to Buddhist-Christian dialogue seemed to be that of Masao Abe who, unlike his predecessors at the Kyoto School, argued that *both* Buddhism *and* Christianity must enter the stage of mutual transformation so that they could successfully meet the challenge of modern nihilism. He acknowledged that Buddhism should improve its vision of time and history, as well as that of ethics and social justice, while Christianity should adopt a more realistic view of God, as that found in the views of Eckhart and Böhme. Unfortunately, Abe's call for a "mutual" transformation of Buddhism and Christianity proved to be addressed mainly to Christians, who should realize the nothingness of God, while there is little, if anything, to change in Buddhism. However, what I found inspiring in Abe's view of a mutual transformation of Buddhism and Christianity is his methodology. When formulating a way in which Buddhism could change he did not use Christian resources to find solutions, but instead searched for them in his own tradition and found them in the *bodhisattva's* double orientation, towards both emptiness and the world of *samsara*.

John Cobb's proposal for Buddhist-Christian dialogue comes from the perspective of Process Theology. He is aware that Buddhist enlightenment and the renewed life in Christ are different goals that cannot easily be reconciled, so he advocates for total pluralism and also proposes a mutual transformation of Buddhism and Christianity, by recognizing the complementarity of the two religious traditions in their capacity to fulfil different needs. In practical terms, Buddhists can learn from Christianity to develop a better sense of history and social action and a way of seeing the Amida Buddha as personal and ethical. What Christians can learn from Buddhism is a new vision of God as emptiness and the dissolution of personhood as ground for developing love. However, Cobb's proposal is rejected by both Buddhists and Christians. On the one hand, Abe criticized Cobb's view of God, for it retains "a trace of dualism," and asked for a complete overcoming of dualism in Process Theology by seeing God as both an actual entity and an actual occasion. On the other hand, the "new Christianity" that would emerge from its interaction with Buddhism is not acceptable by Christians either, for it compromises fundamental Christian doctrines. As such Cobb's proposal indirectly points to comparative theology as a way to surpass these shortcomings and find a way in which Christians and Buddhists would remain true to their own ideals.

In response to the shortcomings encountered in the approach of the founding fathers of Buddhist-Christian dialogue, but also stimulated by Abe's way of dealing with criticism, in the last chapter of this book I have argued for comparative theology as an approach in interfaith dialogue that would truly respect each religious tradition's uniqueness and make dialogue beneficial for all, despite fundamental differences. Given the fact that comparative theology preserves the traditions and resists religious syncretism, while it is still profoundly interested in an in-depth study of other traditions,

I have concluded that it is a more appropriate way of engaging in interfaith dialogue in our pluralist world than the salvation oriented approaches of exclusivism, inclusivism and pluralism. As a confirmation I have shown how it can bear fruit for Christians engaged in Buddhist-Christian dialogue in three specific domains: compassion, prayer, and faith. These are concrete examples of how significant insights to one's own tradition can be gained as a result of dialogue with others. An Orthodox contribution to comparative theology can only be imagined if the rich traditions that engage in dialogue are not corrupted by syncretism, but rather respect the other traditions, learn about their values on their own terms and as a result better know themselves. Although I criticized Knitter's pluralism, I can also confess that "[i]t was only after I began to take seriously and to explore other religious Scriptures and traditions, that I was able to more adequately understand my own."[1] But unlike Knitter, I have done my best to remain faithful to the teachings of Orthodox Christianity.

One of the pioneers of Buddhist-Christian dialogue, Lynn de Silva, argued that "the purpose of dialogue is not to seek for the lowest common denominator; not to create a Parliament of Religions; not to work towards one world religion" but instead to build up local, national and world community.[2] I fully subscribe to this thought. Since we live in multi-religious communities and will never return to a cultural isolation between East and West, the best way to accommodate is by dialogue, and the most appropriate method of dialogue appears to be comparative theology, for it demands preserving the traditions in a multi-cultural and pluralistic society. Conversions are possible and will occur anyway, but at least those who convert will do so honestly and well aware of what other traditions offer. The meeting between Buddhism and Christianity that started in the twentieth century is indeed a remarkable phenomenon that can make a great difference in the further development of the two religions. However, it is up to us to choose if it will lead to a syncretistic good-for-all religion, or to the preserving and enriching of the existing Buddhist and Christian traditions in a world community that respects all religious traditions as they are.

---

1. Knitter, *Without Buddha*, xii.

2. Lynn de Silva, "What is Dialogue?," in *Dialogue* 1/1 (1974) 2.

# Bibliography

Abe, Masao. *Buddhism and Interfaith Dialogue: Part One of a Two-volume Sequel to Zen and Western Thought.* Honolulu: University of Hawaii Press, 1995.

——. "Mahayana Buddhism and Whitehead: A View by a Lay Student of Whitehead's Philosophy." *Philosophy East and West* 25 (1975) 393–405.

——. *Zen and Comparative Studies: Part Two of a Two-Volume Sequel to Zen and Western Thought.* Honolulu: University of Hawaii Press, 1985.

——, ed. *A Zen Life: D. T. Suzuki Remembered.* New York: Weatherhill, 1986.

——. *Zen and the Modern World: A Third Sequel to Zen and Western Thought.* Honolulu: University of Hawaii Press, 2003.

——. *Zen and Western Thought.* Honolulu: University of Hawaii Press, 1985.

Abe, Masao et al. "Buddhist-Christian Dialogue: Past, Present and Future." *Buddhist-Christian Studies* 1 (1981) 13–29.

Abhayasundara, Pranith, ed. *Controversy at Panadura, or Panadura Vadaya.* Colombo, Sri Lanka: The State Printing Corporation, 1990.

Achimescu, Nicolae. *Budism și Creștinism: Considerații privind desăvârșirea omului* [Buddhism and Christianity: Considerations Regarding Human Perfection]. Iași: Tehnopress, 2004. First presented as PhD Thesis at the University of Tübingen, 1993, "Die Vollendung des Menschen in Buddhismus. Bewertung aus orthodoxer Sicht" [Human Perfection in Buddhism. An assessment from an Orthodox perspective], under Prof. Dr. P. Beyerhaus and Prof. Dr. J. Moltmann.

Andrutsos, Hristu. *Dogmatica Bisericii Ortodoxe Răsăritene* [The Dogmatics of the Eastern Orthodox Church]. Translated by Dumitru Stăniloae. Sibiu: Editura Tipografiei Diecezane, 1930.

Aronson, Harvey B. *Love and Sympathy in Theravada Buddhism.* Delhi: Motilal Banarsidass, 1980.

Athanasius the Great. *On the Incarnation of the Word.* Online: www.newadvent.org/fathers/2802.htm.

Baatz, Ursula. *Hugo M. Enomiya-Lassalle: Ein Leben zwischen den Welten* [Hugo M. Enomiya-Lassalle: A Life Between Two Worlds]. Zürich: Benziger, 1998.

Balthasar, Hans Urs von. "Meditation als Verrat [Meditation as Betrayal]." *Geist und Leben* 50/4 (1977) 260–68.

Barnes, Michael, SJ. *Religions in Conversation: Christian Identity and Religious Pluralism.* London: SPCK, 1989.

——. *Theology and the Dialogue of Religions.* Cambridge Studies in Christian Doctrine 8. Cambridge: Cambridge University Press, 2002.

Barth, Karl. *Church Dogmatics*, vol. I, part 2. Edinburgh: T. & T. Clark, 1956.

———. *The Church Dogmatics*, vol. III, part 2. Edinburgh: T. & T. Clark, 1975.

Barth, Karl et al. *Natural Theology: Comprising "Nature and Grace" by Professor Dr. Emil Brunner and the Reply "No!"* Translated by Peter Fraenkel. 1946. Reprinted, Eugene: Wipf & Stock, 2002.

Bartoş, Emil. *Deification in Eastern Orthodox Theology: An Evaluation and Critique of the Theology of Dumitru Stăniloae.* Carlisle, UK: Paternoster, 1999.

Beverley, James. "Interview with the Dalai Lama." *Christianity Today*, June 11, 2001. Online http://www.christianitytoday.com/ct/2001/june11/15.64.html.

Bodhi, Bhikkhu, trans. *The Connected Discourses of the Buddha: A Translation of the Samyutta Nikaya.* Boston: Wisdom, 2000.

Bordeianu, Radu. *Dumitru Stăniloae: Ecumenical Ecclesiology.* Ecclesiological Investigations 13. London: T. & T. Clark, 2011.

Brown, Delwin et al., eds. *Process Philosophy and Christian Thought.* New York: Bobbs-Merrill, 1971.

Brunner, Emil. *Ein offenes Wort: Vorträge und Aufsästze 1917–1934.* Vol. 1. Zürich: Theologischer Verlag, 1981.

Buddha. *The Four Immeasurables: Love, Compassion, Joy and Equanimity.* Online: http://viewonbuddhism.org/immeasurables_love_compassion_equanimity_rejoicing.html.

Buddha. The *Mahavagga.* Online: http://www.sacred-texts.com/bud/sbe13/sbe1312.htm.

Buddhadasa Indapanno, Bhikkhu. *Christianity and Buddhism.* Sinclair Thompson Memorial Lectures, fifth series. Bangkok, 1967.

Buri, Fritz. *The Buddha-Christ as the Lord of the True Self: The Religious Philosophy of the Kyoto School and Christianity.* Translated by Harold H. Oliver. Macon, GA: Mercer University Press, 1997.

Burrell, David B. *Knowing the Unknowable God: Ibn-Sina, Maimonides, Aquinas.* Notre Dame: University of Notre Dame Press, 1987.

Carpenter, James C. "The Christology of John Cobb." Online: http://www.religion-online.org/showarticle.asp?title=2387.

Chariton of Valamo, Igumen. *The Art of Prayer: An Orthodox Anthology.* London: Faber & Faber, 1966.

Clooney, Francis X., SJ. "Comparative Theology: A Review of Recent Books." *Theological Studies* 56 (1995) 521–50.

———. *Comparative Theology: Deep Learning Across Religious Borders.* Malden, MA: Wiley-Blackwell, 2010.

———. *Hindu God, Christian God.* Oxford: Oxford University Press, 2001.

———, ed. *The New Comparative Theology: Thinking Interreligiously in the 21st Century.* London: T. & T. Clark, 2010.

Cobb, John B., Jr. "Amida and Christ: Buddhism and Christianity." Originally delivered at Ryukoku University, Kyoto, Japan, July, 1997. Online: http://www.religion-online.org/showarticle.asp?title=147.

———. "Autobiography." Online: http://www.religion-online.org/showarticle.asp?title=3602.

———. *Beyond Dialogue: Toward a Mutual Transformation of Christianity and Buddhism.* 2nd ed. 1982. Reprinted, Eugene, OR: Wipf & Stock, 1998.

———. "Beyond 'Pluralism.'" Lecture delivered at Bangor Theological Seminary, January 26–27, 2004. Online: http://www.religion-online.org/showarticle.asp?title=3347.

———. "Buddhism and Christianity." Online: http://www.religion-online.org/showarticle.asp?title=3348. Lecture delivered at Bangor Theological Seminary, January 26–27, 2004.

———. *Can Christ Become Good News Again?* St. Louis: Chalice, 1991.

———. *Christ in a Pluralist Age.* 1975. Reprinted, Eugene, OR: Wipf & Stock, 1999.

———. *A Christian Natural Theology: Based on the Thought of Alfred North Whitehead.* London: Lutterworth, 1996.

———. "Faith." *Buddhist-Christian Studies* 14 (1994) 35–41.

———. *God and the World.* 1969. Reprinted, Eugene, OR: Wipf & Stock, 2000.

———. *Questions (June 1998, January 2001, September 2001, August 2002, December 2004, April 2007, May 2007, April 2008, July 2008, September 2008).* Online: http://www.processandfaith.org/writings/ask-dr-cobb/list-by-date.

———. "Reply to Jürgen Moltmann's 'The Unity of the Triune God.'" *St. Vladimir's Theological Quarterly* 28/3 (1984) 173–77.

———. *The Structure of Christian Existence.* Philadelphia: Westminster, 1967.

———. *Transforming Christianity and the World: A Way beyond Absolutism and Relativism.* Faith Meets Faith Series. Maryknoll, NY: Orbis, 1999.

———. "Whitehead and Buddhism." Lecture delivered at the Buddhist College in Budapest, March 6, 2002. Online: http://www.religion-online.org/showarticle.asp?title=1942.

———. "Whitehead's Philosophy and a Christian Doctrine of Man." *Journal of Bible and Religion,* 32 (1964) 209–220.

———. "Who Was Jesus? (Colossians 1:19)." A sermon preached at Highlands United Church of Christ, Vancouver, BC, July 22, 2007. Online: http://www.religion-online.org/showarticle.asp?title=3542.

Cobb, John B., Jr., and David Ray Griffin. *Process Theology: An Introductory Exposition.* Philadelphia: Westminster, 1976.

Cobb, John B. Jr., and Christopher Ives, eds. *The Emptying God: A Buddhist-Jewish-Christian Conversation.* Delhi: Sri Satguru, 1996.

Collins, Steven. *Selfless Persons: Imagery and Thought in Theravada Buddhism.* Cambridge: Cambridge University Press, 1982.

Conze, Edward. *Buddhism: Its Essence and Development.* New York: Harper, 1959.

Corless, Roger, and Paul F. Knitter, eds. *Buddhist Emptiness and Christian Trinity: Essays and Explorations.* New York: Paulist, 1990.

Cornille, Catherine. "Double Religious Belonging: Aspects and Questions." *Buddhist-Christian Studies* 23 (2003) 43–49.

———. *The Im-Possibility of Interreligious Dialogue.* New York: Crossroad, 2008.

———, ed. *Many Mansions? Multiple Religious Belonging and Christian Identity.* Faith Meets Faith Series. Maryknoll, NY: Orbis, 2002.

D'Costa, Gavin, ed. *Christian Uniqueness Reconsidered: The Myth of a Pluralistic Theology of Religions.* Faith Meets Faith Series. Maryknoll, NY: Orbis, 1990.

———. *Christianity and World Religions: Disputed Questions in the Theology of Religions.* Malden, MA: Wiley-Blackwell, 2009.

———. *The Meeting of Religions and the Trinity.* Faith Meets Faith Series. Maryknoll, NY: Orbis, 2000.

Dalai Lama (Tenzin Gyatso). *Activating Bodhicitta: The Awakening Mind & Meditation on Compassion.* Dharamsala, India: Library of Tibetan Works and Archives, 1978.

———. *Ancient Wisdom, Modern World: Ethics for a New Millennium.* Boston: Little, Brown, 1999.

———. *The Good Heart: A Buddhist Perspective on the Teachings of Jesus.* Boston: Wisdom, 1996.

———. *The Heart of Compassion: A Practical Approach to a Meaningful Life.* Twin Lakes, WI: Lotus, 1997.

———. *How to Practice: The Way to a Meaningful Life.* New York: Pocket, 2002.

———. *Kindness, Clarity, and Insight.* Ithaca, NY: Snow Lion, 1984.

———. *Spiritual Advice for Buddhists and Christians.* New York: Continuum, 1998.

———. "The True Expression of Non-violence Is Compassion." Online: http://www. spiritsound.com/bhikshu.html.

———. *Universal Responsibility and the Good Heart.* Dharamsala, India: Library of Tibetan Works and Archives, 1976.

Dalai Lama, and Howard C. Cutler. *The Art of Happiness: A Handbook for Living.* New York: Riverhead, 1998.

Dasgupta, Surendranath. *A History of Indian Philosophy.* Vol. I. Delhi: Motilal Banarsidass, 1975.

Dorrien, Gary. "The Lure and Necessity of Process Theology." *CrossCurrents* 58 (2008) 316–36.

Drew, Rose. *Buddhist and Christian? An Exploration of Dual Belonging.* Routledge Critical Studies in Buddhism. London: Routledge, 2011.

Fodor, Jim, and Frederick Christian Bauerschmidt, eds. *Aquinas in Dialogue: Thomas for the Twenty-First Century.* Directions in Modern Theology. Oxford: Blackwell, 2004.

Franck, Frederick, ed. *The Buddha Eye: An Anthology of the Kyoto School.* New York: Crossroad, 1982.

Fredericks, James L. *Buddhists and Christians: Through Comparative Theology to Solidarity.* Faith Meets Faith Series. Maryknoll, NY: Orbis, 2004.

———. *Faith among Faiths: Christian Theology and Non-Christian Religions.* New York: Paulist, 1999.

Garvey, John. *Seeds of the Word: Orthodox Thinking on Other Religions.* Crestwood, NY: St. Vladimir's Seminary Press, 2005.

Gethin, Rupert. *The Foundations of Buddhism.* Oxford: Oxford University Press, 1998.

Grayling, A. C., ed. *Philosophy 2: Further through the Subject.* Oxford: Oxford University Press, 1998.

Gregory of Nyssa. *The Great Catechism.* Online: http://www.ccel.org/ccel/schaff/npnf 205.xi.ii.xxvi.html.

Griffin, David Ray, and Thomas J. J. Altizer, eds. *John Cobb's Theology in Process.* Philadelphia: Westminster, 1977.

Griffin, David Ray, and Joseph C. Hough Jr., eds. *Theology at the University: Essays in Honor of John B. Cobb.* Albany: SUNY Press, 1991.

Griffiths, Paul J., ed. *Christianity through Non-Christian Eyes.* Faith Meets Faith Series. Maryknoll, NY: Orbis, 1990.

Gross, Rita M., and Terry C. Muck, eds. *Christians Talk about Buddhist Meditation, Buddhists Talk about Christian Prayer.* New York: Continuum, 2003.

Harvey, Peter. *An Introduction to Buddhism: Teachings, History and Practices.* Cambridge: Cambridge University Press, 1990.

——. *An Introduction to Buddhist Ethics: Foundations, Values and Issues.* Cambridge: Cambridge University Press, 2000.

Heim, S. Mark. *The Depth of the Riches: A Trinitarian Theology of Religious Ends.* Grand Rapids: Eerdmans, 2001.

——. *Salvations: Truth and Difference in Religion.* Faith Meets Faith Series. Maryknoll, NY: Orbis, 1995.

Heisig, James. *Dialogues at One Inch above the Ground: Reclamations of Belief in an Interreligious Age.* New York: Crossroad, 2003.

——. *Philosophers of Nothingness.* Honolulu: University of Hawaii Press, 2001.

——. *Sunyata and Kenosis.* Online: http://nirc.nanzan-u.ac.jp/staff/jheisig/pdf/Sunyata_and_Kenosis.pdf.

Henry, Patrick G., and Donald K. Swearer. *For the Sake of the World: The Spirit of Buddhist and Christian Monasticism.* Minneapolis: Fortress, 1989.

Hick, John. *A Christian Theology of Religions: The Rainbow of Faiths.* Louisville: Westminster John Knox, 1995.

——. *God Has Many Names.* Philadelphia: Westminster, 1982.

——. *God and the Universe of Faiths: Essays in the Philosophy of Religion.* 2nd ed. London: Oneworld, 1993.

——. *An Interpretation of Religion: Human Responses to the Transcendent.* New Haven: Yale University Press, 1989.

——, ed. *The Myth of God Incarnate.* London: SCM, 1977.

Hick, John, and Hasan Askari, eds. *The Experience of Religious Diversity.* Farnham, UK: Gower, 1985.

Ică, Ioan I., Jr. ed. *Persoană și Comuniune: Prinos de cinstire Părintelui Profesor Academician Dumitru Stăniloae la împlinirea vârstei de 90 de ani* [Person and Communion: A Token of Honour to Father Professor Dumitru Stăniloae on the Occasion of his 90th Birthday]. Sibiu: Arhiepiscopia Ortodoxă Sibiu, 1993.

Ingram, Paul O. "Faith as Knowledge in the Teaching of Shinran Shonin and Martin Luther." *Buddhist-Christian Studies,* 8 (1988) 23–35.

Ingram, Paul O., and Frederick J. Streng, eds. *Buddhist-Christian Dialogue: Mutual Renewal and Transformation.* 1986. Reprinted, Eugene, OR: Wipf & Stock, 2007.

Ives, Christopher, ed. *Divine Emptiness and Historical Fullness: A Buddhist-Jewish-Christian Conversation with Masao Abe.* Valley Forge, PA: Trinity, 1995.

James, William. *Essays in Radical Empiricism.* Radford, VA: Wilder, 2007.

John Paul II. *Redemptoris missio.* http://www.vatican.va/holy_father/john_paul_ii/encyclicals/documents/hf_jp-ii_enc_07121990_redemptoris-missio_en.html.

Justin Martyr. *The First Apology,* http://www.newadvent.org/fathers/0126.htm.

——. *The Second Apology,* http://www.newadvent.org/fathers/0127.htm.

Katz, Nathan. *Buddhist Images of Human Perfection: The Arahant of the Sutta Pitaka Compared with the Bodhisattva and the Mahasidha.* Delhi: Motilal Banarsidass, 2010.

King, Winston L. "Buddhist-Christian Dialogue Reconsidered." *Buddhist-Christian Studies* 2 (1982) 5–11.

Knitter, Paul F. *Introducing Theologies of Religions.* Maryknoll, NY: Orbis, 2002.

——. *Jesus and the Other Names: Christian Mission and Global Responsibility.* Maryknoll, NY: Orbis, 1996.

———. *One Earth, Many Religions: Multifaith Dialogue and Global Responsibility.* Maryknoll, NY: Orbis, 1995.

———. *Without Buddha I Could not Be a Christian.* Oxford: Oneworld, 2009.

Küng, Hans. *Does God Exist? An Answer for Today.* Translated by Edward Quinn. 1980. Reprinted, Eugene, OR: Wipf & Stock, 2006.

———. *A Global Ethic for Global Politics and Economics.* Translated by John Bowden. London: SCM, 1997.

———. *Global Responsibility. In Search of a New World Ethic.* Translated by John Bowden. 1991. Reprinted, Eugene, OR: Wipf & Stock, 2004.

———. *On Being a Christian.* Translated by Edward Quinn. Garden City, NY: Doubleday, 1976.

———, ed. *Yes to a Global Ethic.* London: SCM, 1996.

Küng, Hans et al. *Christianity and World Religions: Paths of Dialogue with Islam, Hinduism, and Buddhism.* Translated by Peter Heinegg. Maryknoll, NY: Orbis, 1993.

Lee, Kenneth D. "Comparative Analysis of Shinran's Shinjin and Calvin's Faith." *Buddhist-Christian Studies* 24 (2004) 171–90.

Lopez, Donald S., Jr., and Steven C. Rockefeller, eds. *The Christ and the Bodhisattva.* SUNY Series in Buddhist Studies. Albany: SUNY Press, 1987.

Lubac, Henri de. *The Church: Paradox and Mystery.* Translated by James R. Dunn. Staten Island, NY: Alba House, 1969.

———. *Paradoxe et Mystère de l'Eglise.* Paris: Cerf, 1967.

Makransky, John. "Buddhist Perspectives on Truth in Other Religions: Past and Present." *Theological Studies* 64 (2003) 334–61.

Mănăstireanu, Dănuţ. "A Perichoretic Model of the Church, The Trinitarian Ecclesiology of Dumitru Stăniloae." PhD diss., Brunel University, 2005.

May, John D'Arcy, ed. *Converging Ways? Conversion and Belonging in Buddhism and Christianity.* Sankt Ottilien: EOS, 2007.

McFarlane, Thomas J. "Process and Emptiness: A Comparison of Whitehead's Process Philosophy and Mahayana Buddhist Philosophy." 2004. Online: http://www.integralscience.org/whiteheadbuddhism.html.

McGhee, Michael, ed. *Philosophy, Religion and the Spiritual Life.* Royal Institute of Philosophy Supplement 32. Cambridge: Cambridge University Press, 1992.

McGrath, Alister. "The Christian Church's Response to Pluralism." *Journal of Evangelical Theological Society* 35 (1992) 487–501.

Meyendorff, John. "Reply to Jürgen Moltmann's "The Unity of the Triune God."" *St. Vladimir's Theological Quarterly* 28 (1984) 183–88.

Mitchell, Donald W., ed. *Masao Abe: A Zen Life of Dialogue.* Boston: Tuttle, 1998.

Mitchell, Donald W., and James Wiseman, eds. *The Gethsemani Encounter: A Dialogue on the Spiritual Life by Buddhist and Christian Monastics.* New York: Continuum, 1997.

Moltmann, Jürgen. "The Crucified God." *Theology Today* 31 (1974) 6–18.

———. *The Crucified God: The Cross of Christ as the Foundation and Criticism of Christian Theology.* Translated by R. A. Wilson and John Bowden. London: SCM, 1974. Reprinted, 2001.

———. *History and the Triune God: Contributions to Trinitarian Theology.* Translated by John Bowden. London: SCM, 1991.

————. *The Trinity and the Kingdom of God.* Translated by Margaret Kohl. London: SCM, 1981.

Müller, F. Max, trans. *The Larger Sukhavativyuha Sutra.* Online: http://web.mit.edu/stclair/www/larger.html.

————. *The Sacred Books of the East.* Vol. x, part II. Delhi: Motilal Banarsidass, 1965.

Nanamoli, Bhikkhu, and Bhikkhu Bodhi, trans. *The Middle Length Discourses of the Buddha: A Translation of the Majjhima Nikaya.* Boston: Wisdom, 1995.

Navlakha, Suren, trans. *Upanishads.* Ware, UK: Wordsworth, 2000.

Netland, Harold A. *Dissonant Voices: Religious Pluralism and the Question of Truth.* Grand Rapids: Eerdmans, 1991.

————. *Encountering Religious Pluralism: The Challenge to Christian Faith & Mission.* Downers Grove, IL: InterVarsity, 2001.

Nhat Hanh, Thich. *Going Home: Jesus and Buddha as Brothers.* New York: Riverhead, 1999.

————. *The Heart of the Buddha's Teaching.* Berkeley: Parallax, 1998.

————. *Living Buddha, Living Christ.* New York: Riverhead, 1995.

Nishida, Kitaro. *An Inquiry into the Good.* Translated by Masao Abe and Christopher Ives. New Haven: Yale University Press, 1990.

————. *Last Writings: Nothingness and the Religious Worldview.* Translated by David A. Dilworth. Honolulu: University of Hawaii Press, 1987.

————. *A Study of Good.* Translated by V. H. Viglielmo. Tokyo: Printing Bureau of the Japanese Government, 1960.

Nishitani, Keiji. *Religion and Nothingness.* Translated by Jan Van Bragt. Berkeley: University of California Press, 1982.

Odin, Steve. "A Critique of the Kenosis/Sunyata Motif in Nishida and the Kyoto School." *Buddhist-Christian Studies* 9 (1989) 71–86.

Pesala, Bhikku, ed. *The Debate of King Milinda: An Abridgement of the Milinda Panha.* Delhi: Motilal Banarsidass, 1998.

Pieris, Aloysius. *Fire and Water: Basic Issues in Asian Buddhism and Christianity.* Faith Meets Faith Series. Maryknoll, NY: Orbis, 1996.

————. *Love Meets Wisdom: A Christian Experience of Buddhism.* Faith Meets Faith Series. Maryknoll, NY: Orbis, 1988.

Pinnock, Clark. *A Wideness in God's Mercy: The Finality of Jesus Christ in a World of Religions.* Grand Rapids: Zondervan, 1992.

Pinnock, Clark, et al., eds. *The Openness of God: A Biblical Challenge to the Traditional Understanding of God.* Downers Grove, IL: InterVarsity, 1994.

Plato. *Timaeus.* Online: http:// www.ellopos.net/elpenor/physis/plato-timaeus/default.asp.

Race, Alan. *Christians and Religious Pluralism: Patterns in the Christian Theology of Religions.* London: SCM, 1983.

————. *Interfaith Encounter: The Twin Tracks of Theology and Dialogue.* London: SCM, London, 2001.

Rahner, Karl. *Foundations of Christian Faith: An Introduction to the Idea of Christianity.* Translated by William V. Dych. New York: Crossroad, 1997.

————. *Theological Investigations.* London: Darton, Longman & Todd, vol. 6 (1969); vol. 10 (1973); vol. 12 (1974); vol. 17 (1981); vol. 18 (1983, by Crossroad).

Raj, Joseph Jaswant. *Grace in the Saiva Siddhantham and in St. Paul: A Contribution in Inter-faith Cross-cultural Understanding.* Madras: South Indian Salesian Society, 1989.

Ratzinger, Joseph Cardinal. "Letter to the Bishops of the Catholic Church on Some Aspects of Christian Meditation." Online: http://www.ewtn.com/library/curia/cdfmed.htm.

————. "Pro Eligendo Romano Pontifice." 18 April 2005. Online: http://www.vatican.va/gpII/documents/homily-pro-eligendo-pontifice_20050418_en.html.

Riesenhuber, Klaus. "Zen unter Christen in Japan." *Meditation–Zeitschrift für Christliche Spiritualität und Lebensgestaltung* 1 (1999) 23–27.

Russell, Norman. *The Doctrine of Deification in Greek Patristic Thought.* Oxford: Oxford University Press, 2004.

Sanders, John. *No Other Name: An Investigation into the Destiny of the Unevangelized.* Grand Rapids: Eerdmans, 1992.

Schmidt-Leukel, Perry, ed. *Buddhism and Christianity in Dialogue: The Gerald Weisfeld Lectures 2004.* Norwich: SCM, 2005.

————, ed. *Buddhist Attitudes to Other Religions.* St. Otilien: EOS, 2008.

————. *Transformation by Integration: How Inter-faith Encounter Changes Christianity.* London: SCM, 2009.

Shannon, William H., ed. *The Hidden Ground of Love: The Letters of Thomas Merton on Religious Experience and Social Concerns.* New York: Farrar, Straus & Giroux, 1985.

Shaw, Miranda. "William James and Yogacara Philosophy: A Comparative Inquiry." *Philosophy East and West* 37 (1987) 223–44.

Silva, Lynn de. "What is Dialogue?" *Dialogue* 1/1 (1974) 1–16.

Stăniloae, Dumitru. *Ascetică și Mistică Creștină* [Christian Ascetics and Mysticism]. Cluj-Napoca: Cartea Cărții de Știință, 1993.

————. *Chipul Evanghelic al lui Iisus Hristos* [The Image of Jesus Christ in the Gospels]. Sibiu: Editura Centrului Mitropolitan, 1991.

————. *Chipul Nemuritor al lui Dumnezeu* [The Immortal Image of God]. Vol. 1–2. București: Cristal, 1995.

————. *The Experience of God.* Translated by Ioan Ioniță. Brookline: Holy Cross Orthodox Press, 1994. This is a translation of the first part of the first volume of Dumitru Stăniloae's (*Teologia Dogmatica Ortodoxă* [Dogmatic Orthodox Theology].

————. "The Faces of Our Fellow Human Beings." *International Review of Missions* 71 (1982) 29–35.

————. "Fiul și Cuvântul lui Dumnezeu, prin care toate s-au făcut și se refac [The Son and Word of God, through whom all is done and undone]." *Ortodoxia* 35 (1983) 168–76.

————. *Iisus Hristos sau Restaurarea Omului* [Jesus Christ or the Restoration of the Human Being]. Craiova: Omniscop, 1993.

————. "Image, Likeness, and Deification in the Human Person." *Communio* 13 (1986) 64–83.

————. "Liturghia Comunității și Jertfa Interioară în Viziunea Filocalică" [The Liturgy of the Community and Inner Sacrifice in the Filokalian Vision]. *Ortodoxia* 30 (1978) 389–99.

―――. *Orthodoxe Dogmatik.* Translated by Hermann Pitters. Gütersloh: Gütersloher, 1985.

―――. *Poziția D-lui Lucian Blaga față de Creștinism și Ortodoxie* [The Position of Lucian Blaga on Christianity and Orthodoxy]. București: Paideia, 1993.

―――. "Sfânta Treime: Creatoarea, Mântuitoarea și Ținta Veșnică a Tuturor Credincioșilor" [The Holy Trinity: The creator, saviour and eternal goal of all believers]. *Ortodoxia* 38 (1986) 14–42.

―――. *Sfânta Treime sau La început a fost iubirea* [The Holy Trinity, or In the Beginning Was Love]. București: EIBMBOR, 1993.

―――. *Spiritualitate și Comuniune în Liturghia Ortodoxă* [Spirituality and Communion in the Orthodox Liturgy]. Craiova: Mitropolia Olteniei, 1986.

―――. "Starea Primordială a Omului în cele Trei Confesiuni" [The human state in the three confessions]. *Ortodoxia* 8 (1956) 323–57.

―――. *Studii de Teologie Dogmatică Ortodoxă* [Studies in Orthodox Dogmatic Theology]. Craiova: Mitropolia Olteniei, 1991.

―――. *Teologia Dogmatică Ortodoxă* [Dogmatic Orthodox Theology]. Vol. 1–3. București: EIBMBOR, 1978.

―――. *Theology and the Church.* Translated by Robert Barringer. Crestwood, NY: St. Vladimir's Seminary Press, 1980.

―――. *Trăirea lui Dumnezeu în Ortodoxie* [Experiencing God in Orthodoxy]. Cluj-Napoca: Dacia, 1993.

―――. "Viața și Activitatea Patriarhului Dosofteiu al Ierusalimului și Legăturile lui cu Țările Românești" [The Life and Work of Dosoftei of Jerusalem and His Connections with Romanian Principalities]. *Candela* 40 (1929) 208–76.

Sumanashanta, Medagampala. "A Comparison of Buddhist and Christian Perfection." PhD diss., Northwestern University, 1973.

Swidler, Leonard. "A Jerusalem-Tokyo Bridge: Buddhist-Christian Dialogue and the Thought of Seiichi Yagi." In *A Bridge to Buddhist-Christian Dialogue,* edited by Seiichi Yagi and Leonard Swidler, 1–72. New York: Paulist, 1990.

Traer, Robert. "Faith in the Buddhist Tradition." *Buddhist-Christian Studies* 11 (1991) 85–120.

Valea, Ernest. *The Buddha and the Christ: Reciprocal Views.* Charleston, SC: BookSurge, 2009.

Vatican, Encyclical. *Ad Gentes.* Online: http://www.vatican.va/archive/hist_councils/ii_vatican_council/documents/vat-ii_decree_19651207_ad-gentes_en.html.

―――. *Dialogue and Proclamation.* Online: http://www.vatican.va/roman_curia/pontifical_councils/interelg/documents/rc_pc_interelg_doc_19051991_dialogue-and-proclamatio_en.html.

―――. *Dominus Iesus.* Online: http://www.vatican.va/roman_curia/congregations/cfaith/documents/rc_con_cfaith_doc_20000806_dominus-iesus_en.html.

―――. *Lumen Gentium.* Online: http://www.vatican.va/archive/hist_councils/ii_vatican_council/documents/vat-ii_const_19641121_lumen-gentium_en.html.

―――. *Nostra Aetate.* Online: http://www.vatican.va/archive/hist_councils/ii_vatican_council/documents/vat-ii_decl_19651028_nostra-aetate_en.html.

Vempeny, Ishanand. *Krishna and Christ: In the Light of Some of the Fundamental Concepts and Themes of the Bhagavad Gita and the New Testament.* Pune, India: Ishvani Kendra, 1988.

Waldenfels, Hans. *Absolute Nothingness: Foundations for a Buddhist-Christian Dialogue.* Translated by J. W. Heisig. New York: Paulist, 1980.

Walshe, Maurice, trans. *The Long Discourses of the Buddha: A Translation of the Digha Nikaya.* Boston: Wisdom, 1987.

Ward, Keith. *Religion and Human Nature.* Oxford: Clarendon, 1998.

Ware, Kallistos. "The Power of the Name: The Function of the Jesus Prayer." *Cross-Currents* 24 (1974) 184–203.

Webster, John et al., eds. *The Oxford Dictionary of Systematic Theology.* Oxford: Oxford University Press, 2007.

Whitehead, Alfred N. *Adventures of Ideas.* New York: Free Press, 1967.

———. *Process and Reality: An Essay in Cosmology.* Toronto: Free Press, 1969.

———. *Religion in the Making.* New York: Meridian, 1960.

Williams, Paul. *Mahayana Buddhism: The Doctrinal Foundations.* 2nd ed. London: Routledge, 2009.

———. "Response to Mark Siderits' Review." *Philosophy East and West* 50 (2000) 424–53.

———. *Songs of Love, Poems of Sadness: The Erotic Verse of the Sixth Dalai Lama.* London: Tauris, 2004.

———. *Studies in the Philosophy of the Bodhicaryavatara: Altruism and Reality.* Delhi: Motilal Banarsidass, 2000.

Williams, Paul, with Anthony Tribe. *Buddhist Thought: A Complete Introduction to the Indian Tradition.* London: Routledge, 2000.

Yeshe, Thubten. *Silent Mind, Holy Mind: A Tibetan Lama's Reflections on Christmas.* Boston: Wisdom, 1978.

Yusa, Michiko. *Zen & Philosophy: An Intellectual Biography of Nishida Kitaro.* Honolulu: University of Hawaii Press, 2002.

Zernickow, Klaus. "Christliches Zen"—eine vegetarische Fleischkost." *Meditation-Zeitschrift für Christliche Spiritualität und Lebensgestaltung* 1 (1999) 28–31.

# Index

Printed in Great Britain
by Amazon